Fun Programming with Visual Basic™

Que Development Group

Fun Programming with Visual Basic

Copyright© 1992 by Que®

All rights reserved. Printed in the United States of America. No part of this book may be used or reproduced in any form or by any means, or stored in a database or retrieval system, without the written permission of the publisher except in the case of brief quotations in critical articles and reviews. Making copies of any part of this book for any purpose other than your own personal use is a violation of United States copyright laws. For information, address Que Corporation, 11711 N. College Ave., Carmel, IN 46032.

Library of Congress Catalog Card Number: 92-61693

ISBN: 1-56529-106-9

This book and disk set is sold *as is*, without warranty of any kind, either express or implied, respecting the contents of this book, including but not limited to implied warranties for the book's quality, performance, merchantability, or fitness for any particular purpose. Neither Que Corporation nor its dealers or distributors shall be liable to the purchaser or any other person or entity with respect to any liability, loss, or damage caused directly or indirectly by this book.

94 93 92   8 7 6 5 4 3 2 1

Interpretation of the printing code: the rightmost double-digit number is the year of the book's printing; the rightmost single-digit number, the number of the book's printing. For example, a printing code of 92-1 shows that the first printing of the book occurred in 1992.

Trademarks

All terms mentioned in this book that are suspected to be trademarks or service marks have been appropriately capitalized. Que cannot attest to the accuracy of this information. Use of a term in this book should not be regarded as affecting the validity of any trademark or service mark.

Visual Basic is a trademark of Microsoft Corporation.

Publisher
Lloyd J. Short

Associate Publisher
Rick Ranucci

Publishing Manager
Joseph Wikert

Production Editor
Lori Cates

Copy Editor
Judy Brunetti

Technical Editor
David Leithauser

Editorial Assistant
Elizabeth D. Brown

Director of Production and Manufacturing
Jeff Valler

Production Manager
Corinne Walls

Proofreading/Indexing Coordinator
Joelynn Gifford

Production Analyst
Mary Beth Wakefield

Book Designer
Scott Cook

Cover Designer
Dan Armstrong

Graphic Image Specialists
Jerry Ellis
Dennis Sheehan
Susan VandeWalle

Production
Jeff Baker
Claudia Bell
Jodie Cantwell
Paula Carroll
Jay Lesandrini
Sandra Shay
Suzanne Tully
Phil Worthington

Indexers
Joy Dean Lee
Tina Trettin
Sue VandeWalle

Composed in Utopia and MCPdigital by Prentice Hall Computer Publishing.

Screen reproductions in this book were created by means of the program Collage Plus from Inner Media, Inc., Hollis, NH.

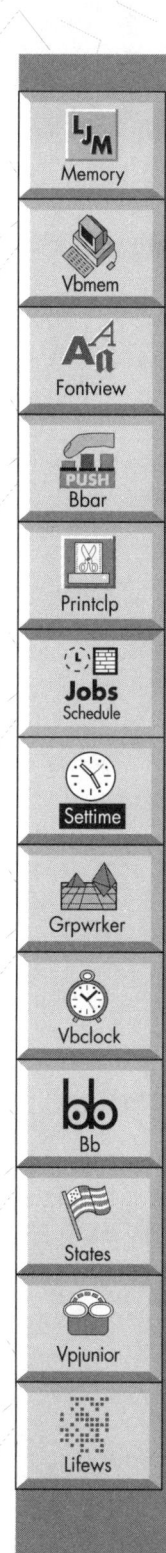

Overview

	Introduction	1
1	Memory Match	7
2	VBMem	37
3	FontView	45
4	ButtonBar Plus	65
5	PrintClip	107
6	Job Scheduler	119
7	SetTime	147
8	GroupWorker	175
9	VBClock	195
10	Blink Blank!	225
11	Name the States	245
12	ViewPoint Jr.	257
13	Life Workshop	281
	Index	331

Contents

Introduction **1**
    Overview 3
    Who Should Use This Book? 3
    What Is in This Book? 4
    Conventions Used in This Book 6
    We Want Your Input 6

1 Memory Match **7**
    Overview 9
        Selecting a Game 9
        High Scores 9
            Viewing High Scores 10
            Beating or Tying a High Score 10
        The *About* Box 10
    Program Operation 11
        Thinking About the Tasks Ahead 12
            Determining the Scope of the Game 12
            How Many Forms Does the Game Require? ... 12
            Does the Game Need a Menuing System? 13
            Should You Use Control Arrays? 13
        The Global Module 15
        The *Board* Form 17
            Creating the Menu Bar 20
            Putting Code Behind the *Board* Form
                and Controls 20
        The *HSENTRY* Form 28
            Putting Code Behind the *HSENTRY* Form 29
        The *High Scores* Form 30
            Putting Code Behind the *High Scores* Form ... 31
        The *About* Form 33
            Putting Code Behind the *About* Form 35

2 VBMem **37**
    Overview 39
    Program Operation 39
        The VBMEM.FRM Code 41
            The Form Load Routine (*Form_Load*) 41
            The Timer Event Routine (*Tmr_Mem*) 41
            The Picture Box Event (*Pic_Pc_Click*) 42
            The Form Resize Event (*Form_Resize*) 42
    Source Code for VBMem 42

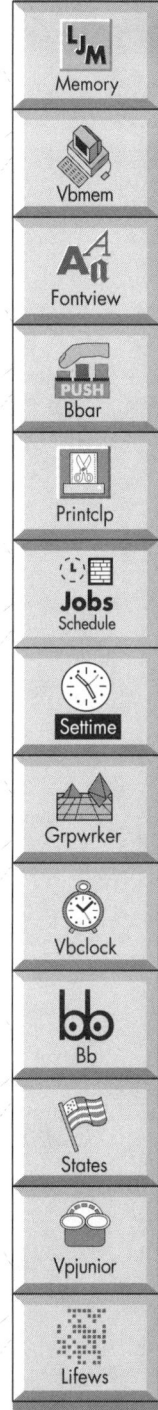

3 FontView 45
Overview 47
Program Operation 49
    Putting the Parts Together: Form and
        Menu Design 49
    Inspecting the FontView Form Code 53
        The Form Load Routine (*Form_Load*) 53
        The Form Resize and Paint Routines
            (*Form_Resize* and *Form_Paint*) 54
        The Size List Box Routine (*Lst_Size_Click*) 54
        The Font List Box Routine
            (*Lst_Face_Click*) 54
        The Italic Option Routine (*Opt_Ital_Click*) 54
        The Bold Option Routine
            (*Opt_Bold_Click*) 55
        The Normal Option Routine
            (*Opt_Norm_Click*) 55
        The *DisplayFace* Routine 55
        The Picture Box Routine (*Picture1_Click*) 55
        The Default Text Routine (*M_DText_Click*) ... 56
        The Exit Routine (*M_Exit_Click*) 56
        The Sample Text Routine (*MSText_Click*) 56
        The Printer Output Routine
            (*M_PrtLst_Click*) 56
        The Screen Load Routine (*M_SFont_Click*) ...57
        The Printer Load Routine (*M_PFont_Click*) ...57
Source Code for *FontView* 58

4 ButtonBar Plus 65
Overview 67
Program Operation 68
    The Global Module (BBARINT.BAS) 69
    The ButtonBar Form (BUTTONBA.FRM) 70
        The General Declarations Section 70
        The *Button_Click* Routine 71
        The *Form_Load* Routine 74
        The *Form_Paint* Routine 76
        The *Form_Resize* Routine 77
        The *Timer1_Timer* Routine 77
        The *Form_MouseMove* Routine 78
        The *Button_GotFocus* Routine 79
        The *Timer2_Timer* Routine 79
        Miscellaneous Resource and
            Memory Routines 80
        The *BarDisplay* Routine 80
        The *Button_DragDrop* Routine 82
        The *KeyHandler* Routine 83
        The *Clear_SystemMenu* Routine 83

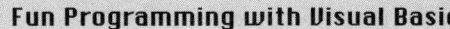

```
The Bar Configuration Form (BARCONFI.FRM) ..... 84
    The Command1_Click Routine ....................... 84
    The Form_Load Routine .............................. 86
    The IconArrange_Click Routine ..................... 89
The BrowseBox Form (BROWSEBOX.FRM) ............. 89
    Core BrowseBox Functions ........................... 92
The IconDisplay Form (ICONDISP.FRM) ................. 95
The Global Routines Module (BBAR.BAS) .............. 96
    The GetMatix Routine ................................ 97
    The WriteDefaultIni Routine ........................ 97
    The GetBBarIni Routine ............................. 101
    The Extractor and ShadowEffects
        Routines ........................................... 103
The License Form (LICENSE.FRM) ....................... 104
Summary ............................................................ 105
```

5 PrintClip **107**
```
Overview ............................................................. 109
    How to Use PrintClip ................................. 109
Program Operation ............................................. 110
    The Load Event ........................................ 111
    The Resize Event ....................................... 111
        Keep the Form Minimized ....................... 112
        Retrieve Clipboard Text ......................... 112
        Break and Print Text Strings .................. 113
    Conclusion ................................................ 116
Source Code for PrintClip .................................... 117
```

6 Job Scheduler **119**
```
Overview ............................................................. 121
    Designing a Utility ..................................... 121
        Designing a Useful Utility ...................... 122
        Making the Interface Intuitively Obvious ..... 122
        Writing Source Code that You Can
            Reuse and Maintain ........................... 122
    Special Features of the Job Scheduler .............. 123
        Using Serial Dates and Times .................. 123
        Using the Timer Control ........................ 123
        Calling the Shell() Function .................... 123
Program Operation ............................................. 123
    Designing the Main Screen ........................... 124
        Drawing the Main Screen Controls ........... 124
        Storing a Job ....................................... 125
        Creating a Job Structure ........................ 125
        Converting from String to Structure
            and Back Again ................................ 126
        Loading the List from a Disk File ............. 130
        Running a Job ..................................... 131
```

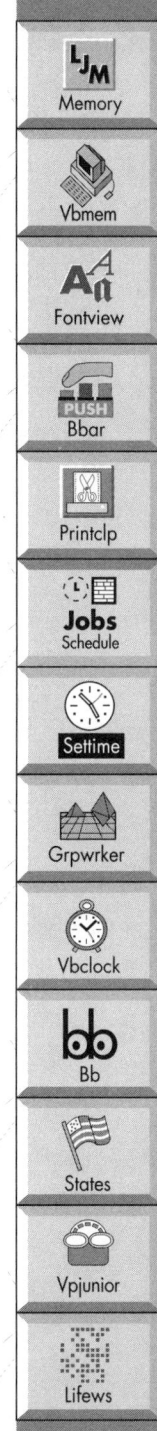

vii

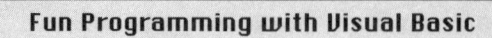

| Deleting a Job from the List 132
| Saving the Job List 132
| Processing the Job List 133
| Designing the *Modify Job* Form 136
| Drawing the Controls 137
| Linking the *File*, *Directory*, and
| *Drive* Controls 137
| Populating the List Boxes 137
| Determining Whether a Job Was Modified ... 138
| Keeping the User from Unloading
| the Form 139
| Adding a Job to the Job List 139
| Modifying a Job in the Job List 140
| Proofing the Application 142
| Disabling Non-Sequiturs and Crashes 142
| Preventing Data Loss 143
| Preventing Program Conflicts 144
| Modifications You Can Make 145

7 SetTime 147

| Overview 149
| Program Operation 151
| The SETTIME.BAS Module 151
| Communications APIs 152
| Private Profile (.INI) APIs 154
| Constants and Global Fields 155
| The OPTFORM.FRM Module 156
| The *Form_Load* Routine 156
| The *Command2* Routine (Quit Button) 157
| The *Command1* Routine (Done Button) 157
| The SETTIME.FRM Module 158
| The *Command1* Routine (Quit Button) 158
| The *CleanUp( )* Procedure 158
| The *Command2* Routine (Start Button) 159
| The *Command4* Routine (Change
| Options Button) 162
| The *Form_Load* Routine 162
| The SETTIME.INI File 163
| Source Code for SetTime 164
| The SETTIME.BAS File 164
| The OPTFORM.FRM File 166
| The SETTIME.FRM File 168
| The SETTIME.INI File 173

8 GroupWorker 175

| Overview 177
| Program Operation 177
| The *Setup* Form 178
| Error Handling 180

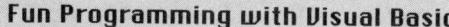
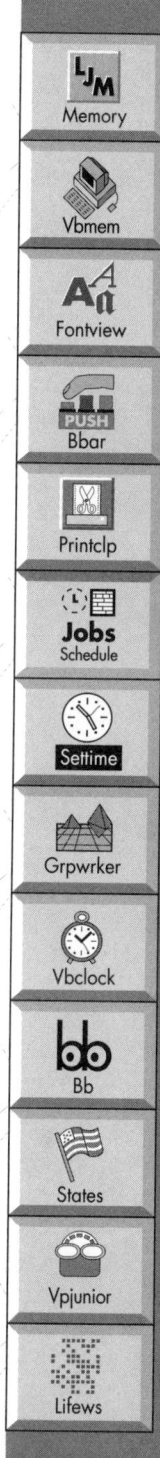

| Processing the Groups 180
     File and Help Menus 181
     Miscellaneous Program Notes 182
     Closing Activities and Thoughts 182
Full Source Code for GroupWorker 183
     GLOBAL.BAS—Global Declarations 183
     MAIN.FRM—*Form2* (Startup Form) 183
     SETUP.FRM—*Form1* 188
     ABOUT.FRM—*Form5* 192
     HELPTXT.FRM—*Form6* 192
     NAGBX.FRM—*Form4* 193
     NAGBOX2.FRM—*Form3* 194

9 VBClock 195

Overview 197
     Options 197
Program Operation 199
     Fundamental Concepts 199
     Keeping VBClock on Top 200
     Floating VBClock with the Active Title Bar 200
     Storing Display Options 201
     Working with the VBCLOCK.INI File 202
     Choosing Fonts and Colors 203
     Moving the Form Without a Title Bar 204
     Timer and Alarm Internals 204
     Manipulating the Pop-up Menu 205
     Conserving Memory 205
     Printing on a Form Versus Using a Label 206
     Using the Picture Box as a Button Bar 206
     Ideas for Further Work 207
     General Rules for Well-Behaved Programs 208
Source Code for VBClock 208
     The Global Listing File 209
     FRM_Clock.FRM 211
     FRM_Disp.FRM 217
     FRM_Opts.FRM 217
     VBCLOCK.BAS 222

10 Blink Blank! 225

Overview 227
     Custom Messages 227
     Miscellaneous Messages 228
     Lunch Messages 228
     Leaving a Message 229
     Retrieving Messages 229
          Using a Password 230
     Setting Display Options 230

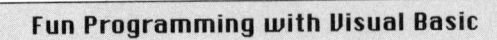

Program Operation 231
　Windows API Functions 231
　Hungarian Notation 232
　Gang Screen 232
　The Global Module 233
　Forms 233
　　frmAbout 233
　　　Declarations 233
　　　Events 233
　　frmBB 234
　　　Declarations 234
　　　Events 234
　　frmBlank 236
　　　Declarations 236
　　　Events 236
　　frmDisplay 237
　　　Declarations 237
　　　Events 237
　　frmEnterMessage 238
　　　Declarations 238
　　　Events 238
　　frmGetNewMessage 239
　　　Declarations 239
　　　Events 239
　　frmLunchMessages 239
　　　Declarations 239
　　　Events 239
　　frmMessages 240
　　　Declarations 240
　　　Events 241
　　frmPassword 241
　　　Declarations 241
　　　Events 241
　　frmWarning 242
　　　Declarations 242
　　　Events 242
　　frmPrintReg 242
　　　Declarations 242
　　　Events 242
　　frmRegistration 242
　　　Declarations 242
　　　Events 242
　The MODULE1.BAS Routines 243

11 Name the States **245**
- Overview 247
- Program Operation 248
  - Windows API 249
  - GLOBAL.BAS Declarations 250
  - Procedural Operation 251
  - Comments and Suggestions 256

12 ViewPoint Jr. **257**
- Overview 259
- Program Operation 260
  - Roll Up Your Sleeves... 261
  - When the Form Loads, the Cradle Will Rock 262
  - API Calls Used in ViewPoint Jr. 265
  - *SendMessage* and the Directory List Box 266
  - Round Robin, or Who Gets Told What 269
  - At Last, the Picture... 272
  - Other Goodies Explained 274
  - The Poor Man's Help System 278

13 Life Workshop **281**
- Overview 283
- Cellular Automata 283
- Using Life Workshop 286
  - Classic Life Experiments 287
  - Hexagonal Life Experiments 289
  - Macrocosmic Experiments 291
- Understanding the Life Workshop Program 292
  - Program Organization 294
  - Program Startup Events 294
  - Programming the Workbench 294
  - Macrocosmic Life 297
  - Help and Miscellaneous 298
- Life Workshop Source Code 298
- Conclusion 329

Index **331**

Fun Programming with Visual Basic

Introduction

Introduction

Overview

Welcome to the world of *Fun Programming with Visual Basic*. We want to emphasize the word *fun*, because that's the approach taken throughout this book. You won't find any boring explanations of all the Visual Basic keywords here! Instead, *Fun Programming with Visual Basic* is filled with some of the most interesting and previously unpublished Visual Basic programs available.

The applications in *Fun Programming with Visual Basic* were gathered from a number of sources, including the Visual Basic forum (MSBASIC) on CompuServe, as well as a handful of electronic bulletin board systems (BBSs) around the country. Each chapter explains the usage and program construction for a different Visual Basic application—as explained by the author of that program.

Who Should Use This Book?

Fun Programming with Visual Basic is aimed at the beginning-to-intermediate Visual Basic programmer. Although you don't need to know the Visual Basic (VB) language inside and out to understand the material in this book, you should have a good understanding of VB fundamentals. For example, you should be familiar with the Visual Basic language and development environment.

If you are just starting out with Visual Basic but are familiar with other BASIC languages (such as QBasic, GW-BASIC, and so on) you need to familiarize yourself with the VB development environment and event-driven architecture. (You can do this by working through a few of the example applications discussed in the Visual Basic documentation set.)

You don't really have to be a programmer at all to get value from this book/disk package. The set includes everything you need to run the bundled applications even if you don't own a copy of Visual Basic! Just follow the installation instructions in the back of the book and you can use all the Windows games/utilities covered in *Fun Programming with Visual Basic* without knowing anything about programming or Visual Basic!

What Is in This Book?

This book contains 13 chapters that serve as insightful documentation for the programs on the bundled disk. Each chapter begins with an explanation of how to use the program. The authors then go into varying levels of detail explaining how they wrote each program with Visual Basic.

We say *varying levels of detail* because some of the programs are short enough to allow the author to explain the program structure on a line-by-line basis. Others, however, are much too long to completely explain in 25-30 pages. For these longer programs, the authors have provided detailed explanations on the most complex portions of their code. Although each nook and cranny of these longer programs is not explained in detail, the fully commented source code is available for your examination on the disk at the back of the book.

Now let's take a quick look at each of the chapters in *Fun Programming with Visual Basic*:

Chapter 1, *Memory Match*, explains the use and structure of a Concentration-like game written by Lou Marino. The object of Memory Match is to turn over pairs of "cards" and find the ones that match. Icons containing flags of the world are used for matching. When the user finds a match, the matched pair remains face up. If a pair does not match, the cards are turned back over. The game continues until all pairs are matched.

Chapter 2, *VBMem*, explains the structure of a simple Visual Basic utility that displays memory usage in real time; the display changes as the system's memory usage does. This program, written by Charles Snider, displays the following system information: Windows operating mode (standard or enhanced), free resources (as a percentage), and free memory (in kilobytes).

Chapter 3, *FontView*, was also written by Charles Snider. FontView is a useful Visual Basic utility that enables you to view and print the fonts that are installed on your system. It is fully compatible with Windows 3.x and all Windows fonts, including TrueType and Adobe Type 1.

Chapter 4, *ButtonBar Plus*, details a slick program launching utility for Windows. Written by Mark J. DiBiasio, the program was designed using a floating toolbar concept. The toolbar consists of 36 buttons arranged in a user-selected matrix. The user can set up each button to launch a program. Each program is represented by an icon of the user's choice. ButtonBar Plus offers the user many advantages over the Windows Program Manager, including a consistent position of the program buttons.

Introduction

Chapter 5, *PrintClip*, was written by Art Krumsee. PrintClip is one of the simplest (yet most powerful) programs included in this book. PrintClip offers a simple and intuitive way to print the contents of the Clipboard—just double-click the PrintClip icon!

Chapter 6, *Job Scheduler*, explains a program that enables you to schedule jobs (or applications) to run on a particular day of the week and at a particular time. Job Scheduler was written by Michael Kosten and offers a handy way to automatically run programs while you are away from your PC.

Chapter 7, *SetTime*, was written by Stephen Pruitt. SetTime serves two purposes. It is primarily a demonstration of programming techniques using Windows API calls for communications and private .INI files. It is also a useful utility to make sure your computer clock is accurate.

Chapter 8, *GroupWorker*, by Dr. Jerry Miller, explains an interesting utility that enables Windows users to create groups of applications, each of which can be launched with a single mouse click.

Chapter 9, *VBClock*, was written by Sarah Holland. The VBClock utility can display the date, time, day of the week, free system resources, and free memory. VBClock also has a simple alarm and message feature.

Chapter 10, *Blink Blank!*, was written by Max Burgstahler. Blink Blank! is a screensaver with a new twist: It's useful. Instead of filling your screen with airborne kitchen appliances, Blink Blank! actually puts your PC to work while you are gone. When you invoke Blink Blank!, you are given the opportunity to display a message on your PC while you are away. If someone wants to leave a message for you while you are away, all they have to do is press the spacebar on your PC and start typing. Blink Blank! can hold up to five messages (of any length) and will display them when you return. You can even print your messages, and they are automatically time-stamped!

Chapter 11, *Name the States*, was written by Dan Lewczyk. Name the States is a Visual Basic program that teaches the names, locations, and capitals of the 50 states.

Chapter 12, *ViewPoint Jr.*, by Barry Seymour, tells about a program that lets you view a variety of graphics files—including several formats not supported by Paintbrush.

Chapter 13, *Life Workshop*, from Ivory Tower Software, allows you to experiment with two-dimensional cellular automata. You can modify the rules and

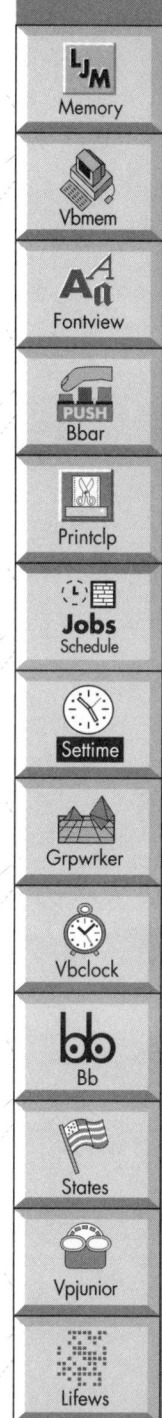

Introduction

observe large colonies of artificial life evolving, or you can assign life to specific cells in the "workbench" and watch different patterns evolve with different sets of rules.

Conventions Used in This Book

All program code and code fragments are indicated by `monospace` type. This includes items that are unique to the Visual Basic language such as events, properties, functions, and so on. Placeholders in code syntax are indicated in *`monospace italic`* type. "Hot keys" that activate menu selections appear in **bold** type in the text.

Some lines of VB code are too long to fit on one line in the book. For those special cases, we have used a line-wrap icon to indicate where two or more lines in the book should appear as one line in your program. For example:

```
↵Function EvalTextEntered (NewDrive As String, TempFileName
    As String) As Integer
```

We Want Your Input

The Que Development Team spent a great deal of time creating *Fun Programming with Visual Basic*. If you would like to give us feedback on this or any other Que programming book, please send your comments to:

Publishing Manager
Que Programming Books
11711 North College Avenue, Suite 141
Carmel, IN 46032

If you are a CompuServe subscriber, please feel free to forward your comments to us electronically at the following CIS address: 76226,632.

We would also like to hear from you if you have written an interesting Visual Basic program that might be appropriate for inclusion in the next edition of this book. Please forward those applications to either our mailing address or our CompuServe address.

Memory Match

by Lou Marino

1

Chapter 1: Memory Match

Overview

The object of Memory Match is to turn over pairs of cards and find the ones that match. Icons containing flags of the world are used for matching. When the user finds a match, the matched pair remains face up. If the pair does not match, the program turns the cards back over. The game continues until all pairs are matched.

Selecting a Game

From the Games menu, select any of the eight available game grids. The program automatically shuffles the cards to create a unique game each time. Figure 1.1 shows a Memory Match game in progress.

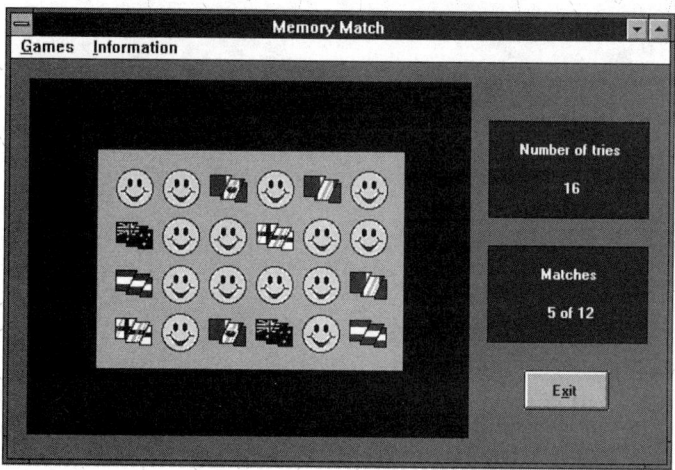

Figure 1.1. A game in progress.

High Scores

Like most games, Memory Match provides a facility for storing, viewing, and inputting high scores. Actually, "high scores" means the lowest number of match tries in a game. This is analogous to golf, in which the person who takes the lowest number of strokes has the highest score.

Viewing High Scores

From the Information menu, select High Scores. A window appears with a listing of people who have achieved a high score. Also included is the high score and the date. Figure 1.2 shows the high scores window.

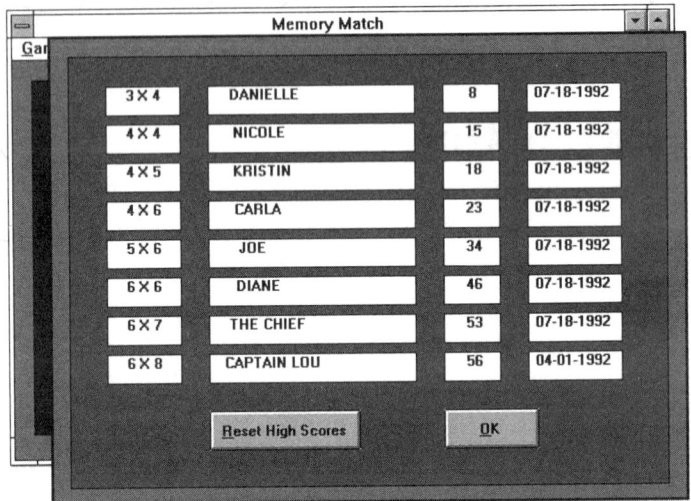

Figure 1.2. The high scores window.

Beating or Tying a High Score

If a player ties or surpasses a high score, a data-entry window appears. Players use this window to enter their names after achieving a high score. The players need only type their names; the program automatically records the score and date. Figure 1.3 shows the New High Score window.

The *About* Box

From the Information menu, select About. The About dialog box appears on the screen. Figure 1.4 shows the Memory Match About dialog box.

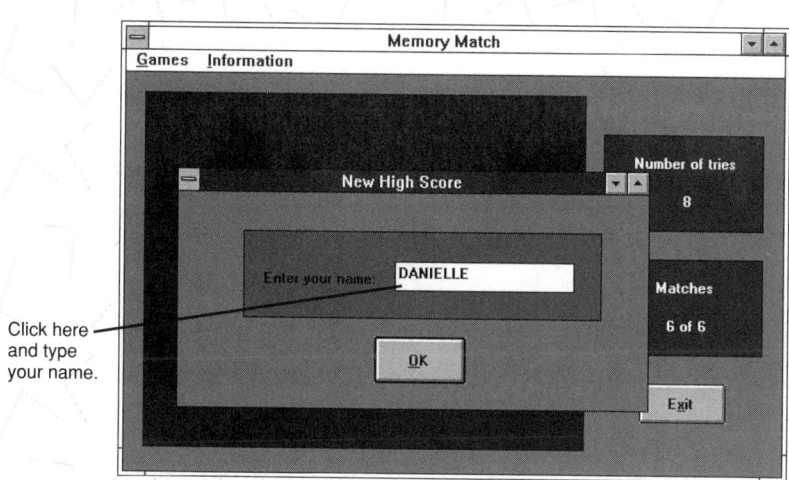

Click here and type your name.

Figure 1.3. Making a new high score entry.

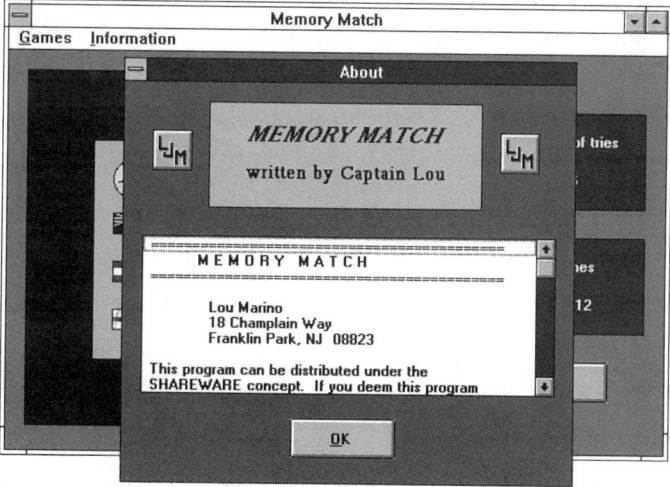

Figure 1.4. The About dialog box.

Program Operation

It's helpful to break a big programming project into smaller pieces, or subprograms. By treating each major operation of the program as a separate entity, you can focus on the details. Take a look at the smaller pieces that make up the Memory Match programming problem.

Thinking About the Tasks Ahead

First, you need to determine the type and scope of the game. After you outline the overall rules of the game, you can reasonably guess the number of required forms. If a significant number of options is presented to the user, your game may need a menuing system.

Lastly, think about any time- and code-saving capabilities Visual Basic provides that you can use to your advantage. For example, control arrays are used in two significant parts of the program.

Determining the Scope of the Game

Each game contains a grid filled with flags of the world. The trick is that all the flags are turned over like a deck of cards placed face down. A player must turn over the cards and match the flags.

Construct the game so that a player can select games ranging from very easy to very difficult. The following eight game grids are included in Memory Match:

Game	Number of Matches
3×4	6
4×4	8
4×5	10
4×6	12
5×6	15
6×6	18
6×7	21
6×8	24

How Many Forms Does the Game Require?

There are three forms that handle the requirements of the game. You know that at least one form is required to contain the actual game, but what other items in addition to the game form are required? Most games keep a record of

the players who have achieved a high score; Memory Match is no exception. You will keep track of the high scores for each of the eight games. The game needs a second form so that players can enter their names after achieving high scores. The third form is necessary to display the list of high scores.

The three forms mentioned will handle the requirements of the game as outlined. An additional form is included that is part of every Windows program—the About form. This last form contains any additional information about the program, version, and author.

Does the Game Need a Menuing System?

Having a selection of eight games is reason enough to consider implementing a pull-down menu system. With additional selections to display high scores and view the About form, the screen becomes a clutter of command buttons if you don't use a menu system.

Should You Use Control Arrays?

Good programmers always think of ways to reduce the memory and program size of an application. The Memory Match application requires that eight different games be available to the player at any time. It is easy to create a form for each game and display only the form for the game that the player selects. Structuring the program in this manner, however, is an inefficient use of resources.

Take a look at the number of picture controls required if each game was created individually using separate forms.

Game	Number of Picture Controls
3×4	12
4×4	16
4×5	20
4×6	24
5×6	30
6×6	36
6×7	42
6×8	48
Total:	228

Adding 228 picture controls to an application significantly increases program size. The most efficient use of memory resources is to make available only the number of controls necessary for the currently selected game.

Like forms, controls can be LOADed and UNLOADed. However, controls have a significant advantage. They can be dynamically created and deleted at runtime. This is achieved by using a control array.

A *control array* is much like any other array used in Visual Basic, such as a string array or an integer array. The major difference is that an array of this kind consists of controls rather than a variable type. Control arrays must be of the same control type, have the same CtlName, and have a unique Index number.

Figure 1.5 is an example of a control array consisting of four command buttons. Notice that the only difference among the command buttons is a unique index.

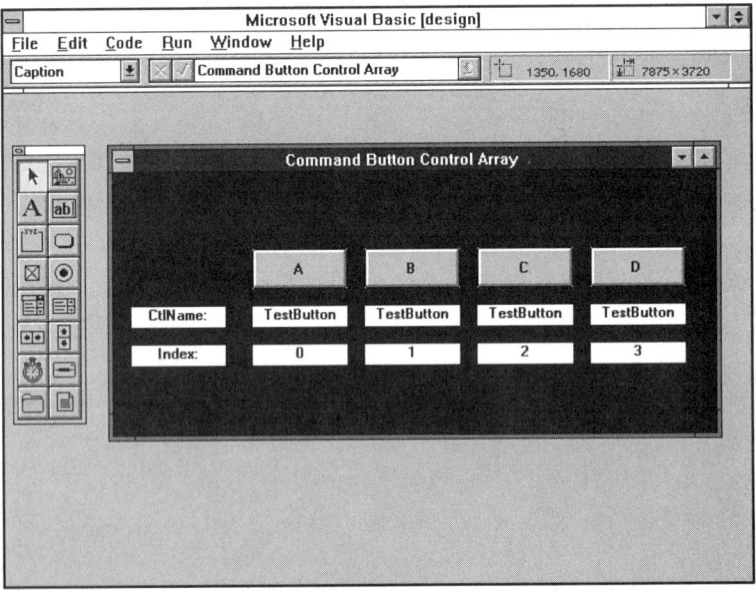

Figure 1.5. The command button control array.

For additional information about control arrays, consult *Visual Basic By Example* (published by Que).

The Global Module

Start Visual Basic and choose New Project from the File menu. From the Project window, highlight GLOBAL.BAS. From the File menu, select Save File As.... When the information box appears, type **MEMORY.GBL**, then click the OK command button to accept the entry. The global module is now named MEMORY.GBL.

Before starting Visual Basic, set the startup directory to your work directory. You do this by highlighting the VB icon, selecting **Properties** from the File menu, and entering your work directory name in the Working Directory field (for example, C:\VB\MMATCH). During development, Visual Basic searches the startup directory for files. You will use several icon and text files for Memory Match. You should also move these files into the default directory.

Figure 1.6 shows the contents of MEMORY.GBL.

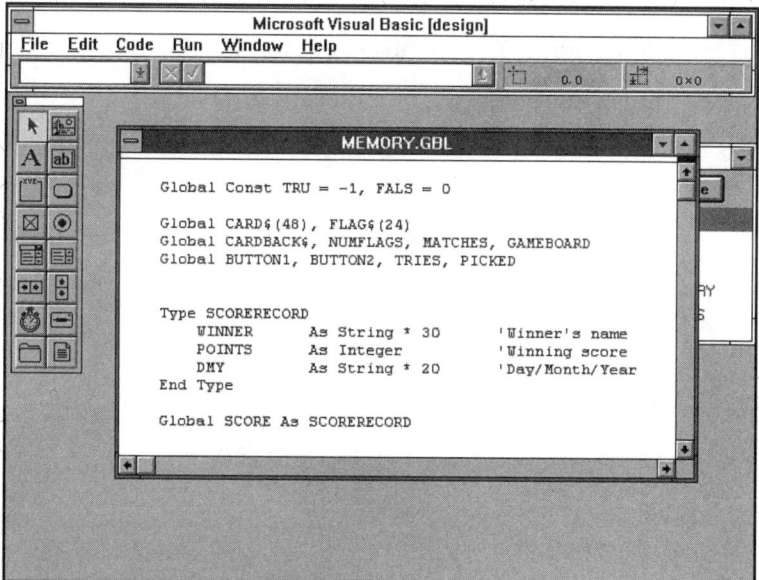

Figure 1.6. The contents of the MEMORY.GBL module.

Chapter 1: Memory Match

The following is an explanation of how each of the MEMORY.GBL variables is used in the program:

- CARD$—A string array with 48 elements. This array holds the names of the flag icons. Because there are 24 different flags, you need twice that amount to hold the matching pairs.

- FLAG$—Array containing the names of the 24 flag icons. These names are randomly placed into the CARD$ array, thus creating a different game each time.

- CARDBACK$—Contains the name of the icon used when the front of the card is face down. Think of this like you would the back of a deck of cards.

- NUMFLAGS—The number of cards needed for the selected game. This is also the number used for dynamically creating the control array (for example, for the 4 × 6 game, NUMFLAGS will be 24).

- MATCHES—The number of successful matched pairs for the current game.

- GAMEBOARD—Used to check if a player has tied or beaten the current high score for the selected game.

- BUTTON1—Index number of the first card of a pair.

- BUTTON2—Index number of the second card of a pair.

- TRIES—A running count of the number of attempts made to match the flags.

- PICKED—Reports if the current selection is the first or second item chosen.

- SCORERECORD—A TYPEd structure is used to read and write records to the high scores file:

    ```
    Type SCORERECORD
            WINNER      As String * 30    'Winner's name
            POINTS      As Integer        'Winning score
            DMY         As String * 20    'Day/Month/Year
    End Type

    Global SCORE As SCORERECORD
    ```

Chapter 1: Memory Match

The *Board* Form

Board is the form used as the playing area for the game. Let's take a step-by-step approach to creating this form.

1. Stretch the form so that you have a generous portion of the screen with which to work.

2. Place a picture control (PICTURE1) within the form and size it to 5655 × 4455. (The sizes of the controls that create this application are suggested. You can, of course, use any size you want.)

3. Select another picture control (PLAYFIELD) from the toolbox and draw a square of 975 × 975 on top of PICTURE1. *Do not* double-click to select this control. By drawing a control on top of another control, a parent-child relationship is established. (The necessity of this relationship is explained later.) Double-clicking to select a control creates a separate object with no relationship to other controls.

4. As in the previous step, select a picture control (MEMORY) and draw a 495 × 495 square centered in PLAYFIELD. PLAYFIELD is now a child of PICTURE1 and a parent of MEMORY.

5. To the right of PICTURE1, place two more picture controls (PICTURE2 and PICTURE3), each having a size of 2055 × 1215.

6. Draw two label controls within PICTURE2 (LABEL1 and NUMTRIES).

7. Similarly, draw two label controls within PICTURE3 (LABEL2 and NUMMATCH).

8. Place a command button on the form.

Figure 1.7 shows a view of the Board form during development.

Table 1.1 is a list of controls needed to create the Board form.

Form/Control	Property	Setting
Form:	BackColor	&H00808080&
	Caption	Memory Match
	FormName	BOARD
Picture:	BackColor	&H00800000&
	CtlName	Picture1

continues

17

Table 1.1. Continued

Form/Control	Property	Setting
Picture:	BackColor	&H00C0C0C0&
	CtlName	PLAYFIELD
Picture:	CtlName	MEMORY
	Index	1
	Picture	FACE03.ICO
Picture:	BackColor	&H00000080&
	CtlName	PICTURE2
Label:	Alignment	2 - Center
	BackColor	&H00000080&
	Caption	Number of tries
	CtlName	LABEL1
	ForeColor	&00FFFFFF&
Label:	Alignment	2 - Center
	BackColor	&H00000080&
	Caption	Number of tries
	CtlName	NUMTRIES
	ForeColor	&00FFFFFF&
Picture:	BackColor	&H00000080&
	CtlName	PICTURE3
Label:	Alignment	2 - Center
	BackColor	&H00000080&
	Caption	Matches
	CtlName	LABEL2
	ForeColor	&00FFFFFF&
Label:	Alignment	2 - Center
	BackColor	&H00000080&
	Caption	Number of tries
	CtlName	NUMMATCH
	ForeColor	&00FFFFFF&
Command:	Caption	E&xit
	CtlName	COMMAND1

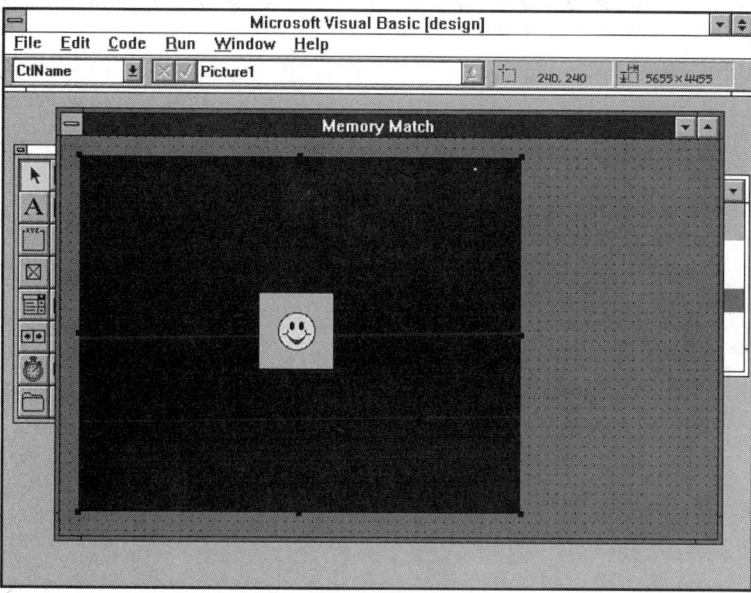

Figure 1.7. Development of the Board form.

Figure 1.8 shows the Board form with added controls.

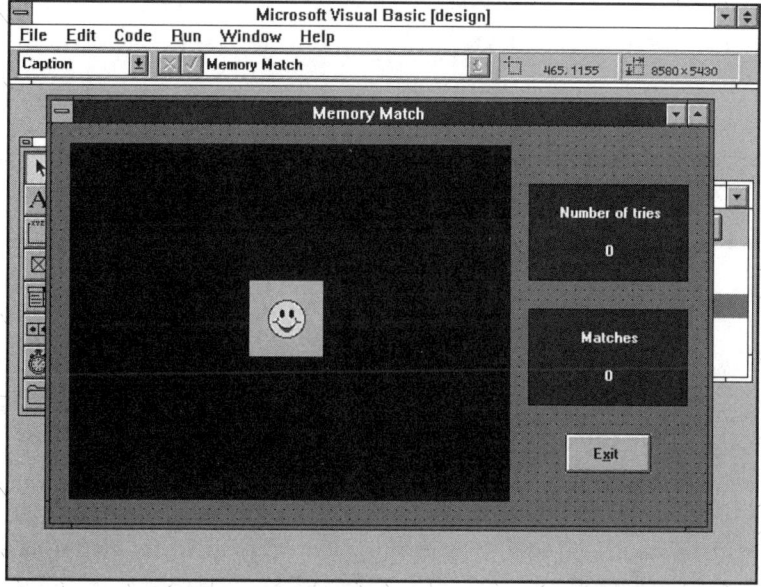

Figure 1.8. The Board form with controls.

Creating the Menu Bar

Create a pull-down menu system for the Board form using the Menu Design Window. To begin work on the menu, select Menu Design Window from the Window menu. Table 1.2 contains the elements needed to build the pull-down menu system.

Caption	Ctlname	Indentation	Index
&Games	GAMES	0	
2 X 2 (2 matches)	JOKE	1	
3 X 4 (6 matches)	GAME	1	1
4 X 4 (8 matches)	GAME	1	2
4 X 5 (10 matches)	GAME	1	3
4 X 6 (12 matches)	GAME	1	4
5 X 6 (15 matches)	GAME	1	5
6 X 6 (18 matches)	GAME	1	6
6 X 7 (21 matches)	GAME	1	7
6 X 8 (24 matches)	GAME	1	8
-	DASH1	1	
&Quit	QUIT	1	
&Information	INFORMATION	0	
&High scores	HISCORE	1	
-	DASH2	1	
&About	PROGINFO	1	

Table 1.2. Elements needed to build the pull-down menu system.

Figure 1.9 shows the Menu Design Window during menu creation.

Figure 1.10 is the Board form with all controls and the menu system.

Putting Code Behind the *Board* Form and Controls

Now that you've added all the necessary controls and the menu system to the Board form, you need to link everything with the powerful Visual Basic programming language.

Chapter 1: Memory Match

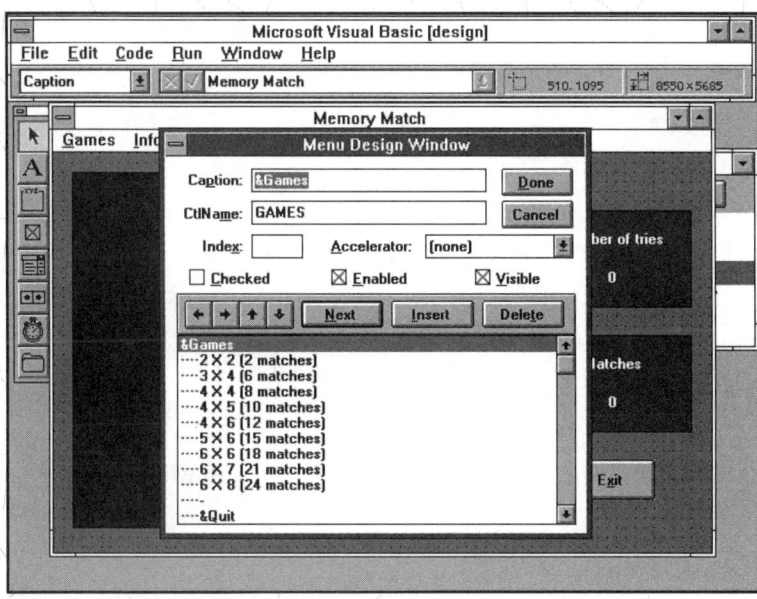

Figure 1.9. Designing the menus for Memory Match.

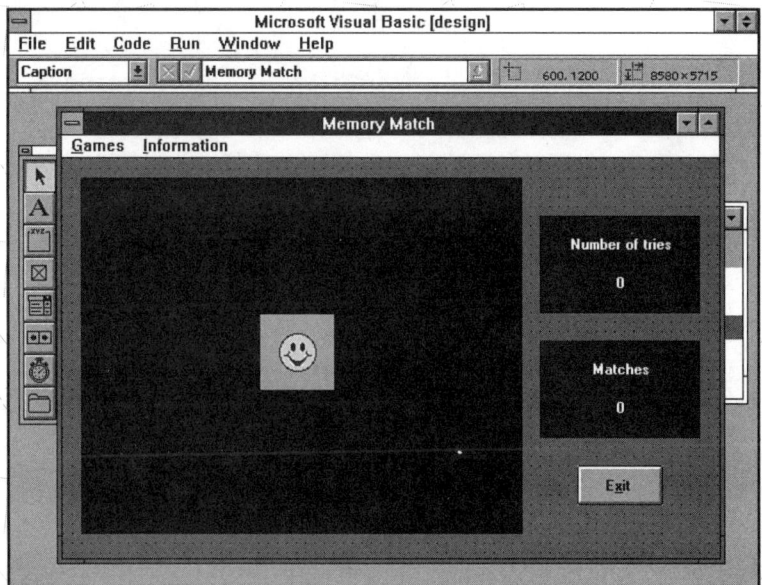

Figure 1.10. The completed main window for Memory Match.

Chapter 1: Memory Match

The following Sub program calls a procedure to randomly place the names of the flag icons into a string array:

```
Sub Form_Load ()
    Call SETUP
End Sub
```

To start a Sub, select New Procedure from the Code menu and choose the Sub option.

All of the icons (.ICO files) are installed as part of the VB setup procedure. The flag icons are in the VB\ICONS\FLAGS subdirectory. The smiling-face icon (FACE03.ICO) is in the VB\ICONS\MISC subdirectory. Copy these icons into your work directory. The following code loads the FLAG$ and CARD$ arrays and performs other miscellaneous initialization/setup operations:

```
Sub SETUP ()

    PICKED = 0

        CARDBACK$ = "FACE03.ICO"



        FLAG$(1)  = "FLGASTRL.ICO":   FLAG$(2)  = "FLGAUSTA.ICO"
        FLAG$(3)  = "FLGBRAZL.ICO":   FLAG$(4)  = "FLGCAN.ICO"
        FLAG$(5)  = "FLGDEN.ICO":     FLAG$(6)  = "FLGFIN.ICO"
        FLAG$(7)  = "FLGFRAN.ICO":    FLAG$(8)  = "FLGGERM.ICO"
        FLAG$(9)  = "FLGIREL.ICO":    FLAG$(10) = "FLGITALY.ICO"
        FLAG$(11) = "FLGJAPAN.ICO":   FLAG$(12) = "FLGMEX.ICO"
        FLAG$(13) = "FLGNETH.ICO":    FLAG$(14) = "FLGNORW.ICO"
        FLAG$(15) = "FLGNZ.ICO":      FLAG$(16) = "FLGPORT.ICO"
        FLAG$(17) = "FLGSPAIN.ICO":   FLAG$(18) = "FLGSWED.ICO"
        FLAG$(19) = "FLGSWITZ.ICO":   FLAG$(20) = "FLGTURK.ICO"
        FLAG$(21) = "FLGUK.ICO":      FLAG$(22) = "FLGUSA01.ICO"
        FLAG$(23) = "FLGUSA02.ICO":   FLAG$(24) = "FLGUSSR.ICO"

    Randomize Timer         'Random numbers will be produced using
                            'the number of seconds past midnight to
                            'seed the random number generator.

    MATCHES = 0             'Reset counters to zero.
    TRIES = 0

    For I = 1 To NUMFLAGS   'Reset CARD$ array to null.
        CARD$(I) = ""
```

Chapter 1: Memory Match

```
    Next

    For I = 1 To NUMFLAGS    'Randomly place icons
                             'into the CARD array
        OK = 0               'to create a different
        Do                   'game each time.
            NUM = Int(NUMFLAGS * Rnd(1) + 1)

            If CARD$(NUM) = "" Then
                X = Int(I * .5 + .5)
                CARD$(NUM) = FLAG$(X)
                OK = 1
            End If

        Loop Until OK

    Next

    NUMMATCH.CAPTION = "0 of" + Str$(NUMFLAGS / 2)

End Sub
```

You must unload the control array before starting a new game. Remember, one control-array object must remain to build new control arrays. The following routine takes care of this initialization and clears all but the first control array element:

```
Sub ICONRESET ()

    If NUMFLAGS Then

        NUMTRIES.CAPTION = "0"      'reset "Number of  tries" counter
        MEMORY(1).VISIBLE = FALS
        MEMORY(1).PICTURE = LoadPicture(ICONDIR$ + "FACE03.ICO")

        For I = 2 To NUMFLAGS       'Unload all control array items
                                    ' except item 1.
            Unload MEMORY(I)
        Next

    End If
```

The MEMORY_Click routine is triggered each time the user clicks a card. Notice that this subprogram has the Static command as part of the procedure definition. When Static is used in a procedure, all values of the variables contained within the subprogram *do not* get reset each time the procedure is called.

In this case, Static is used because you need to keep track of information such as the number of tries, the number of matches, and the currently selected card. If Static was omitted from the procedure, all of the string variables would be set to *null*, and all of the numeric variables would be set to *zero* each time the subprogram was called:

```
Static Sub MEMORY_Click (INDEX As Integer)

CR$ = Chr$(13) + Chr$(10)               'Carriage return + line feed.

If CARD$(INDEX) = "PICKED" Then         'Track cards that are picked.
    Beep
    Exit Sub
End If

If BUTTON1 And INDEX = BUTTON1 Then     'Beep if you click card
    Beep: Beep                          'that is already turned over.
    Exit Sub
End If

PICKED = PICKED + 1                     'Number picked counter.

If PICKED = 1 Then                      'Show flag icons.
    MEMORY(INDEX).PICTURE = LoadPicture(CARD$(INDEX))
    MATCH1$ = CARD$(INDEX)
    BUTTON1 = INDEX
Else
    MEMORY(INDEX).PICTURE = LoadPicture(CARD$(INDEX))
    MATCH2$ = CARD$(INDEX)
    BUTTON2 = INDEX
End If

If PICKED = 2 Then
    PICKED = 0

    TRIES = TRIES + 1                   'Number of tries counter.
    NUMTRIES.CAPTION = Str$(TRIES)

    If MATCH1$ <> MATCH2$ Then
       X = Timer                        'Turn cards back
       While X + 2 > Timer: Wend        'over if not
                                        'a match.
       MEMORY(BUTTON1).PICTURE = LoadPicture(CARDBACK$)
       MEMORY(BUTTON2).PICTURE = LoadPicture(CARDBACK$)
```

Chapter 1: Memory Match

```
            BUTTON1 = 0
            BUTTON2 = 0
        Else
            CARD$(BUTTON1) = "PICKED"       'Leave flags
            CARD$(BUTTON2) = "PICKED"       'showing if a
            MATCHES = MATCHES + 1           'match.

            NUMMATCH.CAPTION = Str$(MATCHES) + " of" + Str$(NUMFLAGS / 2)


    If MATCHES = NUMFLAGS / 2 Then          'Check for end of game.

        'Check if high score for this game was tied or beaten

Open "MMWINNER.FIL" For Random As #1 Len = Len(SCORE)

                    Get #1, GAMEBOARD, SCORE    'There are 8 records
                                                'in the MMWINNER.FIL.
                                                'Each record corresponds
                                                'to each of the 8 games.
                                                'When a game is started,
                                                'the game number is placed
                                                'in the variable GAMEBOARD.
                                                'This variable is used to
                                                'get the high score record
                                                'from the file.

        If SCORE.POINTS = 0 Or TRIES <= SCORE.POINTS Then
                    If TRIES = SCORE.POINTS Then
                            TEXT$ = "You have tied "
                    Else
                            TEXT$ = "You have beaten "
                    End If

        TEXT$ = TEXT$ + "the high score for this game..." + CR$
                ↪TEST$ = TEXT$ +
                "                        Congratulations !!!"
                    MsgBox TEXT$, 64, "New High Score"
                    SCORE.POINTS = TRIES
                    HSENTRY.Show 1
                    Put #1, GAMEBOARD, SCORE
                End If
        Close
```

continues

```
        End If
    End If

End If

End Sub


Sub JOKE_Click ()
    MsgBox "You must be joking.....", 48, "    2 X 2    "
End Sub
```

The GAME_Click procedure sets up the playing grid for the selected game:

```
Sub GAME_Click (INDEX As Integer)

    CR$ = Chr$(13) + Chr$(10)

    If TRIES > 0 And NUMFLAGS / 2 <> MATCHES Then
    ↳  EVAL = MsgBox("Do you want to abandon" + CR$ + _
           "the current game?", 32 + 4, "New game?")
    End If

    If EVAL = 7 Then Exit Sub

    PLAYFIELD.VISIBLE = 0
    Call ICONRESET

    TOPREF = MEMORY(1).TOP
    LEFTREF = MEMORY(1).LEFT

    GAMEBOARD = INDEX

    Select Case INDEX
        Case 1
            NUMFLAGS = 12       '3 X 4
            ROWS = 3
        Case 2
            NUMFLAGS = 16       '4 X 4
            ROWS = 4
        Case 3
            NUMFLAGS = 20       '4 X 5
            ROWS = 4
        Case 4
            NUMFLAGS = 24       '4 X 6
            ROWS = 4
```

Chapter 1: Memory Match

```
        Case 5
            NUMFLAGS = 30          '5 x 6
            ROWS = 5
        Case 6
            NUMFLAGS = 36          '6 X 6
            ROWS = 6
        Case 7
            NUMFLAGS = 42          '6 X 7
            ROWS = 6
        Case 8
            NUMFLAGS = 48          '6 X 8
            ROWS = 6
    End Select

    For I = 1 To NUMFLAGS          'Arrange playing grid.

        If I > ROWS And I Mod ROWS = 1 Then
            LEFTREF = LEFTREF + 600
            TOPREF = MEMORY(1).TOP
        End If

        If I <> 1 Then
            If I Mod ROWS <> 1 Then
                TOPREF = TOPREF + 600
            End If
            Load MEMORY(I)         'Add items to control array.
            MEMORY(I).TOP = TOPREF
            MEMORY(I).LEFT = LEFTREF
        End If

        MEMORY(I).VISIBLE = -1

    Next


    'Adjust the size of the grid background.

    PLAYFIELD.HEIGHT = MEMORY(NUMFLAGS).TOP +
        MEMORY(NUMFLAGS).HEIGHT + 240
    PLAYFIELD.WIDTH = MEMORY(NUMFLAGS).LEFT +
        MEMORY(NUMFLAGS).WIDTH + 240
```

continues

```
'Center the playing grid.

    PLAYFIELD.TOP = (PICTURE1.HEIGHT - PLAYFIELD.HEIGHT) / 2
    PLAYFIELD.LEFT = (PICTURE1.WIDTH - PLAYFIELD.WIDTH) / 2

    PLAYFIELD.VISIBLE = -1
    Call SETUP

End Sub
```

The *HSENTRY* Form

The HSENTRY form is used to capture the name of the person who has just tied or beaten a high score. Table 1.3 contains a chart of the controls needed to build the HSENTRY form.

Table 1.3. Controls needed to build the HSENTRY form.

Form/Control	Property	Setting
Form:	BackColor	&H00808080&
	Caption	New High Score
	FormName	HSENTRY
Picture:	BackColor	&H00808000&
	CtlName	Picture1
Label:	BackColor	&H00808080&
	Caption	Enter your name:
	CtlName	LABEL1
Text:	CtlName	WINNERNAME
Command:	Caption	&OK
	CtlName	COMMAND1

The following is a list of steps used to create the HSENTRY form:

1. From the File menu, select New Form.

2. Place a large rectangular picture control (PICTURE1) in the center of the form.

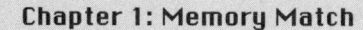

3. Draw a label control (LABEL1) and a text control (WINNERNAME) on PICTURE1.

4. Place a command button on the form. Figure 1.11 shows the completed HSENTRY form.

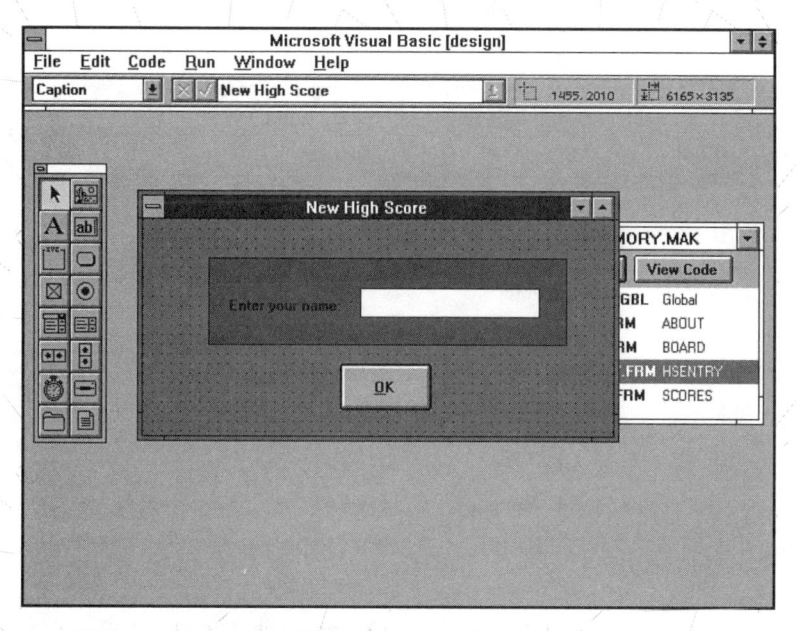

Figure 1.11. The completed HSENTRY form.

Putting Code Behind the *HSENTRY* Form

The following is the only code needed for the HSENTRY form:

```
Sub Command1_Click ()
    SCORE.WINNER = " " + WINNERNAME.TEXT
    SCORE.DMY = " " + Date$
    Unload HSENTRY
End Sub
```

It is important that HSENTRY is called as a *modal* form. Modal forms do not allow continued processing of the program until it is closed. In this case, the result of closing this form provides the name of the new winner.

If HSENTRY were opened as a modeless form, processing would continue after the form was opened. As a result, a blank entry would be created each time because the program would not wait for a name to be entered.

The *High Scores* Form

The High Scores form is used to display a list of those who have the current high score for each of the eight games contained in Memory Match. Each row displays the game grid size, winner name, high score, and date. Table 1.4 is a chart of the controls needed to build the High Scores form.

Table 1.4. Controls needed to build the High Scores form.

Form/Control	Property	Setting	Index
Form:	BackColor	&H00808080&	
	Caption	High Scores	
	FormName	SCORES	
Picture:	BackColor	&H00808000&	
	CtlName	SHOWSCORES	
Label:	CtlName	GAME	1
Label:	CtlName	WINNER	1
Label:	CtlName	POINTS	1
Label:	CtlName	DMY	1
Text:	CtlName	WINNERNAME	
Command:	Caption	&Reset High Scores	
	CtlName	COMMAND1	
Command:	Caption	&OK	
	CtlName	COMMAND2	

The following steps describe how to create the High Scores form:

1. From the File menu, select New Form.

2. Place a large, square picture control (SHOWSCORES) in the center of the form.

3. Draw four separate label controls (GAME, WINNER, POINTS, and DMY) in a row across the top of SHOWSCORES.

4. Draw two command buttons (COMMMAND1 and COMMAND2) along the bottom of SHOWSCORES. Figure 1.12 shows the completed High Scores form.

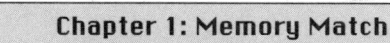

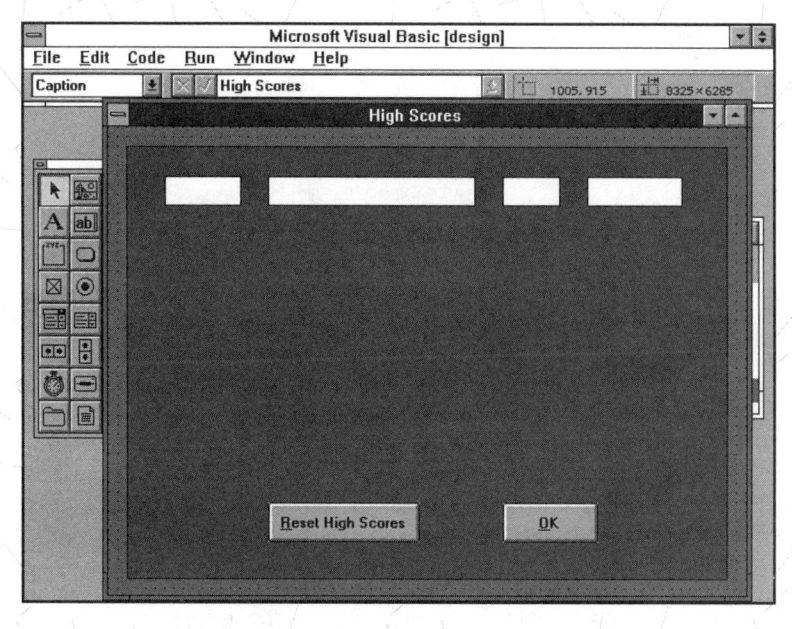

Figure 1.12. The High Scores form shows top scores for each game.

Putting Code Behind the *High Scores* Form

The High Scores form serves two purposes: to display the current high scores and to reset the high scores. You dynamically create four control arrays to hold high score information.

The Form_Load routine, which is in the SCORES.FRM form, calls the DISPLAYSCORES procedure to process the high score information:

```
Sub Form_Load ()
    Call DISPLAYSCORES(TRU)
End Sub
```

The following is the DISPLAYSCORES routine, which creates four control arrays and shows the high scores list:

```
Sub DISPLAYSCORES (NEEDTOLOAD As Integer)

    ReDim CATEGORY$(8)
        CATEGORY$(1) = "3 X 4"
        CATEGORY$(2) = "4 X 4"
        CATEGORY$(3) = "4 X 5"
```

continues

```
CATEGORY$(4) = "4 X 6"
CATEGORY$(5) = "5 X 6"
CATEGORY$(6) = "6 X 6"
CATEGORY$(7) = "6 X 7"
CATEGORY$(8) = "6 X 8"

Open "MMWINNER.FIL" For Random As #1 Len = Len(SCORE)  'open high
                                                       'scores file



For I = 2 To 8                              'Dynamically create four
        If NEEDTOLOAD = TRU Then Load GAME(I)  'control arrays.
        GAME(I).TOP = GAME(I - 1).TOP + 480
        GAME(I).VISIBLE = -1
'Notice that the placement of each item in the control array on the
'form is relative to the previous control in the array. We are using
'480 as spacing between controls.

        If NEEDTOLOAD = TRU Then Load WINNER(I)
        WINNER(I).TOP = WINNER(I - 1).TOP + 480
        WINNER(I).VISIBLE = -1

        If NEEDTOLOAD = TRU Then Load POINTS(I)
        POINTS(I).TOP = POINTS(I - 1).TOP + 480
        POINTS(I).VISIBLE = -1

        If NEEDTOLOAD = TRU Then Load DMY(I)
        DMY(I).TOP = DMY(I - 1).TOP + 480
        DMY(I).VISIBLE = -1
    Next
```

After the control arrays are created and placed on the form, the following For/Next loop is used to read in each of the eight high score records and display them:

```
For I = 1 To 8
        Get #1, I, SCORE
        GAME(I).CAPTION = CATEGORY$(I)
        WINNER(I).CAPTION = SCORE.WINNER
        POINTS(I).CAPTION = Str$(SCORE.POINTS)
        DMY(I).CAPTION = SCORE.DMY
    Next
Close

End Sub
```

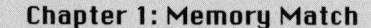

The following section of code shows how to reset the high scores:

```
Sub Command1_Click ()
    CR$ = Chr$(13) + Chr$(10)
```

Do not reset the high scores unless the user confirms the action. The MsgBox function is used here to trap the answer:

```
RESULT = MsgBox("This will erase all of the high scores..." + CR$ +
    Space$(20) + "Are you sure...", 64 + 4 + 256, "Reset High Scores")

    If RESULT <> 6 Then Exit Sub 'The MsgBox function will produce a
                        'return code of 6 if YES was the chosen answer.
                        'If YES was not chosen, the high scores table
                        'will remain unchanged and this sub program
                        'will be exited.
```

If the user chooses YES, a simple For/Next loop is used to fill each of the eight records in the high scores file with null values. After the high scores are cleared, the following block of code calls the DISPLAYSCORES subprogram to show the reset list:

```
Open "MMWINNER.FIL" For Random As #1 Len = Len(SCORE)
        For I = 1 To 8
            SCORE.WINNER = ""
            SCORE.POINTS = 0
            SCORE.DMY = ""
            Put #1, I, SCORE
        Next
    Close
    Call DISPLAYSCORES(FALS)
End Sub
Sub Command2_Click ()
    Unload Scores           'close high scores form
End Sub
```

The *About* Form

Table 1.5 is a list of controls needed to create the last form for Memory Match, the About form.

Table 1.5. Controls needed to create the About form.

Form/Control	Property	Setting
Form:	BackColor	&H00808000&
	Caption	About
	FormName	ABOUT
Picture:	BackColor	&H00C0C0C0&
	CtlName	Picture1
Label:	BackColor	&H00C0C0C0&
	Caption	MEMORY MATCH
	CtlName	LABEL1
	FontItalic	True
	FontSize	13.5
Label:	BackColor	&H00C0C0C0&
	Caption	written by Captain Lou
	CtlName	LABEL2
Command:	Caption	&OK
	CtlName	COMMAND1
List:	CtlName	List1
(optional) Picture:	CtlName	PICTURE2
	Picture	LJM.ICO
(optional) Picture:	CtlName	PICTURE3
	Picture	LJM.ICO

The following steps describe how to create the About form:

1. From the File menu, select New Form.

2. Center a rectangular picture control (PICTURE1) at the top of the form.

3. Draw two label controls (LABEL1 and LABEL2) on PICTURE1.

4. Place a large, square list control just under PICTURE1.

5. Place a command button on the form.

6. Optionally, you can add a custom icon on both sides of PICTURE1. Figure 1.13 shows the completed About form.

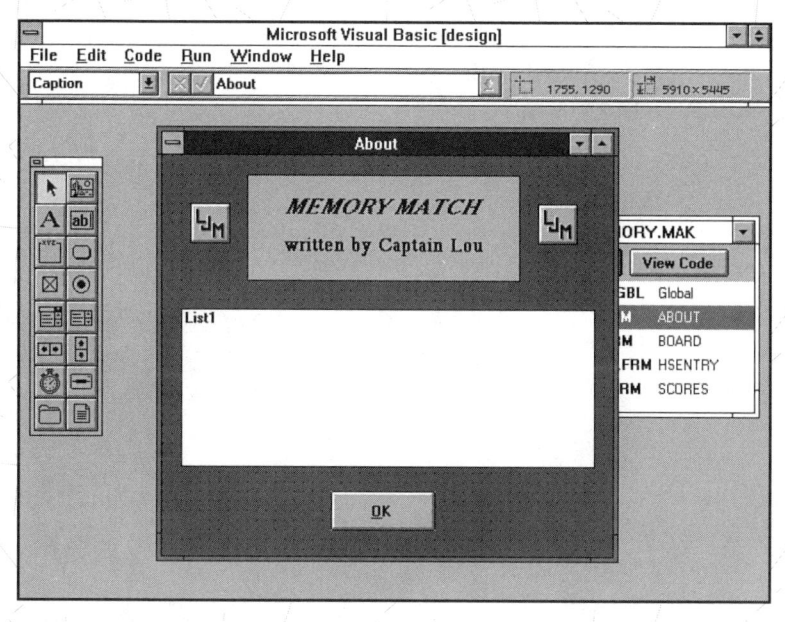

Figure 1.13. The About form.

Putting Code Behind the *About* Form

The About form displays a scrolling text area in the center of the window. The text is placed in the list control using the AddItem method. Any text file can be used as the source file; in this case MMREADME.TXT is used.

```
Sub Form_Load ()
    Open "MMREADME.TXT" For Input As #1
        Do While Not EOF(1)
            Line Input #1, ITEM$
            LIST1.AddItem " " + ITEM$
        Loop
    Close
End Sub
Sub Command1_Click ()
    Unload ABOUT              'close the ABOUT form
End Sub
```

Now that you have a basic understanding of how the Memory Match program works, you should experiment with it on your own. Set breakpoints at some of the locations that you may not fully understand and see how they are invoked, what the values of certain variables are at that point, and so on. You may also want to experiment with extending the code. What about adding even more game grids (8 × 8, 10 × 10, and so on)?

Remember, our goal in publishing *Fun Programming with Visual Basic* is to offer you interesting programs to study for your own use as well as extend or customize for other uses. Be sure to take advantage of the code and techniques presented in this and subsequent chapters when building your own applications.

VBMem

by Charles Snider

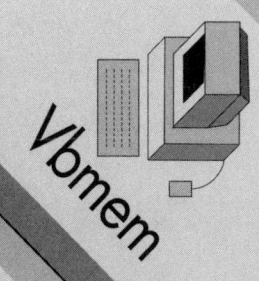

2

Overview

VBMem is a simple Visual Basic utility that displays memory usage in real time; the display changes as the system's memory usage does. VBMem is compatible with Windows 3.1 and later.

When run as a window, VBMem displays the following system information: the Windows operating mode (standard or enhanced), free resources (as a percentage), and free memory (in kilobytes). (See Figure 2.1.) When run as an icon, the program's icon caption displays free memory. Whether you run it windowed or iconized, VBMem displays your system's memory in "real time;" as your system changes, so does VBMem's display—without an annoying flicker!

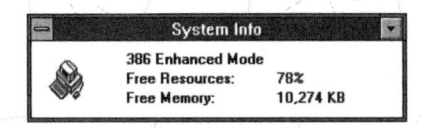

Figure 2.1. The VBMem window.

Many of the About dialog boxes in Windows 3.1 also contain the information VBMem displays; by using VBMem, however, you don't have to go through a menu selection to see the amount of free resources. Send any comments to the author, Charles Snider, CIS 73730,1315.

Program Operation

The VBMEM.FRM contains the following objects (see Figure 2.2):

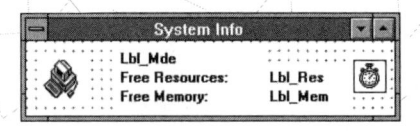

Figure 2.2. The VBMEM.FRM form.

Chapter 2: VBMem

Form   VBMEM.FRM

All settings are default except the following:

> Caption: System Info
>
> FormName: SysInfo
>
> Icon: VBMEM.ICO
>
> MaxButton: False

Label   Label2

All settings are default except the following:

> Caption: Free Resources:

Label   Label3

All settings are default except the following:

> Caption: Free Memory:

Label   Lbl_Mde

Label   Lbl_Res

Label   Lbl_Mem

All settings are default.

Timer   Tmr_Mem

All settings are default except the following:

> Interval: 2000

Picture Box   Pic_Pc

All settings are default except the following:

> Picture: VBMEM.ICO

The VBMEM.FRM Code

VBMem uses three Windows API functions to call information from the system. GetFreeSpace provides the amount of free memory. The GetFreeSystemResources function was added to Windows 3.1, and it provides free system resource information as a combination of the USER and GDI kernels. Finally, GetWinFlags provides Windows configuration information, including the operating mode.

The general declarations section first sets the default data type to integer with the DefInt A-Z statement. This statement is necessary for "good" API calling. You then declare each of the three API functions. The flag checked from GetWinFlags for operating mode is declared as a constant. Finally, two strings store free memory and free resources throughout the program: FreMem and FreRes.

The Form Load Routine (*Form_Load*)

First, you must declare the variables used in the Form_Load procedure. WinFlags is a long integer and must be declared as such. Mode is a string that is used to display Windows' operating mode.

The Move statement then centers the form on the screen. WinFlags retrieves information from the system when it is set equal to GetWinFlags(). The If statement then compares WinFlags with the constant for enhanced mode, WF_ENHANCED. If the result of this comparison is true, Mode is set to 386 Enhanced Mode. If the result is false, Mode is set equal to Standard Mode.

The final section displays the information on the form. You set Label1.Caption equal to Mode. You then obtain free resources by calling GetFreeSystemResources. The return value of GetFreeSystemResources is then converted to a string, formatted to a percent value, and put in Lbl_FreRes.Caption. Similarly, GetFreeSpace returns the amount of free memory. This return value is also converted to a string and formatted before being put into Lbl_FreMem.Caption.

The Timer Event Routine (*Tmr_Mem*)

You use the timer to check the system's free memory and resources periodically to see if either has changed. The interval of two seconds was set at design time. Thus, every two seconds the timer executes the first two statements, calling the two API functions to update FreMem and FreRes with free memory and system resources, respectively.

The If statement then checks to see if the form is minimized (run as an icon) by examining the value of SysInfo.WindowState (SysInfo.WindowState = 1). If the form is minimized, FreMem is obtained again and compared to the current caption of the form. Only if the values differ (FreMem <> SysInfo.Caption) will the caption change, thus reducing any flicker in the display. Note that GetFreeSpace is formatted with KB Free for display as the icon caption.

If the WindowState is not equal to 1, the program is being run as a window and must update both free memory and resources. Again, the newly obtained values are compared to the values in their captions, Lbl_Mem.Caption and Lbl_Res.Caption. The caption changes only if they differ.

The Picture Box Event (*Pic_Pc_Click*)

This procedure displays the "About" information contained in the string Msg$ to a message box when the user clicks the picture box. The string Chr$(13) + Chr$(10) sets a line break. The MsgBox statement contains three arguments:

> Message (Msg$)
>
> The information icon (64)
>
> title$ ("VBMEM v3.1a")

The icon in the picture box was loaded when the control was drawn.

The Form Resize Event (*Form_Resize*)

This procedure changes the form's caption as the program changes from being minimized to being a window (or vice versa). The code is the same as it is in the timer event, except that if the program is not iconized, the form caption is set to System Info.

Source Code for VBMem

The remainder of this chapter lists all the code used to build the VBMem application. You will notice that this program is fairly short. In fact, the listing is just over 50 lines, including many comments. VBMem shows how powerful Visual Basic is and how you can build very useful Windows applications with a fairly small amount of code.

Chapter 2: VBMem

```
' VBMEM v3.1a by Charles K. Snider 7/92
' Send all comments to CompuServe 73730,1315

DefInt A-Z
Declare Function GetFreeSpace Lib "Kernel" (ByVal wFlags) As Long
Declare Function GetFreeSystemResources% Lib "User" (ByVal wType%)
Declare Function GetWinFlags Lib "Kernel" () As Long
Const WF_ENHANCED = &H20
Dim FreMem As String
Dim FreRes As String

Sub Form_Load ()
    Dim WinFlags As Long
    Dim Mode As String
    ' Center window.
    Move (Screen.Width - Width) \ 2, (Screen.Height - Height) \ 2
    ' Get current Windows configuration.
    WinFlags = GetWinFlags()
    If WinFlags And WF_ENHANCED Then
        Mode = "386 Enhanced Mode"
    Else
        Mode = "Standard Mode"
    End If
    ' Get info for initial and display it.
    Lbl_Mde.Caption = Mode
    Lbl_Res.Caption = Format$(GetFreeSystemResources%(0) / 100, "00%")
    Lbl_Mem.Caption = Format$(GetFreeSpace(0) \ 1024, "##,#00") + " KB"
End Sub

Sub Tmr_Mem_Timer ()
    ' Get free memory and resources.
    FreMem = Format$(GetFreeSpace(0) \ 1024, "##,#00") + " KB"
    FreRes = Format$(GetFreeSystemResources%(0) / 100, "00%")
    ' Check if the application is minimized.
    ' If so, display free memory in caption.
    ' Display changes only if memory changes.
    If SysInfo.Windowstate = 1 Then
        FreMem = Format$(GetFreeSpace(0) \ 1024, "##,#00") + " KB Free"
        If FreMem <> SysInfo.Caption Then SysInfo.Caption = FreMem
    Else
        SysInfo.Caption = "System Info"
        If FreRes <> Lbl_Res.Caption Then Lbl_Res.Caption = FreRes
        If FreMem <> Lbl_Mem.Caption Then Lbl_Mem.Caption = FreMem
    End If
End Sub
```

continues

```
Sub Pic_Pc_Click ()
    ' Display About box
    Msg$ = "by Charles Snider" + Chr$(13) + Chr$(10) + _
        "Compuserv 73730,1315"
    MsgBox Msg$, 64, "VBMEM v3.1a"
End Sub

Sub Form_Resize ()
    ' Initial check if the application is minimized.
    ' If so, display free memory in caption.
    If SysInfo.Windowstate = 1 Then
        FreMem = Format$(GetFreeSpace(0) \ 1024, "##,#00") + " KB Free"
        If FreMem <> SysInfo.Caption Then SysInfo.Caption = FreMem
    Else
        SysInfo.Caption = "System Info"
    End If
End Sub
```

FontView

by Charles Snider

Chapter 3: FontView

Overview

FontView is a useful Visual Basic utility that enables you to view and print the fonts installed on your system. It is fully compatible with Windows 3.x and all Windows fonts, including TrueType and Adobe Type 1.

The Windows graphical environment is a natural for fonts. However, remembering what each font looks like, let alone what it prints like, requires as much memory as Windows. Also, the Fonts section of the Control Panel does not enable you to view third-party fonts. This is where FontView steps in. Instead of engaging in the time-consuming process of changing fonts in a document to see what it looks like, simply use FontView to view each font. You can also use FontView to print a list of your fonts for easy reference. The program was designed with simplicity in mind.

After you select FontView to run, an hourglass appears on the screen while the program loads all available fonts to memory. Depending on how many fonts you have installed, this may take anywhere from a few seconds to a few minutes. Remember, TrueType fonts must be loaded into memory; Type 1 fonts are usually stored in a cache somewhere in memory. After the fonts have loaded, the screen appears with a list box containing the fonts on your system (see Figure 3.1).

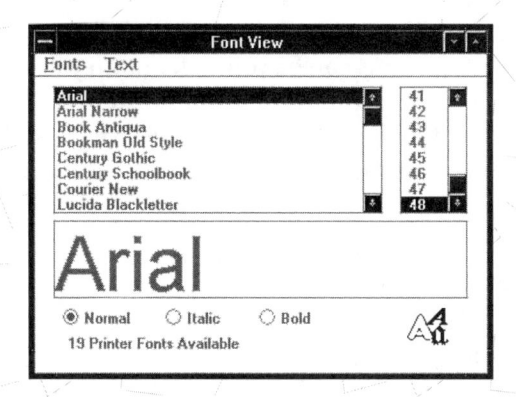

Figure 3.1. FontView lists the installed fonts.

To select a font to view, scroll through the list box that contains the names of the fonts until you reach the one you want. Click the desired font. The picture box near the bottom of the window then displays that font.

To change the point size of the selected font, scroll through the list box on the right that contains the font sizes, and then click the desired value. The maximum value of the font size is 48. To change the displayed font's characteristics, click one of the option buttons below the picture box: Normal (the default), Bold, or Italic. The quantity and type of fonts available (printer versus screen) appear at the bottom of the window. To view the About information, click the icon at the bottom-right corner of the window.

The menu bar contains a few extra options. Under the Fonts menu, you can choose to view either Printer Fonts or Screen Fonts (as explained later in this section). You can also choose to print a sample of each font. After you select this option, the hourglass cursor appears. Again, depending on the number of fonts loaded on your system, printing may take anywhere from several seconds to a few minutes. Under the Text menu, you can choose to enter a user-defined text sample rather than the default text, which is the font's name.

> FontView assumes you have a printer (as well as printer fonts) installed with Windows. It will not run if you do not have a printer installed with Windows.

By default, FontView loads the printer fonts that are on your system. Printer fonts are for printing; screen fonts can be printed, but they don't always look as they appear on-screen. One example is the Windows Terminal font. This screen font, or *raster* font, does not have a "printable" version. Therefore, it prints in the same style as the previously printed font. Because of this convention, FontView prints only printer fonts.

One note for Windows 3.1 users: the fonts that FontView displays are controlled by the TrueType option in the Fonts section of Windows Control Panel. If you select Show Only TrueType Fonts in Applications, FontView shows only TrueType fonts. Similarly, if you have not enabled TrueType fonts in the Control Panel, FontView does not show TrueType fonts.

That's it! FontView gives you a simple and quick way to view and print the fonts installed on your system. Send all comments to the author, Charles Snider, CIS 73730,1315.

Program Operation

FontView is written in 100 percent Visual Basic; there are no Windows API calls or links to DLLs. To help yourself understand the program's code, you should be familiar with the following items in the Visual Basic Language Reference Guide:

- Font properties
- List boxes
- List properties
- Print methods
- Printer objects

The program basically retrieves fonts from the `Printer` object and puts them in a list box. The list box serves as a control array, with each font having a unique index value. That value is passed to either the picture box or printer. It sets that object's font property and is printed to either the screen or the printer. The other objects (option buttons, menu items, and so on) simply modify the font properties or pass values to the item doing the printing. With that understanding, you will find that FontView is not only simple to use, but also easy to program.

Putting the Parts Together: Form and Menu Design

Figure 3.2 shows the design of the main FontView screen.

Figure 3.2. The FontView form.

The main FontView screen consists of the following objects and property values:

Form   FONTVIEW.FRM

All settings are default except the following:

> AutoRedraw: False
>
> BorderStyle: 2 - Sizable
>
> Caption: FontView
>
> FormName: FontView
>
> Height: 4425
>
> Icon: Fontview.ico
>
> MaxButton: False
>
> Width: 5940

List Box   Lst_Face

All settings are default except the following:

> Height: 1590
>
> Sorted: True
>
> Width: 4215

List Box   Lst_Size

All settings are default except the following:

> Height: 1590
>
> Sorted: True
>
> Width: 855

Chapter 3: FontView

Picture Box `Pict_Font`

All settings are default except the following:

>   `AutoRedraw: False`
>
>   `Height: 975`
>
>   `Width: 5295`

Option Button `Opt_Norm`

All settings are default except the following:

>   `Caption: Normal`

Option Button `Opt_Ital`

All settings are default except the following:

>   `Caption: Italic`

Option Button `Opt_Bold`

All settings are default except the following:

>   `Caption: Italic`

Label `Label1`

All settings are default except the following:

>   `Caption: (None)`

Picture Box `Picture1`

All settings are default except the following:

>   `Picture: Fontview.ico`

The menu design window contains the following items (as shown in Figure 3.3):

Fonts Menu:

All settings are default.

>Caption: &Fonts
>Control Name: M_Font
>
>Caption: Prin&ter Fonts
>Control Name: M_PFont
>
>Caption: &Screen Fonts
>Control Name: M_SFont
>
>Caption: -
>Control Name: M_Sep1
>
>Caption: &Print List
>Control Name: M_PrtLst
>
>Caption: -
>Control Name: M_Sep2
>
>Caption: E&xit
>Control Name: M_Exit

Text Menu:

All settings are default.

>Caption: &Text
>Control Name: M_Text
>
>Caption: &Default Text
>Control Name: M_DText
>
>Caption: User &Sample
>Control Name: M_SText

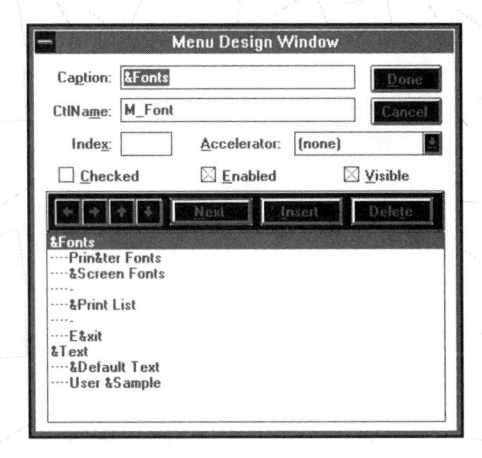

Figure 3.3. The menu design window.

Inspecting the FontView Form Code

The following variables are used throughout the program and must be declared as follows: FaceName and Sample are strings, whereas FaceSize and FaceCount are integers.

The Form Load Routine (*Form_Load*)

This procedure performs the initial loading of the form. The cursor is changed to an hourglass by setting Screen.MousePointer to 11. This informs the user that the program is being loaded. The Move statement centers the form on-screen.

The next section adds the printer fonts to the list box Lst_Face. The program uses the Visual Basic Printer object, which provides access to the system's printer properties. Alternatively, you use the Screen object later to access screen fonts. The printer fonts are retrieved using two nested For loops to remove any duplicate fonts from the list box.

More closely, variable I% is set equal to the Printer.FontCount. The variable x% is set equal to the list box Lst_Face.ListCount. As the first loop (I%) retrieves the next installed printer font, the second loop (x%) checks to see if it is already in the Lst_Face list. A duplicate flag is set to 1 if the condition is true. If the duplicate flag is not equal to 1, the list box AddItem method adds Printer.Fonts(I%) to the list box Lst_Face. The duplicate flag is then set to 0 before the next Printer.FontCount item is retrieved.

The first item is selected in the list box Lst_Face by setting ListIndex to 0. Add the range "6 to 48" of font sizes to the list box Lst_Size by using a For statement. Step 1 indicates that you add every consecutive number. These values are added using the AddItem method. They are also converted to a string using Str$(J%). The list box can contain only string values. You later convert these to integers. The initial font size is set to 42, the last ListIndex in the list box (48 minus 6). Normal font characteristics are set by giving option button Opt_Norm a –1 (TRUE) value.

The total amount of fonts available, FaceCount, is equal to the ListCount of Lst_Face. Label1.Caption is then set to the string Str$(FaceCount) and a description is added. The menu items for printer fonts—M_PFont—and default text—M_DText—are given their default values by setting their Checked properties to –1 (TRUE). Finally, you set the cursor value to 0 to return it to its default value.

The Form Resize and Paint Routines (*Form_Resize* and *Form_Paint*)

The Form_Resize routine calls DisplayFace to repaint the picture box when the form is resized. Alternatively, Form_Paint calls DisplayFace to repaint the picture box after the form is covered by another window.

The Size List Box Routine (*Lst_Size_Click*)

This procedure changes the variable FaceSize$ to the index value of Lst_Size.List selected in the list box. It then calls DisplayFace to change the font size in the picture box to the selected font size. Note that the list box item is a string, and you must convert it to an integer using the Val() function.

The Font List Box Routine (*Lst_Face_Click*)

This procedure changes the variable FaceName$ to the index value of Lst_Face.List selected in the list box. It then calls DisplayFace to display the font in the picture box using the selected font type.

The Italic Option Routine (*Opt_Ital_Click*)

This procedure sets the font attribute of Pict_Font to italic by setting the property of FontBold to 0 (FALSE) and FontItalic to –1 (TRUE). It then calls DisplayFace to change the font in the picture box Pict_Font to display as italic.

The Bold Option Routine (*Opt_Bold_Click*)

This procedure sets the font attribute of Pict_Font to bold by setting the property of FontBold to –1 (TRUE) and FontItalic to 0 (FALSE). It then calls the DisplayFace to change the font in the picture box Pict_Font to display as bold.

The Normal Option Routine (*Opt_Norm_Click*)

This procedure sets the font attribute of Pict_Font to normal by setting the property of FontBold and FontItalic to 0 (FALSE). The normal property is obtained when both of these properties are false. The procedure then calls DisplayFace to change the font in the picture box Pict_Font to display as normal.

The *DisplayFace* Routine

This procedure is contained in the General Declarations part of the form. You create it by choosing New Procedure from the Code menu and entering the name DisplayFace. The procedure changes the Pict_Font picture box's font properties and draws the text to the screen. The FontName must be selected before you can set any of its characteristics (such as bold, italic, or point size).

The Pict_Font.FontName property is set equal to the value of the string FaceName$ from the list box Lst_Face. Both Pict_Font.FontBold and Pict_Font.FontItalic get their values from one of the three option buttons: Opt_Ital, Opt_Bold, or Opt_Norm. The Pict_Font.FontSize property is set equal to the value of the integer FaceSize from the list box Lst_Size.

After the variables are set, the picture box is cleared using the Cls method. The text is selected by comparing the values of the text menu items; either default text or sample text is drawn depending on a –1 (TRUE) return value. The text is then drawn to the picture box by the Pict_Font.Print method.

The Picture Box Routine (*Picture1_Click*)

This procedure displays the About information contained in the string Msg$ to a message box when the picture box is clicked. The string Chr$(13) + Chr$(10) sets a line break. The MsgBox statement contains three arguments:

> Message (Msg$)
>
> The information icon (64)
>
> title$ ("FontView v3.0")

The icon in the picture box was loaded when you drew the control.

The Default Text Routine (*M_DText_Click*)

This procedure sets the text of the picture box `Pict_Font` to the default value. The default is set by having the value of the default text menu item `M_DText.Checked` property set to –1 (TRUE) and the value of the sample text menu item `M_SText.Checked` property set to 0 (FALSE). These values are then used by `DisplayFace`, where the text is selected and subsequently drawn.

The Exit Routine (*M_Exit_Click*)

This procedure terminates the program by calling the `End` statement.

The Sample Text Routine (*MSText_Click*)

This procedure sets the text of the picture box `Pict_Font` to a user-defined sample. The text is set by having the value of the default text menu item `M_DText.Checked` property set to 0 (FALSE) and the value of the sample text menu item `M_SText.Checked` property set to –1 (TRUE). The user's text is retrieved via an input box. The string `Sample$` is set equal to the return value of the input box. If the input box returns a null string (" "), the menu values are set back to the default sample. These values are then used by `DisplayFace` where the text is selected and subsequently drawn.

The Printer Output Routine (*M_PrtLst_Click*)

This procedure sends the list of fonts to the printer. It first sets an error trap using the `On Error Resume Next` statement. Then it checks to see if the screen fonts are loaded into the list box by checking the value of `M_Sfont`. If the value is –1 (TRUE), a message box is displayed indicating that screen fonts cannot be printed. You then use an `Exit Sub` statement to back out of the routine. If the value of `M_Sfont` is 0 (FALSE), printer fonts are loaded in the list box and printing can continue.

The next step changes the mouse cursor to the hourglass. A header is defined via the `Header$` string and sent to the printer with the `Printer.Print` statement, along with a blank line using the `Chr$(13) + Chr$(10)` string. The value of `M_SText.Checked` is examined to determine the setting of the variable `Sample$`. If `M_SText.Checked` is –1 (TRUE), the sample text is printed; if it is 0 (FALSE), the value of `Sample$` is set to null. A `For` loop retrieves each font from the list box `Lst_Face`. The property `Printer.FontName` controls the type of font to be printed.

It is set equal to each item from the list box (K%). The remaining Printer statements set the font attributes to normal (Printer.FontBold = 0 and Printer.FontItalic = 0) and the font size (Printer.FontSize = 14). The next font is then printed with the next value of the list box (K%).

After the For statement is complete, the printer font is returned to its default value. The number of fonts is printed by obtaining the value of the ListCount. The Printer.EndDoc statement ends the call to the printer, and the cursor is set back to its default (0).

The Screen Load Routine (*M_SFont_Click*)

This procedure selects the screen fonts and adds them to the list box Lst_Face. It first looks at the checked property of the screen fonts menu item M_SFonts to see if the screen fonts are currently loaded. If a −1 (TRUE) value is returned, the routine is exited. If printer fonts are loaded, the routine continues.

The menu item for printer fonts M_PFonts.Checked value is set to 0 (FALSE) and the menu item for screen fonts M_SFonts.Checked value is set to −1 (TRUE). The cursor is then set to an hourglass (11). The previous contents of the list box are removed using the RemoveItem method. A Do loop starts with the number Lst_Face.ListCount and continues until it reaches 0.

The rest of the procedure adds the screen fonts to the list box using the same method in the Form_Load procedure. This is accomplished by replacing the Printer object with the Screen object. After the fonts are loaded, the Lst_Face.Index is set to the first item (0) and the cursor is returned to its default (0). Note that by selecting the first item in the list box, the picture box Pict_Face changes automatically. Then the variable FaceCount is set to the number of fonts in the list. Finally, Label1.Caption is updated, converting the integer FaceCount to a string.

The Printer Load Routine (*M_PFont_Click*)

This procedure performs the same function as M_SFont_Click, except that it loads printer fonts into the list box Lst_Face.

Source Code for *FontView*

The remainder of this chapter lists the Visual Basic source code for the FontView program. The GLOBAL.BAS module is empty because there is no need to declare global variables, types, or constants. All the code for FontView is contained in one form, FONTVIEW.FRM.

```
GLOBAL.BAS Module  - none

FONTVIEW.FRM Form  - below

' FontView v3.0 by Charles K. Snider 04/92
' Send all comments to: CompuServe 73730,1315

' Declare variables.
Dim FaceName As String
Dim Sample As String
Dim FaceSize As Integer
Dim FaceCount As Integer

Sub Form_Load ()
    On Error Resume Next
    Screen.MousePointer = 11
    ' Center on-screen.
    Move (Screen.Width - Width) \ 2, (Screen.Height - Height) \ 2
    ' Get list of printer fonts and add to list box.
    For I% = 0 To Printer.FontCount - 1
        For x% = 0 To Lst_Face.ListCount - 1
            If Printer.Fonts(I%) = Lst_Face.List(x%) Then
                Duplicate = 1
            End If
        Next x%
    If Duplicate <> 1 Then Lst_Face.AddItem Printer.Fonts(I%)
    Duplicate = 0
    Next I%
    ' Select first item in list box.
    Lst_Face.ListIndex = 0
    ' Add list of font sizes to list box.
    For J% = 6 To 48 Step 1
        Lst_Size.AddItem Str$(J%)
    Next J%
    ' Select initial font size in list box.
    Lst_Size.ListIndex = 42
    ' Select normal font characteristic (TRUE).
    Opt_Norm.Value = -1
```

Chapter 3: FontView

```vb
    ' Get total amount of fonts and display in label.
    FaceCount = Lst_Face.ListCount
    Label1.Caption = Str$(FaceCount) + " Printer Fonts Available"
    ' Check menu option.
    M_PFont.Checked = -1
    M_DText.Checked = -1
    Screen.MousePointer = 0
End Sub

Sub Form_Resize ()
    ' Repaint picture when form is resized.
    DisplayFace
End Sub

Sub Form_Paint ()
    ' Repaint picture box after covered by another window.
    DisplayFace
End Sub

Sub Lst_Size_Click ()
    ' Set variable to item chosen in list box.
    FaceSize = Val(Lst_Size.List(Lst_Size.ListIndex))
    ' Display it.
    DisplayFace
End Sub

Sub Lst_Face_Click ()
    ' Set variable to item chosen in list box.
    FaceName$ = Lst_Face.List(Lst_Face.ListIndex)
    ' Display it.
    DisplayFace
End Sub

Sub Opt_Ital_Click ()
    ' Set font attribute to italic (TRUE) and turn bold off (FALSE).
    Pict_Font.FontBold = 0
    Pict_Font.FontItalic = -1
    ' Display it.
    DisplayFace
End Sub

Sub Opt_Bold_Click ()
    ' Set font attribute to Bold (TRUE) and turn Italic off (FALSE).
    Pict_Font.FontBold = -1
    Pict_Font.FontItalic = 0
    ' Display it.
```

continues

```
        DisplayFace
End Sub

Sub Opt_Norm_Click ()
  ' Set font attribute to Normal by setting Bold and Italic to FALSE(0)
    Pict_Font.FontBold = 0
    Pict_Font.FontItalic = 0
    ' Display it.
    DisplayFace
End Sub

Sub DisplayFace ()
    ' To display selected font.
    On Error Resume Next
    ' Get font, option, and size.
    Pict_Font.FontName = FaceName$
    Pict_Font.FontBold = Opt_Bold.Value
    Pict_Font.FontItalic = Opt_Ital.Value
    Pict_Font.FontSize = FaceSize
    ' Clear picture box.
    Pict_Font.Cls
    ' Display it.
    If M_DText.Checked = -1 Then Pict_Font.Print ; FaceName$
    If M_SText.Checked = -1 Then Pict_Font.Print ; Sample$
End Sub

Sub Picture1_Click ()
    ' Display "About Box".
    Msg$ = "FontView by Charles Snider" + Chr$(13) + Chr$(10) +
        "Compuserve 73730,1315"
    MsgBox Msg$, 64, "FontView v3.0"
End Sub

Sub M_DText_Click ()
    M_DText.Checked = -1
    M_SText.Checked = 0
    DisplayFace
End Sub

Sub M_Exit_Click ()
    End
End Sub

Sub M_SText_Click ()
    M_DText.Checked = 0
    M_SText.Checked = -1
```

Chapter 3: FontView

```vb
        Sample$ = InputBox$("Please enter sample text:")
        If Sample$ = "" Then
            M_DText.Checked = -1
            M_SText.Checked = 0
            Sample$ = FaceName
        End If
        DisplayFace
End Sub

Sub M_PrtLst_Click ()
    ' Print routine sends sample of each font to the printer.
    ' Set Error trap.
    On Error Resume Next
    ' Check to see if screen is checked. If so, exit sub.
    If M_SFont.Checked = -1 Then
        Msg$ = "You may not print Screen fonts. Please select
            'Printer' from the Fonts menu."
        MsgBox Msg$, 48, "FontView"
        Exit Sub
    End If
    ' Change mouse cursor to hourglass.
    FontView.MousePointer = 11
    ' Print header.
    Header$ = "Sample Printer Fonts - Font Viewer v3.0"
    Printer.Print Header$ + Chr$(13) + Chr$(10)
    ' Get fonts and send each to printer.
    If M_SText.Checked = 0 Then Sample$ = ""
    For K% = 0 To Lst_Face.ListCount - 1
        Printer.FontName = Lst_Face.List(K%)
        Printer.FontBold = 0
        Printer.FontItalic = 0
        Printer.FontSize = 14
        Printer.Print Lst_Face.List(K%) + " " + Sample$
    Next K%
    ' Restore printer font to default.
    Printer.FontSize = 10
    Printer.FontName = Screen.Fonts(0)
    ' Print number of available fonts.
    Printer.Print Chr$(13) + Chr$(10) + "Number Of Fonts: ";
        Lst_Face.ListCount
    ' End printing.
    Printer.EndDoc
    ' Restore cursor to default.
    FontView.MousePointer = 0
End Sub
```

continues

Chapter 3: FontView

```
Sub M_SFont_Click ()
    ' Check if already selected.
    If M_SFont.Checked = -1 Then Exit Sub
    M_PFont.Checked = 0
    M_SFont.Checked = -1
    FontView.MousePointer = 11
    ' Remove previous contents of list.
    Do While Lst_Face.ListCount
        Lst_Face.RemoveItem 0
    Loop
    ' Get list of screen fonts and add to the list box.
    For I% = 0 To Screen.FontCount - 1
        For x% = 0 To Lst_Face.ListCount - 1
            If Screen.Fonts(I%) = Lst_Face.List(x%) Then
                Duplicate = 1
            End If
        Next x%
    If Duplicate <> 1 Then Lst_Face.AddItem Screen.Fonts(I%)
    Duplicate = 0
    Next I%
    ' Select first item in list box.
    Lst_Face.ListIndex = 0
    FontView.MousePointer = 0
    FaceCount = Lst_Face.ListCount
    Label1.Caption = Str$(FaceCount) + " Screen Fonts Available"
End Sub

Sub M_PFont_Click ()
    ' Check if already selected.
    If M_PFont.Checked = -1 Then Exit Sub
    M_PFont.Checked = -1
    M_SFont.Checked = 0
    FontView.MousePointer = 11
    ' Remove previous contents of list.
    Do While Lst_Face.ListCount
        Lst_Face.RemoveItem 0
    Loop
    ' Get list of printer fonts and add to the list box.
    For I% = 0 To Printer.FontCount - 1
        For x% = 0 To Lst_Face.ListCount - 1
            If Printer.Fonts(I%) = Lst_Face.List(x%) Then
                Duplicate = 1
            End If
        Next x%
    If Duplicate <> 1 Then Lst_Face.AddItem Printer.Fonts(I%)
    Duplicate = 0
```

Chapter 3: FontView

```
    Next I%
    ' Select first item in list box.
    Lst_Face.ListIndex = 0
    FontView.MousePointer = 0
    FaceCount = Lst_Face.ListCount
    Label1.Caption = Str$(FaceCount) + " Printer Fonts Available"
End Sub
```

Chapter 3: FontView

ButtonBar Plus

by Mark J. DiBiasio

Chapter 4: ButtonBar Plus

Overview

ButtonBar Plus is a program-launching utility for Microsoft Windows 3.1. The program was designed with a floating toolbar concept, consisting of 36 buttons arranged in a user-selected matrix. Each button can be set up to launch a program and is represented by an icon of the user's choice.

FUN PROGRAMMING NOTE: To use ButtonBar Plus with Windows 3.0, you need the SHELL.DLL file from Microsoft. This file is available on CompuServe. In addition, Windows 3.0 users must place the THREED.VBX file (included with ButtonBar Plus) in the \WINDOWS\SYSTEM directory.

ButtonBar Plus offers the user many advantages over the Windows Program Manager, including a consistent position of the program buttons. Other ButtonBar features include program-launching options that allow the user to choose (from a list box) a file to load with a selected program, launch a program in a "minimized" condition, and load a program using an environment variable. The purpose of ButtonBar is to produce a visually consistent interface that is easy to configure and quick to use. Figure 4.1 shows the ButtonBar Plus window. The title bar contains the name of the program that the cursor is over (in this case, Calculator).

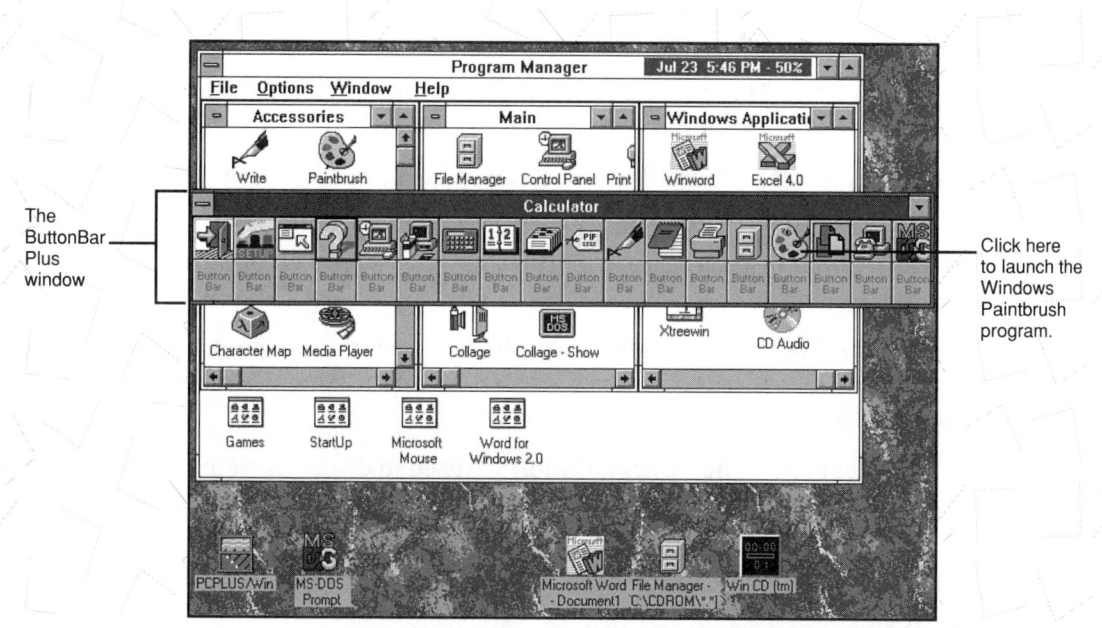

Figure 4.1. The ButtonBar Plus window. Just click an icon to launch the corresponding program.

Program Operation

Programming Notes:

ButtonBar Plus employs a number of special programming techniques that use Windows API functions to supplement Visual Basic functions. ButtonBar uses API calls to track the mouse pointer screen position, capture embedded icons, find ButtonBar's starting directory, read and write ButtonBar configuration files, and get system memory statistics. These API functions can be applied to any program where a similar programming requirement exists.

To load ButtonBar Plus into the design mode of Visual Basic, you need the Microsoft Visual Basic Toolkit.

When you run ButtonBar Plus in Visual Basic design mode, you must comment out four lines of code in the BUTTONBA.FRM Form_Load routine. These lines are preceded by a "Programmer's Note" comment.

ButtonBar Plus consists of seven forms and one custom control. The following list briefly describes each form's function:

BBARINT.BAS—This module contains global constants, variables, and API function declarations available to all forms.

BUTTONBA.FRM—ButtonBar is the main form of this program. All program functions start from the subroutines located in this form.

BARCONFI.FRM—The BarConfig form controls user preferences, button setup, and icon linking.

BROWSE.FRM—The BrowseBox is a multipurpose form used for viewing file directories and selecting programs, icons, and program-launching functions.

ICONDISP.FRM—The IconDisplay form is used to display the embedded icons available to the user from a Windows program that is in the process of being set up in BarConfig form.

BBAR.BAS—This module contains subroutines available on a global basis.

Chapter 4: ButtonBar Plus

LICENSE.FRM—This form is displayed when the program starts up.

THREED.VBX—This custom control allows the use of three-dimensional enhanced buttons, frames, radio buttons, and check boxes. This is a custom control file from the Microsoft Visual Basic Professional Toolkit.

The code description in this chapter consists of annotations for each of the major pieces of the ButtonBar Plus application.

The Global Module (BBARINT.BAS)

The following is the source code for the global module, which includes an assortment of global constants, variables, and API function declarations:

```
'BBARINT FORM
'ButtonBar Plus
'(c) Copyright 1992 - Mark J. DiBiasio

Global Const Ver$ = "1.01"
Global Const Modal = 1
Global BBARINI As String
Global MaxIcon As Integer
Global IconWide As Integer
Global IconHigh As Integer
Global ScreenWide As Integer
Global FormChange As Integer
Global LaunchLine(36, 4) As String
Global COLCount As Integer
Global RowCount As Integer
Global BarDir As String
Global ScreenDivsor As Integer
Global WinShutDown As Integer
Global Minimize As Integer
Global IconDirectory As String
Global ButtonIconPath As String
Global ButtonCMDPath As String
Global RunProgramBox As Integer
Global LoadWithFile As Integer
Global Arange As Integer
Global Moveicon As Integer
Global IconMessage As Integer
Global WindowsProgram As Integer
Global Const TRU = -1
Global Const FALS = 0
Global Const WHITE = &HFFFFFF
```

continues

```
Global Const DARKGREY = &H808080
Global Const KEY_F1 = &H70
Global Const TotalIcons = 36

Type PointAPI
    X As Integer
    y As Integer
End Type

'API CALL Declarations ------------------------------------------------
Declare Function GetFocus Lib "User" () As Integer
Declare Function GetWindowsDirectory Lib "Kernel" (ByVal Buff$, ByVal
    sizeBuf%) As Integer
Declare Function GetPrivateProfileString Lib "Kernel" (ByVal
    lpApplicationName As String, ByVal lpKeyName As String, ByVal
    lpDefault As String, ByVal lpReturnedString As String, ByVal nSize
    As Integer, ByVal lpFileName As String) As Integer
Declare Function WritePrivateProfileString Lib "Kernel" (ByVal
    lpApplicationName As String, ByVal lpKeyName As String,
    ByVal lpString As String, ByVal lplFileName As String) As Integer
Declare Sub GetCursorPos Lib "User" (LpPoint As PointAPI)
```

The ButtonBar Form (BUTTONBA.FRM)

The ButtonBar form is the main program module. All program events stem from a user action or from a timer set to perform a given function at a certain interval. The general section contains the module-level declared variables and API declarations.

The General Declarations Section

```
'BUTTONBAR FORM
'ButtonBar Plus
'(c) Copyright 1992 - Mark J. DiBiasio

DefInt A-Z
'Navigation key codes
Const KEY_END = &H23
Const KEY_HOME = &H24
Const KEY_LEFT = &H25
Const KEY_UP = &H26
Const KEY_RIGHT = &H27
Const KEY_DOWN = &H28
Const MF_BYPOSITION = &H400
```

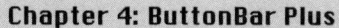

```
Dim IconRow As Integer, IconFormMax As Integer, StartIcon As Integer
Dim WhoHas As Integer
Dim CpPoint   As PointAPI

'API CALL Declarations ----------------------------------------------
Declare Function ExitWindows% Lib "user" (ByVal dwReserved&, ByVal
    wReturnCode%)
Declare Function GetActiveWindow Lib "User" () As Integer
Declare Function GetMessagePos& Lib "User" ()
Declare Function WindowFromPoint Lib "User" (ByVal MPos&)
Declare Function GetParent Lib "User" (ByVal hWnd)
Declare Function GetNextWindow Lib "User" (ByVal hWnd, ByVal wCMD)
Declare Function GetFreeSpace Lib "Kernel" (ByVal wFlags As Integer)
    As Long
Declare Function GetModuleHandle Lib "Kernel" (ByVal ModName$)
Declare Function GetHeapSpaces& Lib "Kernel" (ByVal Hmodule)
Declare Function GetModuleFileName Lib "Kernel" (ByVal Hmodule,
    ByVal lpFileName$, ByVal nSize%)
Declare Function GetSystemMenu Lib "User" (ByVal hWnd As Integer,
    ByVal bRevert As Integer) As Integer
Declare Function RemoveMenu Lib "User" (ByVal hMenu As Integer, ByVal
    nPosition As Integer, ByVal wFlags As Integer) As Integer
```

The *Button_Click* Routine

The Button_Click routine initiates an action, depending on which button was clicked:

```
Sub Button_Click (Index As Integer)
On Error GoTo errorhandler
PState% = 1      'Set launch program state to normal.

Select Case Index
Case 1 'Exit program button
'Write program exit location & matrix to BBAR.INI for next startup.
Y% = WritePrivateProfileString("ButtonBar", ByVal "Matrix",
    ByVal Str$(ColCount) + "-" + Str$(RowCount), BarDir + "\" + BBARINI)
Y% = WritePrivateProfileString("ButtonBar", ByVal "Position",
    ByVal Str$((ButtonBar.top)) + "," + Str$((ButtonBar.left)),
    BarDir +  "\" + BBARINI)
Empty% = DoEvents()
If WinShutDown Then RetVal% = ExitWindows(0, 0) Else End

Case 2 'ButtonBar Setup & Configuration
'Disable first three buttons so user can't change their functions.
For z% = 1 To 3
```

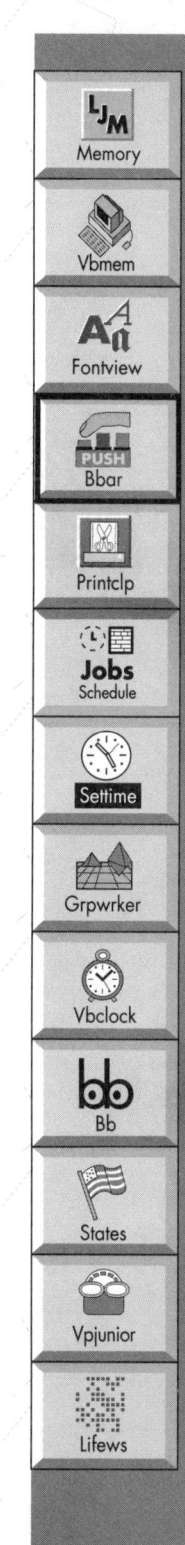

continues

Chapter 4: ButtonBar Plus

```
        Button(z%).enabled = FALS
Next z%
Load Barconfig
Barconfig.Show

Case 3 'Run a program button.
'Load/Run a Program Box
RunProgramBox = TRU
BrowseBox.Show Modal 'Show BrowseBox in modal state.
If Minimize Then ButtonBar.windowState = 1 'Minimize ButtonBar.

Case Else 'Any other button pressed.
'Start of ReArrange a Button Location routine.
If Moveicon Then
    StartIcon = Index
    Button(Index).DragIcon = DragIcon.picture   'Set starting button
                                                'DragIcon.
    Button(Index).DragMode = 1                  'Place button in drag mode.
    Exit Sub
End If

'User selects which button configuration to edit.
If Barconfig.visible = TRU Then
    Barconfig.Label1.caption = Str$(Index)
    Barconfig.picture1.picture = ButtonBar.Button
        (Val(Barconfig.Label1.caption)).picture
    For X% = 1 To 4
    Barconfig.Entry(X%).text=
        LaunchLine((Val(Barconfig.Label1.caption)), X%)
    Next X%
    Barconfig.SetFocus
    Exit Sub
End If

 'Begin program launch routine.

            LaunchApp$ = LaunchLine(Index, 2)
            RunProg$ = ""

CheckEnvironment:
'Look to see if a user variable is in the program line and parse
' it if it is there.
If InStr(LaunchApp$, "%") > 0 Then
    FirstSign% = InStr(LaunchApp$, "%")
    SecondSign% = InStr(FirstSign% + 1, LaunchApp$, "%")
    EnvVarible$ = Mid$(LaunchApp$, FirstSign% + 1,
        (SecondSign%-FirstSign%) - 1)
```

```
        LaunchApp$ = Left$(LaunchApp$, FirstSign% - 1) +
            Environ$(EnvVarible$) + Mid$(LaunchApp$, SecondSign% + 1)
End If
'Loop back if more than one variable is present.
If InStr(LaunchApp$, "%") > 0 Then GoTo CheckEnvironment

'Show User Commandline Input box
If InStr(LaunchApp$, "@") > 0 Then
        CMDLine$ = InputBox$("Enter Command Line to Load Designated
            Program with:", "Load Program Option", "", screen.width \ 3,
            screen.height \ 3)
        If Len(RTrim$(CMDLine$)) > 0 Then LaunchApp$ = Mid$(LaunchApp$,
            1, InStr(LaunchApp$, "@") - 1) + CMDLine$ Else Exit Sub
End If

'Show BrowseBox for user to select which file to load with this program.
If InStr(LaunchApp$, "?") > 0 Then
    LoadWithFile = TRU
    RunProgrneBox = FALS
    BrowseBox.DriveBox.drive = Left$(LaunchLine(Index, 3), 2)
    BrowseBox.DirBox.Path = LaunchLiCH(Index, 3)
'See if there is a file pattern set.
    If InStr(LaunchApp$, "*") > 0 Then
        BrowseBox.FileBox.Pattern = Mid$(LaunchApp$,
            InStr(LaunchApp$, "*"))
    Else
        BrowseBox.FileBox.Pattern = "*.*"
    End If
BrowseBox.caption = "Load Selection (" + BrowseBox.FileBox.Pattern + ")"
BrowseBox.Show Modal  'STOP here until user picks a file.

RunProg$ = RTrim$(ButtonCMDPath) 'Selected file.

    If Len(RunProg$) > 0 Then 'Remove ? mark and file pattern
                              'before running application.
        LaunchApp$ = Mid$(LaunchApp$, 1, InStr(LaunchApp$, "?") - 1)
            + RunProg$
    Else
        LaunchApp$ = Mid$(LaunchApp$, 1, (InStr(LaunchApp$, "?") - 1))
    End If
End If

'Run program in iconized state.
If InStr(LaunchApp$, "#") > 0 Then
    PState% = 7
    LaunchApp$ = Mid$(LaunchApp$, 1, (InStr(LaunchApp$, "#") - 1))
End If
```

continues

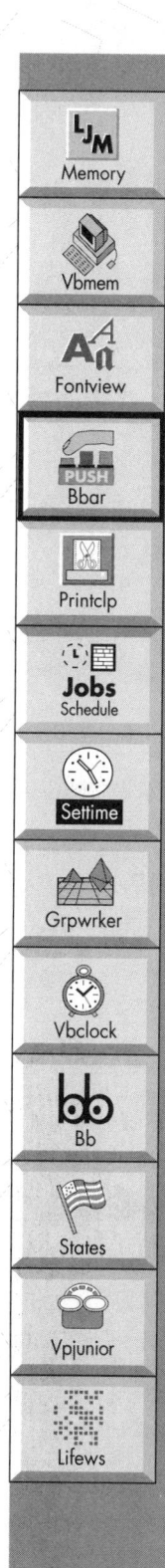

```
'If working directory has a user environmental variable, parse it out.
If InStr(LaunchLine(Index, 3), "%") > 0 Then
    FirstSign% = InStr(LaunchLine(Index, 3), "%")
    SecondSign% = InStr(FirstSign% + 1, LaunchLine(Index, 3), "%")
    EnvVarible$ = Mid$(LaunchLine(Index, 3), FirstSign% + 1,
        (SecondSign% - FirstSign%) - 1)
    LaunchLine(Index, 3) = Left$(LaunchLine(Index, 3), FirstSign% - 1) +
        Environ$(EnvVarible$) + Mid$(LaunchLine(Index, 3), SecondSign% + 1)
End If

screen.mousepointer = 11
If Len(LaunchLine(Index, 3)) > 0 Then
    ChDrive Left$(LaunchLine(Index, 3), 2)  'Change drive to request
                                            'location.
    ChDir LaunchLine(Index, 3)              'Change directory.
End If
If Minimize And PState% = 1 Then ButtonBar.windowState = 1
Call BarDisplay
Empty% = Shell(RTrim$(LaunchApp$), PState%) 'Load program.
screen.mousepointer = 0
End Select

Exit Sub

errorhandler:
        If Len(RTrim$(LaunchLine(Index, 2))) < 1 Then
                Msg$ = "This Button has not been Configured!!"
        Else
                Msg$ = Error$(Err)
        End If
        Beep
        MsgBox Msg$, 0, "ButtonBar Error"
        screen.mousepointer = 0
        Exit Sub
        Resume Next
End Sub
```

The *Form_Load* Routine

When the user starts ButtonBar, the Form_Load routine performs all program initialization. This includes showing the introductory screen, checking the user's screen resolution, setting button dimensions, and reading the BBAR.INI file:

Chapter 4: ButtonBar Plus

```
Sub Form_Load ()
License.Show           'Load Intro form.
License.Refresh
ButtonBar.windowState = 0
ButtonBar.top = 0
ButtonBar.left = 0
screen.mousepointer = 11
Clear_SystemMenu ButtonBar 'Remove unwanted items from System Menu.

' Check what display resolution is being used and tailor buttons
' for best appearance.
ScreenWide = screen.width
Select Case ScreenWide

    Case Is > 12000                     '1024x768 pixel display.
        For Y% = 1 To 36
         ButtonBar.Button(Y%).BevelWidth = 3
        Next Y%
        ScreenDivsor = 12
        Button(1).width = (ScreenWide / 18) + 12
        Button(1).height = Button(1).width

    Case Is = 12000                     '800x600 pixel display.
        ScreenDivsor = 15
        Button(1).width = (ScreenWide / 18) + 12
        Button(1).height = 685

    Case Is < 12000                     '640x480 pixel display.
        For Y% = 1 To 36
           ButtonBar.Button(Y%).BevelWidth = 1
           ButtonBar.Button(Y%).AutoSize = 1
        Next Y%
        ScreenDivsor = 15
        Button(1).width = (ScreenWide / 18) + 12
        Button(1).height = Button(1).width
End Select


   BarDir = "c:\windows"        'Default directory.
'Programmer's Note: While in the VB Design mode, it will be necessary
' to rem the next four lines. Otherwise you will get an Illegal
' Function Call message.

   Hmodule = GetModuleHandle("BBAR.EXE")   'Locate which directory
                                           'ButtonBar was launched from.

   Buff$ = Space$(255)
```

continues

```
    TChars% = GetModuleFileName(Hmodule, Buff$, 255)
    BarDir = Left$(Buff$, TChars% - 9)

    BBARINI = "BBAR.INI"

    CMD$ = Command$                 'Load ButtonBar with a custom .INI file
        If Len(CMD$) > 0 Then       ' based on an environmental variable.
            If InStr(CMD$, "%") > 0 Then
                Env$ = Mid$(CMD$, 2, InStr(2, CMD$, "%") - 2)
                BBARINI = Environ$(Env$) + ".INI"
            Else
                BBARINI = Left$(CMD$, 8) + ".INI"
            End If
        End If


GetBBarIni        'Load BBar.INI settings.

IconWide = Button(1).width - 16
IconHigh = Button(1).height - 16

If ColCount = 0 Then
    IconFormMax = ScreenWide \ IconWide
Else
    IconFormMax = ColCount
End If

Call GetMatix(IconFormMax, IconRow)      'Get BBar Button layout.
Call ArrangeBar(IconFormMax, IconRow)    'Execute layout.

'Set Default Menu Name for 1st two Buttons
If WinShutDown Then LaunchLine(1, 1) = "Exit Windows"
    Else LaunchLine(1, 1) = "Exit ButtonBar Program"
LaunchLine(2, 1) = "ButtonBar Configuration & Button Setup"

WhoHas = hWnd     'Get ButtonBar window's handle number.
Empty% = DoEvents()
screen.mousepointer = 0
Unload License
End Sub
```

The *Form_Paint* Routine

When the paint command is issued by Windows, ButtonBar's `Form_Paint` routine redraws button layout:

```
Sub Form_Paint ()
If ButtonBar.windowState <> 1 Then
    IconFormMax = ((ButtonBar.width) \ IconWide)
    Call GetMatix(IconFormMax, IconRow)    'Get closest matrix.
    Call ArrangeBar(IconFormMax, IconRow)  'Arrange BBar to new matrix.
Else
FormChange = TRU
End If
Call BarDisplay
End Sub
```

The *Form_Resize* Routine

If the user restores ButtonBar from a minimized state or adjusts the width of the button display, flags are set for a complete ButtonBar redraw when Windows issues the next paint command. This process is handled by the Form_Resize routine:

```
Sub Form_Resize ()
ButtonBar.AutoReDraw = TRU
ButtonBar.ForeColor = &HFFFFFF

ButtonBar.caption = "ButtonBar"
If ButtonBar.windowState = 1 Then
    ButtonBar.Timer1.enabled = FALS 'If minimized don't do timing loop.
    Arange = TRU
    ButtonBar.Refresh
Else
    ButtonBar.Timer1.enabled = TRU
End If


If Arange Then Exit Sub
If FormChange Then
 FormChange = FALS
 Form_Paint
End If
End Sub
```

The *Timer1_Timer* Routine

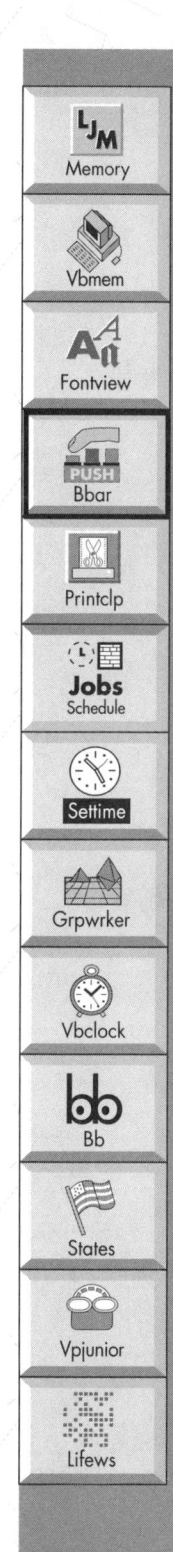

The Timer1_Timer routine uses API calls to determine which button the mouse pointer is currently on. Command buttons do not send cursor position messages, so it is necessary to ask Windows for the current mouse pointer location. The API calls in this subroutine perform this function and then send the result to the `Form_MouseMove` subroutine. The purpose of this routine is to place the button title in the ButtonBar `caption` so that the user knows what program this button launches:

```
Sub Timer1_Timer ()
'This Timer loop occurs every 250ms.
Arange = FALS
MyPos& = GetMessagePos&()            'See where the MousePointer is.
Wnd = WindowFromPoint(MyPos&)        'Get the handle of the window
                                     'the mouse is over.
NowHas = GetParent(Wnd)              'Get parent window.
    If WhoHas = NowHas Then          'If parent window = ButtonBar
        HasFocus = GetActiveWindow() 'get active window.
          Call GetCursorPos(CpPoint) 'Get current MousePointer position.
          xpos! = CSng(CpPoint.X): ypos! = CSng(CpPoint.y)
            If HasFocus = WhoHas Then   'If active window = ButtonBar
                'Which button is the mouse over.
                Call Form_MouseMove(0, 0, xpos!, ypos!)
            End If
    End If
End Sub
```

The *Form_MouseMove* Routine

The `Form_MouseMove` routine is the destination of the `Timer1_Timer` subroutine. Coordinates sent to this routine provide the mouse pointer position, relative to where ButtonBar is located on-screen. From that point, it is possible to identify the button and place its title in the ButtonBar `caption`.

```
Sub Form_MouseMove (Button As Integer, Shift As Integer,
    X As Single, y As Single)
        On Error Resume Next
        Static OldSpot

        'Locate which button the MousePointer is over.

        xpos = ((((X * ScreenDivsor) - ButtonBar.left) \ (IconWide)) + 1)
        ypos = ((((y * ScreenDivsor) - (ButtonBar.top + 360)) \
            (IconHigh)) + 1)

        Select Case RowCount
                Case 1
                    Spot = xpos
                Case 2
                    Spot = ((ypos - 1) * 18) + xpos
```

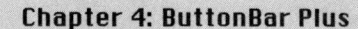

```
                Case 3
                    Spot = ((ypos - 1) * 12) + xpos
                Case 4
                    Spot = ((ypos - 1) * 9) + xpos
                Case 6
                    Spot = ((ypos - 1) * 6) + xpos
                Case 9
                    Spot = ((ypos - 1) * 4) + xpos
                Case 12
                    Spot = ((ypos - 1) * 3) + xpos
            End Select

    'Place program title name in ButtonBar caption.
    If OldSpot <> Spot Then
        If Spot > 0 And Spot <= 36 Then
            ButtonBar.caption = LaunchLine(Spot, 1)
            OldSpot = Spot
            If Len(RTrim$(ButtonBar.caption)) = 0 _
                Then ButtonBar.caption = "ButtonBar"
            Exit Sub
            End If
        End If
End Sub
```

The *Button_GotFocus* Routine

The `Button_GotFocus` routine performs the same functions as the previous two subroutines—the only difference is that this event is generated by changing the button focus with the keyboard cursor keys (as opposed to the mouse).

```
Sub Button_GotFocus (Index As Integer)
ButtonBar.caption = LaunchLine(Index, 1)  'Change caption to program
                                          ' title.
End Sub
```

The *Timer2_Timer* Routine

`Timer2_Timer` is the second `Timer` function in ButtonBar. It is active when ButtonBar has been minimized (see the `BarDisplay` function):

```
Sub Timer2_Timer ()
'This Timer loop happens every 11 seconds.
Call BarDisplay
End Sub
```

continues

Miscellaneous Resource and Memory Routines

The following routines in BUTTONBA.FRM use standard Windows API calls to get system resources and available memory statistics:

```
Function GetFreeResources (ModuleName$)
    rInfo& = GetHeapSpaces&(GetModuleHandle(ModuleName$))
    Totalr& = HiWord&(rInfo&)
    FreeR& = LoWord(rInfo&)
    GetFreeResources = FreeR& * 100 \ Totalr&
End Function

Function HiWord& (LongInt&)
    Temp& = LongInt& \ &H10000
    If Temp& < 0 Then Temp& = Temp& + &H10000
    HiWord& = Temp&
End Function

Function LoWord& (LongInt&)
    Temp& = LongInt& Mod &H10000
    If Temp& < 0 Then Temp& = Temp& + &H10000
    LoWord& = Temp&
End Function

Sub GetMemory (FreeMem As Long)
    FreeMem = GetFreeSpace(0)
End Sub

Sub GetResource (ResFree As Integer)
FreeUser = GetFreeResources("User")
FreeGDI = GetFreeResources("GDI")
    If FreeUser <= FreeGDI Then
            ResFree = FreeUser
    Else
            ResFree = FreeGDI
    End If
End Sub
```

The *BarDisplay* Routine

The BarDisplay routine paints the time in a box when ButtonBar is an icon. Painting to an iconized form is similar to painting to a form in its normal state:

```
Sub BarDisplay ()
Static Chime%
GetMemory FreeSpace&   'See how much free memory.
```

Chapter 4: ButtonBar Plus

```
GetResource TFree       'See how much free resources.

If ButtonBar.windowState <> 0 Then
    If IconMessage Then
        ButtonBar.caption = "Res: " + Format$(TFree, "00") + "%" +
            Chr$(13) + "Ram: " + Format$(FreeSpace& \ 1024, "#,###") + "K"
        ButtonBar.icon = DragIcon.DragIcon    'Piggy-backed the Time Icon
                                              'on the DragIcon--keeps
                                              'program smaller.
        ButtonBar.AutoReDraw = FALS
        ButtonBar.fillcolor = &H0&            'Black.
        Cls                                   'Clear the Icon.
        ButtonBar.ForeColor = QBColor(12)     'Set Fore Color to Red.
        Line (1, 260)-(530, 500), , B         'Draw Box on Icon.
        ButtonBar.ForeColor = QBColor(10)     'Set Fore Color to
                                              'Bright Green.
        CurrentX = (635 - TextWidth(Format$(Now, "h:mma/p"))) \ 2:
            Currenty = 280
        Print Format$(Now, "H:MM  a/p")
        ButtonBar.AutoReDraw = TRU
    Else
        ButtonBar.caption = "Res: " + Format$(TFree, "00") + "%" +
            Chr$(13) + "Ram: " + Format$(FreeSpace& \ 1024, "#,###") + "K"
    End If
End If


    If IconMessage Then
            Select Case Minute(Now) 'Chime on the hour and half hour.
                Case 0
                    If Chime% = 0 Then Beep
                    Chime% = 1            'Only chime once.
                Case 30
                    If Chime% = 0 Then Beep
                    Chime% = 1
                Case Else
                    Chime% = 0
            End Select
    End If

End Sub
```

The Button_DragDrop routine allows the user to change the location of a button on the bar. This event is initiated by selecting **Re**Arrange Icons in the **B**utton Layout menu of the BarConfig form. The user clicks the target button once to identify it as the target, then clicks the target again and holds the mouse

81

button. The mouse pointer changes to the drag icon, and the user drags and drops the icon to the destination button. The target and destination button configuration and icons are then swapped.

The *Button_DragDrop* Routine

```
Sub Button_DragDrop (Index As Integer, Source As Control,
    X As Single, y As Single)
'ReArrange buttons on ButtonBar routine.

            Static TempButton(1, 4) As String       'Set up a string for
                                                    'temporary storage.

            Button(StartIcon).DragMode = 0
            Button(Index).DragMode = 0
            For z% = 1 To 4
               TempButton(1, z%) = LaunchLine(Index, z%)  'Temp holds
                                                          'destination
                                                          'button info.

              'Swap starting to destination.
              LaunchLine(Index, z%) = LaunchLine(StartIcon, z%)

              'Swap temp to start position.
              LaunchLine(StartIcon, z%) = TempButton(1, z%)

            Next z%
            'Load icon files to button.
            Button(Index).picture = LoadPicture(LaunchLine(Index, 4))
            'Load icon files to button.
            Button(StartIcon).picture = LoadPicture(LaunchLine(StartIcon, 4))

            Button(StartIcon).DragIcon = LoadPicture()    'Erase DragIcon.
            If Len(LaunchLine(StartIcon, 4))<1
               Then Button(StartIcon).picture =
               ButtonBar.DefaultIcon.picture
            'Write changes to BBar.INI file.
            LN = StartIcon
            Y% = WritePrivateProfileString("ButtonBar", ByVal "Button #" +
               Str$(LN), ByVal LaunchLine(LN, 1) + "¦" + LaunchLine(LN, 2)
               + "¦" + LaunchLine(LN, 3) + "¦" + LaunchLine(LN, 4),
               BarDir + "\" + BBARINI)
            LN = Index
            Y% = WritePrivateProfileString("ButtonBar", ByVal "Button #"
               + Str$(LN), ByVal LaunchLine(LN, 1) + "¦" +
               LaunchLine(LN, 2) + "¦" + LaunchLine(LN, 3) + "¦" +
               LaunchLine(LN, 4), BarDir + "\" + BBARINI)
```

```
End Sub

Sub Button_KeyDown (Index As Integer, Keycode As Integer,
    Shift As Integer)
Call KeyHandler(Index, Keycode, Shift)
End Sub
```

The *KeyHandler* Routine

The KeyHandler routine processes keyboard input. The keys it handles are F1, Home, End, and the cursor keys.

```
Sub KeyHandler (Index, Keycode, Shift)
On Error Resume Next
If Keycode = Key_F1 Then Empty% = Shell("Winhelp.exe BBar.hlp", 1)

    'KeyBoard navigation of ButtonBar.
    Select Case Keycode
        Case KEY_HOME
            Button(1).SetFocus
        Case KEY_END
            Button(36).SetFocus
        Case KEY_LEFT
            Button(Index - 1).SetFocus
        Case KEY_RIGHT
            Button(Index + 1).SetFocus
        Case KEY_UP
            Button(Index - ColCount).SetFocus
        Case KEY_DOWN
            Button(Index + ColCount).SetFocus
    End Select
End Sub
```

The *Clear_SystemMenu* Routine

The Clear_SystemMenu subroutine removes unnecessary items from the System menu:

```
Sub Clear_SystemMenu (A_Form As Form)
    HSysMenu = GetSystemMenu(A_Form.hWnd, 0)
    r = RemoveMenu(HSysMenu, 8, MF_BYPOSITION)    'Switch to
    r = RemoveMenu(HSysMenu, 7, MF_BYPOSITION)    'separator bar.
    r = RemoveMenu(HSysMenu, 6, MF_BYPOSITION)    'Close
    r = RemoveMenu(HSysMenu, 5, MF_BYPOSITION)    'separator bar.
    r = RemoveMenu(HSysMenu, 4, MF_BYPOSITION)    'Maximize.
End Sub
```

The Bar Configuration Form (BARCONFI.FRM)

The `BarConfig` form allows the user to set up buttons to launch a program, rearrange buttons on the bar, and set user preferences for program operation.

The *Command1_Click* Routine

Clicking one of the four buttons in the `Command1_Click` routine enables the user to set up a new button, clear a button configuration, save a configuration, or exit from the form. The user selects which button to edit by clicking it with the mouse pointer:

```
Sub Command1_Click (Index As Integer)
On Error GoTo Errorhandler
Select Case Index            'Select a button.
  Case 1      'Browse Button
    RunProgramBox = FALS
    BrowseBox.Show
    BarConfig.enabled = FALS   'Disable BarConfig form so user can't do
                               'anything while BrowseBox is on-screen.

         While BrowseBox.visible   'Put program in loop so no more
                                   'code is executed until
     Empty% = DoEvents()           'BrowseBox function is finished.
      Wend


          Unload IconDisplay
          BarConfig.enabled = TRU    'Enable BarConfig form.

          If Len(ButtonCMDPath) > 0 Then
              Entry(2).text = ButtonCMDPath     'Program path
                                                ' and name.

  'Parse out working directory name.
          For I% = 1 To Len(Entry(2).text)
              If InStr(I%, Entry(2).text, "\") >= 3
                  Then Section% = InStr(I%,
                  Entry(2).text, "\")
          Next I%
        If Section% > 3 Then Entry(3).text =
              Left$(Entry(2).text, Section% - 1)
        Else Entry(3).text = Left$(Entry(2).text, Section%)
      End If
```

Chapter 4: ButtonBar Plus

```
            If Len(ButtonIconPath) > 0 Then Entry(4).text = _
                ButtonIconPath
            If Not WindowsProgram Then picture1.picture = _
                LoadPicture((Entry(4).text))

            'Place selected program name in Title field--
            'in case user forgets to type it in.
            If Len(LTrim$(Entry(1).text)) < 1 Then
                Entry(1).text = Mid$(Entry(2).text, Section% + 1)
                If Len(LTrim$(Entry(1).text)) > 0 _
                    Then Entry(1).text = UCase$(Left$(Entry(1).text, _
                    InStr(Entry(1).text, ".") - 1))
            End If

            Unload BrowseBox
            ButtonIconPath = ""
            ButtonCMDPath = ""
            Entry(1).SetFocus
            'Select the text in title field - reminds user
            'to type own.
            If Len(Entry(1).text) > 0 Then
                Entry(1).SelStart = 0
                Entry(1).SelLength = Len(Entry(1).text)
            End If

Case 2          'Clear all fields.
    Entry(1).text = ""
    Entry(2).text = ""
    Entry(3).text = ""
    Entry(4).text = ""
    picture1.picture = LoadPicture()

Case 3          'Save selection to BBAR.INI file.
            LN = (Val(label1.caption))
            LaunchLine(LN, 1) = Entry(1).text
            LaunchLine(LN, 2) = UCase$(Entry(2).text)
            LaunchLine(LN, 3) = UCase$(Entry(3).text)
            LaunchLine(LN, 4) = UCase$(Entry(4).text)
            Y% = WritePrivateProfileString("ButtonBar", _
                ByVal "Button #" + Str$(LN), ByVal _
                LaunchLine(LN,1) + "|" + LaunchLine(LN, 2) + "|" + _
                LaunchLine(LN, 3) + "|" + LaunchLine(LN, 4), BarDir + _
                "\" + BBARINI)
            ButtonBar.Button(Val(label1.caption)).picture = _
                picture1.picture
```

continues

```
        'Save icon to .BMP file.
    If Len(RTrim$(LaunchLine(LN, 4))) > 0
        Then SavePicture picture1.picture, LaunchLine(LN, 4)

Case 4           'Close BarConfig form and reset.
     For z% = 1 To 3
           ButtonBar.Button(z%).enabled = TRU 'Enable first three
                                              'buttons on ButtonBar.
     Next z%

     Entry(1).SetFocus
     BarConfig.Hide
     picture1.picture = ButtonBar.Button(4).picture

         For X% = 1 To 4
             Entry(X%).text = LaunchLine(4, X%)
         Next X%
         label1.caption = "4"
         ButtonBar.Timer1.enabled = TRU
         IconArrange.checked = FALS
         MoveIcon = FALS
         WindowsProgram = FALS
    End Select

Exit Sub
Errorhandler:
    MsgBox Error$(Err)
    Resume Next
End Sub
```

The *Form_Load* Routine

The Form_Load routine initializes the BarConfig form:

```
Sub Form_Load ()
'Set BarConfig screen position.
BarConfig.left = (Screen.width - BarConfig.width) \ 2
BarConfig.top = (Screen.height - BarConfig.height) \ 2
icon = LoadPicture()
BarConfig.caption = "Button Configuration Menu"
User_Setup(1).checked = WinShutDown      'Set check mark if true.
User_Setup(2).checked = Minimize         'Set check mark if true.
User_Setup(3).checked = IconMessage      'Set check mark if true.

'Set BarConfig starting entry.
label1.caption = "4"
```

Chapter 4: ButtonBar Plus

```
picture1.picture = ButtonBar.Button(4).picture
For X% = 1 To 4
    Entry(X%).text = LaunchLine(4, X%)
Next X%
End Sub

Sub Entry_GotFocus (Index As Integer)
Panel3D3(Index).shadowColor = 1   'Change box with focus to black.
End Sub

Sub Entry_LostFocus (Index As Integer)
Panel3D3(Index).shadowColor = 0
End Sub

Sub User_Setup_Click (Index As Integer)
Select Case Index

    Case 1                          'End Windows on exit.
        If User_Setup(1).checked = FALS Then
            User_Setup(1).checked = TRU
            WinShutDown = TRU
            LaunchLine(1, 1) = "Exit Windows"
        Else
            User_Setup(1).checked = FALS
            WinShutDown = FALS
            LaunchLine(1, 1) = "Exit Program"
        End If
        Y% = WritePrivateProfileString("ButtonBar", ByVal
            "WinShutDown", ByVal Str$(WinShutDown), BarDir + "\" +
            BBARINI)

    Case 2              ' Minimize ButtonBar after program launch.
        If User_Setup(2).checked = FALS Then
            User_Setup(2).checked = TRU
            Minimize = TRU
        Else
            User_Setup(2).checked = FALS
            Minimize = FALS
        End If
        Y% = WritePrivateProfileString("ButtonBar", ByVal
            "MinimizeOnUse", ByVal Str$(Minimize), BarDir + "\"
            + BBARINI)

    Case 3              'Show current time on ButtonBar icon & chime.
        If User_Setup(3).checked = FALS Then
            User_Setup(3).checked = TRU
            IconMessage = TRU
```

continues

Chapter 4: ButtonBar Plus

```
            Else
                User_Setup(3).checked = FALS
                IconMessage = FALS
                ButtonBar.icon = ButtonBar.DefaultIcon.Dragicon
            End If
            Y% = WritePrivateProfileString("ButtonBar", ByVal
                "IconShowTime", ByVal Str$(IconMessage), BarDir +
                "\" + BBARINI)

        Case 5                          'Show program information.
            cf$ = Chr$(13) + Chr$(10)
            Panel3d1.visible = FALS
            Advertise$ = "ButtonBar Plus" + cf$ + "Version " + ver +
                cf$ + cf$ + "by Mark  DiBiasio"+ cf$ + " Copyright 1992
                - All Rights Reserved" + cf$ + cf$ + cf$ + cf$ + "DataDesign
                Systems, Inc." + cf$ + "dba Software City" + cf$
            Advertise$ = Advertise$ + "15958-B Shady Grove Road" + cf$ +
                "Gaithersburg, Maryland 20877" + cf$ +
                "Tel. (301) 670-0818  Fax. (301) 330-5087"
            Label4.caption = Advertise$
            Ok.visible = TRU
            Label4.visible = TRU
            Advertise$ = ""
        End Select

End Sub

Sub Form_Resize ()
Entry(1).SetFocus
End Sub

Sub OK_Click ()
'Hidden button behind BarConfig form.
Ok.visible = FALS       'Hide.
Label4.visible = FALS   'Hide.
Panel3d1.visible = TRU  'Show.
End Sub

Sub Form_KeyDown (Keycode As Integer, Shift As Integer)
    If Keycode = Key_F1 Then
      Empty% = Shell("Winhelp.exe BBar.hlp", 1)
    End If

End Sub

Sub Command1_KeyDown (Index As Integer, Keycode As Integer,
    Shift As Integer)
```

Chapter 4: ButtonBar Plus

```
If Keycode = Key_F1 Then Empty% = Shell("Winhelp.exe BBar.hlp", 1)

End Sub

Sub Entry_KeyDown (Index As Integer, Keycode As Integer, Shift As Integer)
If Keycode = Key_F1 Then Empty% = Shell("Winhelp.exe BBar.hlp", 1)
End Sub
```

The *IconArrange_Click* Routine

The `IconArrange_Click` routine sets the flag so that the user can rearrange button locations:

```
Sub IconArrange_Click ()
        If IconArrange.checked = FALS Then
            IconArrange.checked = TRU
            MoveIcon = TRU                  'Enable icon rearrange--
                                            'see ButtonBar.Button().
        Else
            IconArrange.checked = FALS
            For X% = 4 To 36
                ButtonBar.Button(X%).dragMode = 0
                ButtonBar.Button(X%).Dragicon = LoadPicture()
                                 'Remove all Dragicon pictures.
            Next X%
            MoveIcon = FALS
        End If

End Sub

Sub Help_Click ()
Empty% = Shell("Winhelp.exe BBar.hlp", 1)
End Sub
```

The *BrowseBox* Form (BROWSEBOX.FRM)

The `BrowseBox` form is used anytime you need to access the file directories. This routine hides and shows controls depending on which mode that `ButtonBar` has set. The primary modes are

- Running a program
- Selecting a program while configuring a button
- Selecting an icon file to be linked to a DOS program

89

```
'BrowseBox FORM
'ButtonBar Plus
'(c) Copyright 1992 - Mark J. DiBiasio

Const RUNCAPTION = "&Run"
Const EXITCAPTION = "&Apply"
Const LOADCAPTION = "&Load"
Const SELECTCAPTION = "&Select"

Sub DriveBox_Change ()
On Error GoTo DriveError
    DirBox.path = DriveBox.drive
    Exit Sub

DriveError:
    If Err = 68 Then
    Beep
    MsgBox "Error Reading Drive!", 16, "Drive Error"
    Else
    MsgBox Error$(Err)
    End If
    Resume Next

End Sub

Sub DirBox_Change ()
 On Error Resume Next
    FileBox.path = DirBox.path
    If FileBox.ListCount Then
        FileBox.SetFocus
        FileBox.ListIndex = 0
    End If
End Sub

Sub FileBox_Click ()
On Error GoTo GotError
    'View the icon.
    If IconBox.Visible Then
        If Right$(FileBox.FileName, 3) = "ico" Or
            Right$(FileBox.FileName, 3) = "bmp" Then
            IconBox.Picture = LoadPicture(FileBox.path + "\" +
                FileBox.FileName)
        End If
    End If
    If SelectButton.caption = EXITCAPTION Then SelectButton.caption =
        SELECTCAPTION
```

Chapter 4: ButtonBar Plus

```
Exit Sub
GotError:
    MsgBox Error$(Err)
    Resume Next
End Sub

Sub FileBox_DblClick ()
    SelectButton_Click
End Sub

Sub Form_Load ()
left = (Screen.width - width) \ 2                      'Set screen position.
top = (Screen.height - height) \ 2
IconBox.left = (IconPanel.width - IconBox.width) \ 2   'Center IconBox in panel.
IconBox.top = (IconPanel.height - IconBox.height) \ 2
Empty% = DoEvents()                                    'Give Windows a moment.
    FileBox.Pattern = "*.exe;*.bat;*.pif;*.com"
    If RunProgramBox Then                              'Run a program.
        BrowseBox.caption = "Select File to Execute"
        ProgramSelect.Visible = FALS
        IconSelect.Visible = FALS
        IconBox.Visible = FALS
        IconPanel.Visible = FALS
        SelectButton.caption = RUNCAPTION
    Else
        BrowseBox.caption = "Select Command File"
        SelectButton.caption = SELECTCAPTION
        ProgramSelect.Value = TRU
    End If
    If LoadWithFile Then                               'Hide unused controls.
        ProgramSelect.Visible = FALS
        IconSelect.Visible = FALS
        IconBox.Visible = FALS
        IconPanel.Visible = FALS
    End If

    Screen.MousePointer = 0              'Set mouse pointer to normal.

End Sub

Sub FileBox_PathChange ()

    If Not RunProgramBox Then SelectButton.caption = "&Select"

End Sub
```

continues

Chapter 4: ButtonBar Plus

```
Sub Form_Paint ()

    Call ShadowEffect(DirBox)     'Add three-dimensional effect.
    Call ShadowEffect(DriveBox)
    Call ShadowEffect(FileBox)


End Sub
```

Core *BrowseBox* Functions

The next several routines make up the core of the BrowseBox form functions. The caption of the Select button determines the action taken by the SelectButton_Click subroutine:

```
Sub SelectButton_Click ()

    If Len(DirBox.path) > 3 Then       'If user selects other than the
                                       'root directory.
        PathMarker$ = "\"
    Else
        PathMarker$ = ""
    End If

  Select Case SelectButton.caption 'Select based on mode of BrowseBox.
    Case SELECTCAPTION                 'Selected program to be
                                       'configured as a button.
       If FileBox.FileName <> "" Then
           If IconBox.Visible Then
             ↪ ButtonIconPath = FileBox.path + PathMarker$ +
                   FileBox.FileName
           Else
             ↪ ButtonCMDPath = FileBox.path + PathMarker$ +
                   FileBox.FileName
              IconDisplay.Show Modal
              BrowseBox.ProgramSelect.Refresh
              BrowseBox.IconSelect.Refresh
              If ButtonIconPath = "" Then IconSelect.Value = TRU
           End If
              SelectButton.caption = EXITCAPTION
              Call SelectButton_Click
       End If
    Case RUNCAPTION                            'Selected Run A Program box.
        RunProgramBox = FALS
        ChDir FileBox.path
     ↪ If Len(FileBox.FileName) > 0 Then TaskID% = Shell(FileBox.path +
           PathMarker$ + FileBox.FileName, 1)
```

Chapter 4: ButtonBar Plus

```
        Unload BrowseBox
    Case LOADCAPTION            'Run a program with a selected file.
        RunProgramBox = FALS
        LoadWithFile = FALS
        ButtonCMDPath = FileBox.path + PathMarker$ + FileBox.FileName
        Unload BrowseBox
    Case Else                   'Choose an icon to be placed
                                'on the button.
        If ButtonIconPath = "" Then
            MsgBox "Please Select an Icon File!"
            Exit Sub
        End If
        Unload BrowseBox
    End Select
End Sub

Sub CancelButton_Click ()
ButtonIconPath = ""         'Clear all flags and variables.
ButtonCMDPath = ""
RunProgramBox = FALS
LoadWithFile = FALS
Unload BrowseBox

End Sub

Sub Form_KeyDown (Keycode As Integer, Shift As Integer)
    If Keycode = Key_F1 Then
       Empty% = Shell("Winhelp.exe BBar.hlp", 1)
    End If

End Sub

Sub SelectButton_KeyDown (Keycode As Integer, Shift As Integer)
If Keycode = Key_F1 Then Empty% = Shell("Winhelp.exe BBar.hlp", 1)

End Sub

Sub DirBox_KeyDown (Keycode As Integer, Shift As Integer)
If Keycode = Key_F1 Then Empty% = Shell("Winhelp.exe BBar.hlp", 1)
End Sub

Sub FileBox_KeyDown (Keycode As Integer, Shift As Integer)
If Keycode = Key_F1 Then Empty% = Shell("Winhelp.exe BBar.hlp", 1)

End Sub
```

continues

```
Sub DriveBox_KeyDown (Keycode As Integer, Shift As Integer)
If Keycode = Key_F1 Then Empty% = Shell("Winhelp.exe BBar.hlp", 1)
End Sub

Sub IconSelect_Click (Value As Integer)

    DriveBox.drive = Left$(IconDirectory, 2)
    DirBox.path = IconDirectory
    FileBox.Pattern = "*.ico;*.bmp"
    SelectButton.caption = SELECTCAPTION
    IconBox.Visible = TRU
    IconPanel.Visible = TRU
    BrowseBox.caption = "Select Icon File"

End Sub

Sub ProgramSelect_Click (Value As Integer)
On Error Resume Next

If Not LoadWithFile Then                                    'Choose a program.
    FileBox.Pattern = "*.bat;*.pif;*.exe;*.com"             'FilePattern for
                                                            'executables.
    SelectButton.caption = SELECTCAPTION
    IconBox.Visible = FALS
    IconPanel.Visible = FALS
    BrowseBox.caption = "Select Command File"
    DriveBox.drive = Left$(BarDir, 2)
    If Len(Barconfig.entry(3).text) > 3 Then    'Edit an existing entry,
                                                'so go to its directory.
        DriveBox.drive = Left$(Barconfig.entry(3).text, 2)
        DirBox.path = Barconfig.entry(3).text
    Else
        DriveBox.drive = Left$(BarDir, 2)       'Start at ButtonBar
                                                'default directory.
        DirBox.path = BarDir
    End If
Else
    SelectButton.caption = LOADCAPTION
    IconBox.Visible = FALS
    IconPanel.Visible = FALS
    BrowseBox.caption = "Load Selection (" + FileBox.Pattern + ")"
End If

End Sub
```

The *IconDisplay* Form (ICONDISP.FRM)

This form is used to display the embedded icons in a program file when the user is configuring a new button. A routine called Extractor (located in BBAR.BAS) uses an API call to paint the available icons to the IconDisplay form, enabling the user to select which icon to use.

```
'ICONDISPLAY FORM
'ButtonBar Plus
'(c) Copyright 1992 - Mark J. DiBiasio

Sub Form_Load ()
'Set screen position.
IconDisplay.left = BrowseBox.left + BrowseBox.Panel3D2.left
IconDisplay.top = (BrowseBox.top + BrowseBox.Panel3D2.top +
   BrowseBox.Panel3D2.Height) + 395
Call Extractor(ButtonCMDPath) 'Get icons from selected program.
End Sub


Sub A_Icon_Click (Index As Integer)
BarConfig.Picture1.picture = A_Icon(Index).image 'Place selected icon to
                                                 'picture on BarConfig.
ButtonIconPath = IconDirectory + "\" +
   Left$(BrowseBox.FileBox.FileName, InStr(BrowseBox.FileBox.FileName,
   ".")) + "bmp"
WindowsProgram = TRU 'This is a Windows program.
Unload IconDisplay
End Sub

Sub Command3D1_Click ()
ButtonIconPath = ""
WindowsProgram = FALS
Unload IconDisplay
End Sub

Sub Form_Paint ()
If Not WindowsProgram Then IconDisplay.Hide
End Sub
```

The Global Routines Module (BBAR.BAS)

The BBAR.BAS module contains global subroutines. The ArrangeBar routine performs the button alignment task. ArrangeBar sorts and aligns the buttons, and resets the ButtonBar form dimensions according to the matrix.

```
'BBAR BAS
'ButtonBar Plus
'(c) Copyright 1992 - Mark J. DiBiasio

DefInt A-Z
Const coW_HINSTANCE = (-6)
Declare Function GetWindowWord Lib "User" (ByVal hWnd As Integer,
    ByVal nIndex As Integer) As Integer
Declare Function ExtractIcon Lib "SHELL.DLL" (ByVal lpHandle
    As Integer, ByVal lpExe As String, ByVal lpiconindex
    As Integer) As Integer
Declare Function DrawIcon Lib "USER" (ByVal lpHandle As Integer,
    ByVal xcoord As Integer, ByVal ycoord As Integer,
    ByVal HIcon As Integer) As Integer

Sub ArrangeBar (IconFormMax As Integer, IconRow As Integer)
ButtonBar.Hide                      'Hiding ButtonBar speeds arrangement.
Arange = TRU                        'Set Arange flag.
ButtonBar.Timer1.enabled = FALS     'Turn off main timer.
Start = 1: Finish = IconFormMax
For X% = 1 To IconRow               'Start main loop.
    For Y% = Start To Finish        'Do secondary loop moving buttons
                                    'to new position based on new matrix.
      ButtonBar.Button(Y%).width = IconWide + 20
      ButtonBar.Button(Y%).Height = IconHigh + 20
      ButtonBar.Button(Y%).left = RowLeft
      ButtonBar.Button(Y%).top = RowTop
      RowLeft = RowLeft + IconWide
    Next Y%
   Start = Finish + 1: Finish = Finish + IconFormMax: RowLeft = 0: RowTop =
       RowTop + IconHigh
   If Finish > TotalIcons Then Finish = TotalIcons
Next X%
ButtonBar.Height = (RowCount * IconHigh) + 396   'Make allowance for
                                                 'menu bar height.
ButtonBar.width = (ButtonBar.Button(ColCount).left +
    ButtonBar.Button(ColCount).width) + 80  'Add for Windows border width
ButtonBar.Timer1.enabled = TRU                   'Reactivate main timer.
ButtonBar.Show
```

```
FormChange = TRU
Arange = FALS
End Sub
```

The *GetMatix* Routine

When the user resizes the ButtonBar form, the following routine sets the Bar matrix to the approximate form width set by the user:

```
Sub GetMatix (Col As Integer, Row As Integer)
'Find the closest column count.
Select Case Col
    Case 1 To 3
        Col = 3
        Row = 12
    Case 4 To 5
        Col = 4
        Row = 9
    Case 6 To 8
        Col = 6
        Row = 6
    Case 9 To 11
        Col = 9
        Row = 4
    Case 12 To 17
        Col = 12
        Row = 3
    Case Else
        Col = 18
        Row = 2
    End Select
ColCount = Col
RowCount = Row

End Sub
```

The *WriteDefaultIni* Routine

The WriteDefaultIni routine is called when ButtonBar is executed for the first time, using API calls to write a private .INI file:

```
Sub WriteDefaultIni ()
    'Used only when a BBAR.INI doesn't exist.

    Y% = WritePrivateProfileString("ButtonBar", ByVal "Matrix",
        ByVal Str$(18) + "-" + Str$(2), BarDir + "\" + BBARINI)
```

continues

Chapter 4: ButtonBar Plus

```
      Y% = WritePrivateProfileString("ButtonBar", ByVal "Position",
          ByVal Str$(0) + "," +  Str$(0), BarDir + "\" + BBARINI)
      Y% = WritePrivateProfileString("ButtonBar", ByVal "WinShutDown",
          ByVal Str$(0), BarDir + "\" + BBARINI)
      Y% = WritePrivateProfileString("ButtonBar", ByVal "MinimizeOnUse",
          ByVal Str$(-1), BarDir + "\" + BBARINI)
      Y% = WritePrivateProfileString("ButtonBar", ByVal "Icon Show Time",
          ByVal Str$(-1), BarDir + "\" + BBARINI)
      Y% = WritePrivateProfileString("ButtonBar", ByVal "ICONDirectory",
          ByVal BarDir +  "\BBARICON", BarDir + "\" + BBARINI)
   ICONDirectory = BarDir + "\BBARICON"
   LN = 3
   LaunchLine(LN, 1) = "Run A Program"
   LaunchLine(LN, 2) = ""
   LaunchLine(LN, 3) = BarDir
   LaunchLine(LN, 4) = ""
      Y% = WritePrivateProfileString("ButtonBar", ByVal "Button #" +
          Str$(LN), ByVal LaunchLine(LN, 1) + "¦" + LaunchLine(LN, 2)
          + "¦" + LaunchLine(LN, 3) + "¦" + LaunchLine(LN, 4), BarDir +
          "\" + BBARINI)
   LN = 4
   LaunchLine(LN, 1) = "ButtonBar Help"
   LaunchLine(LN, 2) = "WinHelp BBAR.HLP"
   LaunchLine(LN, 3) = BarDir
   LaunchLine(LN, 4) = ICONDirectory + "\WINHELP.ICO"
      Y% = WritePrivateProfileString("ButtonBar", ByVal "Button #" +
          Str$(LN), ByVal LaunchLine(LN, 1) + "¦" + LaunchLine(LN, 2)
          + "¦" + LaunchLine(LN, 3) + "¦" + LaunchLine(LN, 4), BarDir +
          "\" + BBARINI)
   LN = 5
   LaunchLine(LN, 1) = "Control Panel"
   LaunchLine(LN, 2) = "Control.exe"
   LaunchLine(LN, 3) = BarDir
   LaunchLine(LN, 4) = ICONDirectory + "\CONTROL.ICO"
      Y% = WritePrivateProfileString("ButtonBar", ByVal "Button #"
          + Str$(LN), ByVal LaunchLine(LN, 1) + "¦" + LaunchLine(LN, 2) +
          "¦" + LaunchLine(LN, 3) + "¦" + LaunchLine(LN, 4), BarDir +
          "\" + BBARINI)
   LN = 6
   LaunchLine(LN, 1) = "Windows Setup"
   LaunchLine(LN, 2) = "Setup.Exe"
   LaunchLine(LN, 3) = BarDir
   LaunchLine(LN, 4) = ICONDirectory + "\SETUP.ICO"
      Y% = WritePrivateProfileString("ButtonBar", ByVal "Button #"
          + Str$(LN), ByVal LaunchLine(LN, 1) + "¦" + LaunchLine(LN, 2)
          + "¦" + LaunchLine(LN, 3) + "¦" + LaunchLine(LN, 4), BarDir +
          "\" + BBARINI)
```

Chapter 4: ButtonBar Plus

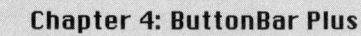

```
LN = 7
LaunchLine(LN, 1) = "Calculator"
LaunchLine(LN, 2) = "Calc.Exe"
LaunchLine(LN, 3) = BarDir
LaunchLine(LN, 4) = ICONDirectory + "\CALC.ICO"
Y% = WritePrivateProfileString("ButtonBar", ByVal "Button #"
    + Str$(LN), ByVal LaunchLine(LN, 1) + "¦" + LaunchLine(LN, 2) +
    "¦" + LaunchLine(LN, 3) + "¦" + LaunchLine(LN, 4), BarDir +
    "\" + BBARINI)
LN = 8
LaunchLine(LN, 1) = "Calendar"
LaunchLine(LN, 2) = "Calendar.Exe"
LaunchLine(LN, 3) = BarDir
LaunchLine(LN, 4) = ICONDirectory + "\CALENDAR.ICO"
Y% = WritePrivateProfileString("ButtonBar", ByVal "Button #"
    + Str$(LN), ByVal LaunchLine(LN, 1) + "¦" + LaunchLine(LN, 2) +
    "¦" + LaunchLine(LN, 3) + "¦" + LaunchLine(LN, 4), BarDir +
    "\" + BBARINI)
LN = 9
LaunchLine(LN, 1) = "Card File"
LaunchLine(LN, 2) = "Cardfile.Exe"
LaunchLine(LN, 3) = BarDir
LaunchLine(LN, 4) = ICONDirectory + "\CARDFILE.ICO"
Y% = WritePrivateProfileString("ButtonBar", ByVal "Button #"
    + Str$(LN), ByVal LaunchLine(LN, 1) + "¦" + LaunchLine(LN, 2) +
    "¦" + LaunchLine(LN, 3) + "¦" + LaunchLine(LN, 4), BarDir +
    "\" + BBARINI)
LN = 10
LaunchLine(LN, 1) = "PIF Editor"
LaunchLine(LN, 2) = "PifEdit.exe ?*.pif"
LaunchLine(LN, 3) = BarDir
LaunchLine(LN, 4) = ICONDirectory + "\PIF.ICO"
Y% = WritePrivateProfileString("ButtonBar", ByVal "Button #" +
    Str$(LN), ByVal LaunchLine(LN, 1) + "¦" + LaunchLine(LN, 2) +
    "¦" + LaunchLine(LN, 3) + "¦" + LaunchLine(LN, 4), BarDir +
    "\" + BBARINI)
LN = 11
LaunchLine(LN, 1) = "Windows Write"
LaunchLine(LN, 2) = "Write.exe ?*.wri"
LaunchLine(LN, 3) = BarDir
LaunchLine(LN, 4) = ICONDirectory + "\WRITE.ICO"
Y% = WritePrivateProfileString("ButtonBar", ByVal "Button #"
    + Str$(LN), ByVal LaunchLine(LN, 1) + "¦" + LaunchLine(LN, 2) +
    "¦" + LaunchLine(LN, 3) + "¦" + LaunchLine(LN, 4), BarDir +
    "\" + BBARINI)
LN = 12
```

continues

```
        LaunchLine(LN, 1) = "Note Pad"
        LaunchLine(LN, 2) = "NotePad.exe ?"
        LaunchLine(LN, 3) = BarDir
        LaunchLine(LN, 4) = ICONDirectory + "\NOTEPAD.ICO"
        Y% = WritePrivateProfileString("ButtonBar", ByVal "Button #"
            + Str$(LN), ByVal LaunchLine(LN, 1) + "¦" + LaunchLine(LN, 2) +
            "¦" + LaunchLine(LN, 3) + "¦" + LaunchLine(LN, 4), BarDir +
            "\" + BBARINI)
        LN = 13
        LaunchLine(LN, 1) = "Print Manager"
        LaunchLine(LN, 2) = "Printman.exe"
        LaunchLine(LN, 3) = BarDir
        LaunchLine(LN, 4) = ICONDirectory + "\PRINTMAN.ICO"
        Y% = WritePrivateProfileString("ButtonBar", ByVal "Button #"
            + Str$(LN), ByVal LaunchLine(LN, 1) + "¦" + LaunchLine(LN, 2) +
            "¦" + LaunchLine(LN, 3) + "¦" + LaunchLine(LN, 4), BarDir +
            "\" + BBARINI)
        LN = 14
        LaunchLine(LN, 1) = "File Manager"
        LaunchLine(LN, 2) = "Winfile.exe"
        LaunchLine(LN, 3) = BarDir
        LaunchLine(LN, 4) = ICONDirectory + "\WINFILE.ICO"
        Y% = WritePrivateProfileString("ButtonBar", ByVal "Button #" +
            Str$(LN), ByVal LaunchLine(LN, 1) + "¦" + LaunchLine(LN, 2) +
            "¦" + LaunchLine(LN, 3) + "¦" + LaunchLine(LN, 4), BarDir +
            "\" + BBARINI)
        LN = 15
        LaunchLine(LN, 1) = "Paint Brush"
        LaunchLine(LN, 2) = "Pbrush.exe ?*.bmp;*.pcx"
        LaunchLine(LN, 3) = BarDir
        LaunchLine(LN, 4) = ICONDirectory + "\PBRUSH.ICO"
        Y% = WritePrivateProfileString("ButtonBar", ByVal "Button #"
            + Str$(LN), ByVal LaunchLine(LN, 1) + "¦" + LaunchLine(LN, 2) +
            "¦" + LaunchLine(LN, 3) + "¦" + LaunchLine(LN, 4), BarDir +
            "\" + BBARINI)
        LN = 16
        LaunchLine(LN, 1) = "System Editor"
        LaunchLine(LN, 2) = "Sysedit.exe"
        LaunchLine(LN, 3) = BarDir + "\system"
        LaunchLine(LN, 4) = ICONDirectory + "\SYSEDIT.ICO"
        Y% = WritePrivateProfileString("ButtonBar", ByVal "Button #" +
            Str$(LN), ByVal LaunchLine(LN, 1) + "¦" + LaunchLine(LN, 2) +
            "¦" + LaunchLine(LN, 3) + "¦" + LaunchLine(LN, 4), BarDir +
            "\" + BBARINI)
        LN = 17
        LaunchLine(LN, 1) = "Terminal"
```

Chapter 4: ButtonBar Plus

```
    LaunchLine(LN, 2) = "Terminal.exe"
    LaunchLine(LN, 3) = BarDir
    LaunchLine(LN, 4) = ICONDirectory + "\TERMINAL.ICO"
    Y% = WritePrivateProfileString("ButtonBar", ByVal "Button #" +
        Str$(LN), ByVal LaunchLine(LN, 1) + "¦" + LaunchLine(LN, 2) +
        "¦" + LaunchLine(LN, 3) + "¦" + LaunchLine(LN, 4), BarDir +
        "\" + BBARINI)
    LN = 18
    LaunchLine(LN, 1) = "MS Dos Window"
    LaunchLine(LN, 2) = "C:\Command.Com"
    LaunchLine(LN, 3) = "c:\"
    LaunchLine(LN, 4) = ICONDirectory + "\DOS.ICO"
    Y% = WritePrivateProfileString("ButtonBar", ByVal "Button #"
        + Str$(LN), ByVal LaunchLine(LN, 1) + "¦" + LaunchLine(LN, 2) +
        "¦" + LaunchLine(LN, 3) + "¦" + LaunchLine(LN, 4), BarDir +
        "\" + BBARINI)

    For g% = 19 To 36
        Y% = WritePrivateProfileString("ButtonBar", ByVal "Button #" +
            Str$(g%), ByVal "", BarDir + "\" + BBARINI)
    Next g%
    GetBBarIni 'Once this file is written--now read it!
End Sub
```

The *GetBBarIni* Routine

The GetBBarIni routine uses API calls to read the ButtonBar settings saved previously in a private .INI file.

```
Sub GetBBarIni ()
On Error GoTo ErrorTrap
    'READ BBAR.INI file.
    Buf$ = String$(1024, 0)
    BufSize% = Len(Buf$)
    Y% = GetPrivateProfileString("ButtonBar", ByVal
        "Matrix", "Error", Buf$, BufSize%, BarDir + "\" + BBARINI)
    If InStr(Buf$, "Error") > 0 Then
        Call WriteDefaultIni           'If no file exists.
        Exit Sub
        End If

    'This flag is manually placed in BBAR.INI for some SuperVga cards
    'that give you font size choices.
    Y% = GetPrivateProfileString("ButtonBar", ByVal
        "ScreenFont", "Error", Buf$, BufSize%, BarDir + "\" + BBARINI)
    Temp$ = Left$(Buf$, InStr(Buf$, Chr$(0)) - 1)
```

continues

```
If Temp$ = "SMALL" Then ScreenDivsor = 15

'Flag--close windows on program exit.
Y% = GetPrivateProfileString("ButtonBar", ByVal "WinShutDown",
    "Error", Buf$, BufSize%, BarDir + "\" + BBARINI)
Temp$ = Left$(Buf$, InStr(Buf$, Chr$(0)) - 1)
WinShutDown = Val(Temp$)

'Flag--minimize ButtonBar on program execution.
Y% = GetPrivateProfileString("ButtonBar", ByVal "MinimizeOnUse",
    "Error", Buf$, BufSize%, BarDir + "\" + BBARINI)
Temp$ = Left$(Buf$, InStr(Buf$, Chr$(0)) - 1)
Minimize = Val(Temp$)

'Flag--turn minimized ButtonBar into a clock.
Y% = GetPrivateProfileString("ButtonBar", ByVal "IconShowTime",
    "Error", Buf$, BufSize%, BarDir + "\" + BBARINI)
Temp$ = Left$(Buf$, InStr(Buf$, Chr$(0)) - 1)
IconMessage = Val(Temp$)

For X% = 3 To 36        'GET button definitions.
Y% = GetPrivateProfileString("ButtonBar", ByVal "Button #" + Str$(X%),
    Error", Buf$, BufSize%, BarDir + "\" + BBARINI)
Temp$ = Left$(Buf$, InStr(Buf$, Chr$(0)) - 1)
If Temp$ = "Error" Then
    ButtonBar.Button(X%).picture = ButtonBar.DefaultIcon.picture
    GoTo skip
End If

'Parse out each line for Button setup— "¦" is the separator.
LaunchLine(X%, 1) = Mid$(Temp$, 1, InStr(Temp$, "¦") - 1)
        If Len(LTrim$(LaunchLine(X%, 1))) < 1 Then
            ButtonBar.Button(X%).picture =
                ButtonBar.DefaultIcon.picture
            GoTo skip
        End If

Temp$ = Mid$(Temp$, InStr(Temp$, "¦") + 1)
LaunchLine(X%, 2) = Mid$(Temp$, 1, InStr(Temp$, "¦") - 1)
Temp$ = Mid$(Temp$, InStr(Temp$, "¦") + 1)
LaunchLine(X%, 3) = Mid$(Temp$, 1, InStr(Temp$, "¦") - 1)
Temp$ = Mid$(Temp$, InStr(Temp$, "¦") + 1)
    If Len(Temp$) > 0 Then LaunchLine(X%, 4) = Mid$(Temp$, 1)
        If X% > 2 And Len(LTrim$(LaunchLine(X%, 4))) > 3 Then
        'Load icons into buttons.
            ButtonBar.Button(X%).picture =
                LoadPicture(LaunchLine(X%, 4))
```

Chapter 4: ButtonBar Plus

```
            End If
skip:
Next X%

    'Get last ButtonBar matrix.
    Y% = GetPrivateProfileString("ButtonBar", ByVal "Matrix",
        "Error", Buf$, BufSize%, BarDir + "\" + BBARINI)
    Temp$ = Left$(Buf$, InStr(Buf$, Chr$(0)) - 1)
    ColCount = Val(Mid$(Temp$, 1, InStr(Temp$, "-") - 1))

    'Get last screen position
    Y% = GetPrivateProfileString("ButtonBar", ByVal "Position",
        "Error", Buf$, BufSize%, BarDir + "\" + BBARINI)
    Temp$ = Left$(Buf$, InStr(Buf$, Chr$(0)) - 1)
    ButtonBar.top = Val(Mid$(Temp$, 1, InStr(Temp$, ",") - 1))
    Temp$ = Mid$(Temp$, InStr(Temp$, ",") + 1)
    ButtonBar.left = Val(Temp$)

    'Get icon storage directory.
    Y% = GetPrivateProfileString("ButtonBar", ByVal "IconDirectory",
        "Error", Buf$, BufSize%, BarDir + "\" + BBARINI)
    Temp$ = Left$(Buf$, InStr(Buf$, Chr$(0)) - 1)
    ICONDirectory = Temp$

Exit Sub
ErrorTrap:
    If Err <> 5 Then MsgBox Error$(Err) + Chr$(13) + LaunchLine(X%, 4)
    Resume Next
End Sub
```

The *Extractor* and *ShadowEffects* Routines

The Extractor routine uses a special technique to retrieve and draw embedded icons located in a windows program. The ShadowEffects routine is used to add a three-dimensional look to the objects displayed by ButtonBar Plus.

```
Sub Extractor (ExeFile$)
    'This extracts embedded icons from a Windows program.
    Handle% = IconDisplay.hWnd
    'Get instance handle of IconDisplay window.
    Inst% = GetWindowWord(Handle%, GWW_HINSTANCE)
    'Pull icons from target file if they exist.
    For z% = 0 To 5
        HIcon% = ExtractIcon(Inst%, ExeFile$, z%)   'See func. dec.
        IconDisplay.A_icon(z%).Cls
        Draw% = DrawIcon(IconDisplay.A_icon(z%).hdc, 0, 0,
            HIcon%) 'Paint Icon
```

continues

```
            'Refresh after paint *** MUST DO ***
            'otherwise it won't work!!!
            IconDisplay.A_icon(z%).Refresh
      Next z%
      'HIcon% returns a 1 if the program is a non-Windows program.
      If HIcon% <> 1 Then WindowsProgram = TRU Else WindowsProgram = FALS
End Sub

Sub ShadowEffect (Target_Control As Control)
   'Add three-dimensional effect to target control.
   Dim Target_Offset As Single
   screen.ActiveForm.scalemode = Pixels
   Target_Offset = 1
   screen.ActiveForm.DrawWidth = 2
   screen.ActiveForm.ForeColor = WHITE
   screen.ActiveForm.Line (Target_Control.left - Target_Offset,
      Target_Control.top + Target_Control.Height + Target_Offset)
      -(Target_Control.left + Target_Control.width + Target_Offset,
      Target_Control.top + Target_Control.Height + Target_Offset)
   screen.ActiveForm.Line -(Target_Control.left + Target_Control.width +
      Target_Offset, Target_Control.top - Target_Offset)
      screen.ActiveForm.ForeColor = DARKGREY
   screen.ActiveForm.Line -(Target_Control.left - Target_Offset,
      Target_Control.top - Target_Offset)
   screen.ActiveForm.Line -(Target_Control.left - Target_Offset,
      Target_Control.top + Target_Control.Height)
   End Sub
```

The *License* Form (LICENSE.FRM)

The License form is loaded during program startup, and displays the program version, title, and license information:

```
'License Form
'ButtonBar Plus
'(c) Copyright 1992 - Mark J. DiBiasio

Sub Form_Load ()
left = (Screen.width - width) \ 2
top = (Screen.height - height) \ 2
Label1.caption = Label1.caption + " V" + ver
AuthorLabel.caption = "By Mark J. DiBiasio" + Chr$(13) +
    " Copyright 1992  -   All Rights Reserved"
```

```
ShareWareLabel.caption = "This product is protected by the
    copyright laws of the United States as well other
    principalities. No portion of this product, source code or
    design, may be sold, copied or included in another product"
ShareWareLabel.caption = ShareWareLabel.caption +
    " without the written permission of the author."
ShareWareLabel2.caption = "Using this product means that you have
    read and have agreed to abide by the terms of the ButtonBar Plus
    License Agreement."
End Sub

Sub Form_Paint ()
'Title Screen Delay.
Start! = Timer
    While Timer < Start! + 2
        Empty% = DoEvents()
    Wend
End Sub
```

Summary

While I programmed ButtonBar Plus, I paid particular attention to keeping the program size to a minimum and execution speed as fast as possible. Removing the default icon and drag icon from secondary forms, reusing variables and forms whenever possible, doing form resizing when the form is hidden, and keeping the global module as small as possible are a few of the ways to accomplish this without limiting the program's functionality.

The ButtonBar Plus program and source code included with this book remain the property of Mark J. DiBiasio. No portion of the source code or design can be used, included with other programs written for profit, or sold without the written permission and/or compensation of the author. The purpose of including source code and executable software with this book is to educate the reader; however, if readers wish to use this software, they must register the software with the author and pay a license fee. The license fee schedule is as follows:

License this copy of ButtonBar Plus V1.01	$15.00
License this copy of ButtonBar Plus V1.01 and receive one copy of ButtonBar Plus Advanced	$25.00

ButtonBar Plus Advanced Edition supports 66 user-configurable buttons and includes other enhancements not found in the Plus version.

Chapter 4: ButtonBar Plus

PrintClip

by Art Krumsee

Chapter 5: PrintClip

Overview

Like most Windows users, I had ideas for several utilities within weeks of the Windows 3.0 release. One of the most basic was a quick and easy way to print a small block of text from an application. Occasionally, I wanted to print a paragraph from a word processing document. Specifically, I wanted to print an E-mail message I read online using Terminal and other communications packages. The only choice I had was to copy the text to the Clipboard, load Notepad, paste the text to Notepad, and then print it from Notepad and return to Terminal. This was hardly a convenient option.

Because I had written many DOS utilities over the years, my inability to put together a Windows utility to meet my needs was very frustrating. I had casual programming experience in BASIC, Pascal, and C, but none of that prepared me for my first perusal of the Windows Software Developer's Kit manuals. After a few hours of browsing, I was overwhelmed. It would take at least three months of full-time work to develop the expertise to write simple Windows applications in C. Unfortunately, because I'm not a professional programmer, my supervisior had other ideas about how I would spend my work hours.

The next moment of hope came with the release of Turbo Pascal for Windows. I upgraded my old copy of Turbo Pascal and began reading the manuals. I worked through the introductory manuals; for the first time, I understood the basic concepts of object-oriented programming. I worked through the tutorial and created a sample Windows application. To learn the Turbo Pascal ObjectWindows API, however, would take four to six weeks of study.

Fortunately, Microsoft released Visual Basic at about the same time. Within hours, I was writing simple applications. Within a few days, I had completed my first utility. Perhaps most impressively, I finished the PrintClip application in less than 40 lines of code.

How to Use PrintClip

PrintClip is a simple but useful Windows application. When you load PrintClip, an icon appears at the bottom of the screen. You can keep it in the Windows StartUp group or on the Run line in Windows 3.1. When you double-click PrintClip, it checks for text in the Windows Clipboard. If it finds text, it sends it to the default Windows printer. Regardless of whether the printer is a dot-matrix printer, an HP LaserJet, or a PostScript printer, the text appears formatted in 80-column lines.

If you want to print from the Windows Terminal application, highlight the text you want to print using the mouse, select **C**opy from the Terminal **E**dit menu, and then double-click the PrintClip icon.

PrintClip can also help you print text from non-Windows applications. If the DOS character-mode application is running full-screen, just press Alt-Enter to drop it into a window. Then highlight the text you want to print, select **C**opy from the Windows Control **E**dit menu (the box with the dash in it, located in the upper-left corner of every Windows window) and then double-click the PrintClip icon. This is particularly helpful if your only printer is a PostScript printer and your DOS applications don't support PostScript.

Program Operation

PrintClip is based on less than 40 lines of Visual Basic code. But that doesn't mean that developing PrintClip was without challenges. Perhaps the most difficult task was developing an application that had no form. PrintClip always appears as an icon—never as a form. Visual Basic is built around the concept of code attached to forms, with objects on those forms.

After reading through the documentation and checking with other Visual Basic developers on CompuServe, I realized that PrintClip had to have a form. Visual Basic applications just don't function without forms. This brought me to the second phase of the problem: What was I going to do with the form? I first tried keeping it minimized (as an icon) using the form's `Resize` event. As soon as the user clicks the icon, the `Resize` event is triggered. The first thing I put in the `Resize` event was a statement to reduce the form back to an icon (`WindowState=1`). Unfortunately, the code in the `Resize` event is not really processed until after the form is drawn on-screen. Even a blank form takes a few moments to draw. I was left with a distracting paint/erase sequence on-screen every time I double-clicked the PrintClip icon.

My next thought was to make the form very small. Windows can paint and clear a pixel-sized form in milliseconds, I reasoned. But a Visual Basic form can't be that small. It has to have a title bar and it has to be wide enough to hold the control button and the minimize/maximize buttons. Even a form this large was distracting; however, I learned that a small form painted and cleared much faster than a big one.

Next, I tried dragging the form as far off-screen as I could, leaving just the lower-right corner displayed at the top of the screen. This helped because

Windows doesn't try to paint parts of the form it can't display. This led to the final solution: leave the form in the middle of the screen during development, but include a statement in the code that moves it off-screen as part of the load process. Because the form's name is PrintClip, I added the statement `PrintClip.Left=-5000`. This moves the form off-screen to the left before it is displayed. From the perspective of the user, the PrintClip application has no form.

You may recall that PrintClip has a form that is invisible to the user. Figure 5.1 shows the actual form that contains the code.

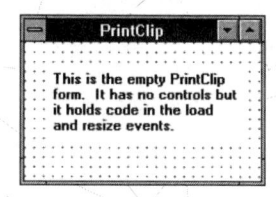

Figure 5.1. The "invisible" PrintClip form.

Let's explore the pieces of Visual Basic code that drive the PrintClip utility.

The *Load* Event

The code in the Load event is extremely simple. It positions the form off-screen and then minimizes it to an icon. The code reads as follows:

```
Sub Form_Load ()
    windowstate = 1
    printclip.left = -5000
End Sub
```

The *Resize* Event

The code in the Resize event is considerably more complex. The code has several functions:

1. To minimize the form immediately so that it stays iconized.

2. To check for the presence of text in the Clipboard. If text is in the Clipboard, retrieve it. If there is no text in the Clipboard, display an error message.

3. To break the text into 80-column lines if they are longer than 80 lines. (This is important, because the text in Windows applications usually includes carriage returns only at the end of paragraphs.)

4. To print each line of text.

Keep the Form Minimized

The skeletal code for maintaining a minimized state is as follows:

```
If WindowState <> 1 Then
    WindowState = 1
    .
    .
    .
    Code for Retrieving and processing Clipboard text
    .
    .
    .
End If
```

The first lines of code check to see if the form is minimized; if not, the lines minimize the form. Specifically, if the value of the WindowState property is not 1, the routine sets it to 1.

The initial check of the WindowState property is required because setting the WindowState to 1 generates another call to the Resize event. If you want to see an application run out of stack space quickly, create a Resize event for a form that just sets WindowState to 1. After the first resize, the window is resized repeatedly until the program crashes. The If WindowState condition checks to ensure that none of the following code is executed unless the PrintClip icon is double-clicked.

Retrieve Clipboard Text

The skeletal code for retrieving the Clipboard text is as follows:

```
If Clipboard.GetFormat(1) Then
    temp$ = Clipboard.GetText(1)
    .
    .
    .
    Code for formatting and printing text
    .
    .
    .
```

```
Else
    Msg$ = "There is no text on the Clipboard."
    MsgBox Msg$ , 0, "PrintClip Error"
End If
```

Visual Basic provides functions for inserting, retrieving, and checking the contents of the Clipboard. PrintClip uses two of them: `GetFormat()` and `GetText()`. Because PrintClip prints only text, the `GetFormat()` function is critical. `GetFormat()` returns a value of TRUE if the Clipboard holds data of the desired type. The following is a list of possible types:

Clipboard Format	Value
CF_LINK	&HBF00
CF_TEXT	1
CF_BITMAP	2
CF_METAFILE	3
CF_DIB	8

By passing a value of 1 to the `GetFormat()` function, PrintClip checks to see if there is any text in the Clipboard.

If there is text in the Clipboard, the second line retrieves it and stores it in the variable `temp$`. As with the `GetFormat()` function, a value of 1 specifies that you want text to be returned from the Clipboard.

If there is no text in the Clipboard to print, PrintClip uses the Visual Basic `MsgBox` statement to report this to the user. The first parameter is a text string that contains the message to be displayed. The second parameter determines how many and what kind of buttons to display below the error message. This example uses the simplest value—zero—which causes only an OK button to be displayed. The third parameter of the `MsgBox` statement specifies the title that appears in the title bar of the message box.

Break and Print Text Strings

The following code fragment breaks the text into 80-column strings and prints them:

```
cr$ = Chr$(13)
While Len(temp$) > 80
    If InStr(temp$, cr$) > 80 Or InStr(temp$, cr$) = 0 Then
```

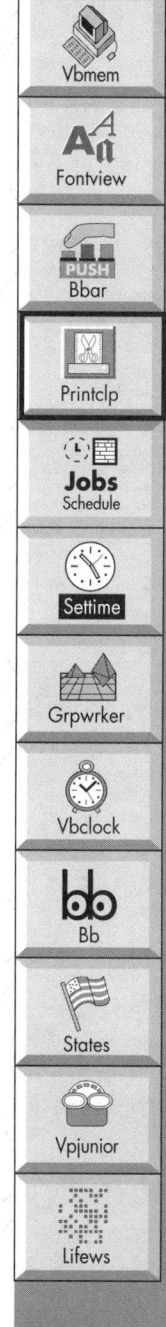

continues

```
            counter = 80
            While Mid$(temp$, counter, 1) <> " " and counter > 1
                counter = counter - 1
            Wend
            If counter = 1 Then counter = 80
            prstr$ = Left$(temp$, counter)
            temp$ = Right$(temp$, Len(temp$) - counter)
        Else
            prstr$ = Left$(temp$, InStr(temp$, cr$) - 1)
            temp$ = Right$(temp$, Len(temp$) - (InStr(temp$, cr$) + 1))
        End If
        printer.Print prstr$
Wend
printer.Print temp$
printer.EndDoc
```

The first line establishes the variable cr$, which holds the value chr$(13) (a carriage return). The cr$ variable will be used to look for carriage returns within the text copied from the Clipboard. Next, the code immediately opens a While...Wend loop to process temp$. In each iteration of the loop, a piece of temp$ will print and be removed from the front of temp$ until temp$ is 80 or fewer characters long. At that time, the program breaks out of the loop and processes the last two lines, printing the rest of temp$ and closing the print job.

Within the While...Wend loop, PrintClip immediately checks to see if and where there are carriage returns within temp$. If there is a carriage return within the first 80 characters, PrintClip executes the statements in the Else portion of the If statment:

```
            prstr$ = Left$(temp$, InStr(temp$, cr$) - 1)
            temp$ = Right$(temp$, Len(temp$) - (InStr(temp$, cr$) + 1))
```

These lines are fairly typical examples of the flexible string processing possible with Visual Basic's string functions. Here's a summary of each of the string manipulation routines used in this portion of the program:

Left$(x,y)—returns the leftmost y characters of the string specified in variable x.

Right$(x,y)—returns the rightmost y characters of the string specified in variable x.

Len(x)—returns the length in characters of the string specified in variable x.

InStr(x,y)—returns the location of the string y within the string specified by variable x.

Chapter 5: PrintClip

The first of these two lines of code sets the variable `prstr$` equal to the leftmost portion of `temp$`, up to (but not including) the carriage return. It uses `InStr` to determine where the carriage return is and then subtracts 1 from that value to exclude the carriage return.

The second line uses the `Right$` function to cut off the portion of `temp$` just printed. It uses `Len()` to determine the total length of the string and `InStr()` to determine the length of portion just printed. By subtracting the second from the first, the program determines how many characters should remain in the string. The `Right$` function keeps only the rightmost characters and assigns them to `temp$`.

What happens if there is no carriage return in the first 80 characters of `temp$`? Because you don't want PrintClip to break a line by cutting a word in half, you must search for a space near the end of the first 80 characters in `temp$`. The line can then be broken at that space:

```
counter = 80
While Mid$(temp$, counter, 1) <> " " and counter > 1
    counter = counter - 1
Wend
If counter = 1 Then counter = 80
```

This block of code begins by setting the variable `counter` to a value of 80. It then opens a `While...Wend` loop having its condition based on another Visual Basic string function: `Mid$()`. `Mid$(x,y,z)` returns `z` characters from string `x` starting at position `y`.

PrintClip's loop begins with `Mid$` returning the 80th character within `temp$` and checking to see if it is a space. If it is a space, the loop ends. If not, `counter` is decremented (reduced in value by 1) and the loop resumes. This time, however, it checks to see if the 79th character is a space. The loop continues until a space is found.

If the first 80 characters of the text contain neither a space nor a carriage return, the `While...Wend` loop also ends if the value of `counter` falls to 1. In this case, the line immediately following the loop resets the counter to 80. This will cause the first 80 characters of this unbroken block of characters to print on a single line.

When the location of the space has been found and stored in the variable `counter`, PrintClip uses a familiar block of code to define the string to be printed, and to eliminate the printed text from `temp$`. This code is virtually the same as the block that identified the carriage return in `temp$`; however, you use the variable `counter` to know where to break the string. The first line assigns to the variable `prstr$` the leftmost characters of `temp$` up to the space. The second line uses `Right$` to keep all of `temp$` except the characters just assigned to `prstr$`:

```
    prstr$ = Left$(temp$, counter)
    temp$ = Right$(temp$, Len(temp$) - counter)
```

After assigning a value to `prstr$` and truncating `temp$`, PrintClip exits the `If...Then...End If` condition and prints the line of text it identified:

```
        printer.Print prstr$
    Wend
```

After printing this line, PrintClip encounters the `Wend`, which returns it to the beginning of the loop if the length of `temp$` is more than 80 characters. If the length of `temp$` is 80 characters or fewer, the `While...Wend` loop ends and the last two lines are executed:

```
    printer.Print temp$
    printer.EndDoc
```

The first of these lines prints the remaining contents of `temp$`. The second closes the print job, releasing the job to the Windows Print Manager for final processing.

Conclusion

Although PrintClip's code is brief and its function is simple, it serves as an excellent example of the ease with which you can create useful applications in Visual Basic. It also provides excellent examples of complex string processing. Effective use of functions such as `Left$()`, `Mid$()`, `Instr()`, and `Len()` allow the programmer to manipulate text in many situations, including output formatting, data-entry editing, search and replace, and so on.

PrintClip also illustrates a highly functional technique for creating Visual Basic applications that appear to be without an associated form. This technique is useful whenever there is a need for a tool that operates automatically by clicking an icon.

More importantly, PrintClip is a handy utility to use every day in Windows. It functions quickly and unobtrusively with any application that copies text to the Clipboard.

Source Code for PrintClip

The PrintClip program contains the fewest number of lines of code of any program included in this book. Even though PrintClip was built with less than 40 lines of code and requires no Global code, it is a very powerful and handy tool. Here is the complete code listing for the PrintClip program:

```
Sub Form_Resize ()
If windowstate <> 1 Then
    windowstate = 1

    If Clipboard.GetFormat(1) Then      'Is there text in the clipboard?
        temp$ = Clipboard.GetText(1)    'Get text from Clipboard
        cr$ = Chr$(13)

        While Len(temp$) > 80
            If InStr(temp$, cr$) > 80 Or InStr(temp$, cr$) = 0 Then
                'Find a space at the right end of the first
                    80 characters in temp$
                counter = 80
                While Mid$(temp$, counter, 1) <> " " And counter > 1
                    counter = counter - 1
                Wend
                If counter = 1 Then counter = 80
                'Define prstr$ as the portion of temp$ up to the space
                prstr$ = Left$(temp$, counter)
                temp$ = Right$(temp$, Len(temp$) - counter)
            Else
                prstr$ = Left$(temp$, InStr(temp$, cr$) - 1)
                temp$ = Right$(temp$, Len(temp$) -
                    (InStr(temp$, cr$) + 1))
            End If
            printer.Print prstr$
        Wend

        printer.Print temp$
        printer.EndDoc
    Else
        Msg$ = "There is no text on the Clipboard."
        MsgBox Msg$, 0, "PrintClip Error"' Display error message.
    End If

End If
End Sub
Sub Form_Load ()
    windowstate = 1
    printclip.left = -5000
End Sub
```

Chapter 5: PrintClip

Job Scheduler

by Michael Kosten

6

Chapter 6: Job Scheduler

Overview

Old-timers to computer programming recall an era before interactive applications such as word processing and spreadsheets. The programmer had to specify a program's input before the program's execution. This was first done with a batch of punch cards, and later in an electronic job file. Computer operators queued and ran the program, and you received the output hours or days later. If you made a mistake on the input, you went through the entire process again.

Minicomputers and mainframe computers still make this distinction between an interactive session and a batch job requiring no run-time user input. Often, batch jobs of resource-intensive operations and system backups are performed at night and at regular intervals. So, the ability to schedule jobs is usually part of minicomputer operating systems.

Because the operating system frequently supplied with PCs (DOS) was designed for a single user running one interactive program, DOS can't schedule jobs. The concept of batch jobs is maintained in .BAT files, such as AUTOEXEC.BAT, which runs automatically when the computer is booted. With Windows, which can run several programs simultaneously, scheduling jobs is possible. Although it is still quite a horse race, Windows is evolving into an operating system that may become the backbone of corporate world computing, supporting powerful servers and networked workstations. In this environment, job scheduling is critical.

The Visual Basic Job Scheduler utility schedules jobs to run on a particular day of the week and at a particular time. To do this requires three components: a list of jobs and times they are to be run, a clock, and a method of launching jobs. In Visual Basic, these are the List Box and Timer controls and the Shell() function. Visual Basic is such a high-level language that writing a scheduling program is easy. The challenge lies in designing a utility that is simple for others to use but still well-featured.

Designing a Utility

Applications come and go, out-gunned and out-featured by fierce competition. But the fame of a good utility is pervasive and lasting, if not lucrative. Utilities demand elegance; because they need to do only one thing well, elegance is achievable. Here are three simple rules by which to write a utility program.

Designing a Useful Utility

Write generic or useful utilities to use for many situations; however, do not "kitchen sink" a utility by adding too many features. This is espccially true in the Windows environment. In the DOS world, where a user can run only one program at a time (and maybe one utility, such as SideKick, as a TSR), applications are laden with features. A word processor might include a calendar application, a spreadsheet, or a communications interface. Windows users can design their desktops with their choice of a word processor, spreadsheet, or calendar program. Data-exchange protocols like dynamic data exchange (DDE) make it possible for these applications to share data with each other, even if they come from different developers. A good utility needs to do only one thing well, and, if appropriate, it should be able to interact with other Windows applications.

Making the Interface Intuitively Obvious

Intuitive is a popular buzzword in the computer world, and for good reason. Today, users are much less patient about learning a program. (I hate to think what results a survey on manual-reading would return.) The user (someone other than yourself) should be able to figure out a utility by looking at the screen, exploring menus, and clicking a few buttons. As a corollary, you should add safeguards so that the user is warned against doing something disastrous. Also, reduce keyboard entry to a minimum; the mouse is quickly becoming a necessity for working in the Windows environment.

Writing Source Code that You Can Reuse and Maintain

Writing modular code includes organizing frequently used code into separate functions and subroutines. This helps make the code more readable and reduces the size of a program. Another advantage is that you can build a personal library of functions that you can use in other programs. Whenever a portion of code may be useful in other programs, it's a good idea to write it as a user-defined function. This also helps make the source code easier to maintain. If there is a bug in a function, you need to change it in only one place.

Special Features of the Job Scheduler

Even if you don't have an urgent need for a job scheduler, this utility is a great example of some of the powerful—and maybe under-utilized—features of Visual Basic that you can use in many other programs.

Using Serial Dates and Times

In many programming languages, dealing with times and dates can be troublesome. Visual Basic, however, makes time- and date-handling easy with the introduction of time and date serials, like those found in spreadsheet applications. In another language, if you wanted to display the date a week from today, you might need to keep a table of the days in each month—and then account for leap years! In Visual Basic, you need only convert a date to a serial, add seven, and then convert it back to a date. It could be even simpler; for example, `Format$(Now+7,"ddddd")` returns the date a week from today as a string.

Using the *Timer* Control

The `Timer` might be the most interesting control in Visual Basic. It simplifies programming that is quite difficult in other languages. The `Timer` executes code at predetermined intervals. This enables you to create a utility that works in the background without draining the computer's resources.

Calling the *Shell()* Function

`Shell()` executes a program. It is similar to choosing **File | Run** from the Windows Program Manager, except you have more control of the window style.

Program Operation

Now let's take a look at the forms and code that make up the Job Scheduler and then explore some modifications you can make to the program.

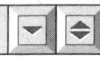

Designing the Main Screen

The opening screen of the utility, a form named `FormJobList`, appears in the Visual Basic design mode as shown in Figure 6.1.

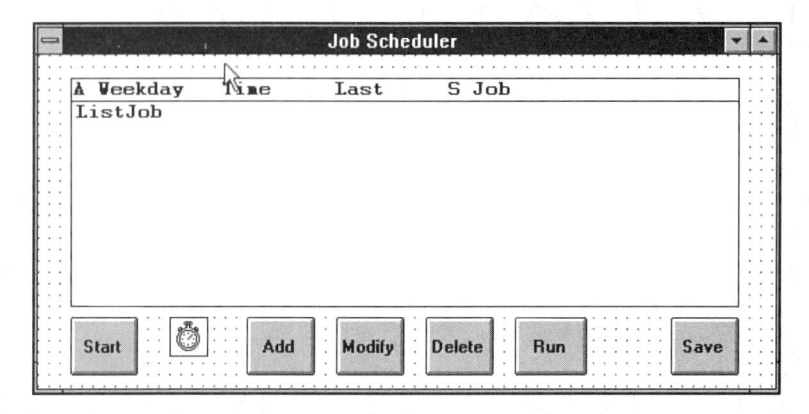

Figure 6.1. The initial Job Scheduler form.

Drawing the Main Screen Controls

It is a good idea to start programming by drawing all the main screen controls. Included is a list box control, `ListJob`, which contains one item for each scheduled job. As described by the label above the list box, each list item contains

- An active flag
- The weekday the job is scheduled
- The time the job is scheduled
- The date the job last ran
- The path of the job file (as space permits)
- The name of the job file (as space permits)
- The parameters of the job file (as space permits)

The *S* column holds the window style (1, 2, 3, 4, or 7) as described in the Visual Basic `Shell()` function. This determines whether the job runs in a normal, minimized, or maximized window.

The user navigates the utility with six command button controls. `CommandAdd` and `CommandModify` load the `FormModifyJob` form, where the user adds or changes a job in the `ListJob` control. `CommandDelete` deletes the current item from the list. `CommandRun` calls the `Shell()` function for the current list item, which is useful for testing. `CommandSave` writes the current list to a disk file—DEFAULT.SCH in the Windows directory. This file is automatically loaded into `ListJob` at the start of the program. `CommandStart` enables the `Timer` control `TimerJob`—represented on the design screen by a stopwatch—and disables all other controls. There is no control to unload the utility; the user must use the Close option from the system control box in the upper-left corner of the screen.

Storing a Job

The core object of the program is a job. Each control processes a job or the job list. You can store all the pertinent information about a job as a string, as displayed in the `ListJob` control. You can then use the `Mid$` function to extract information from the string. If a job is stored in the string `sJob`, a subroutine for calling the `Shell()` function might be written like this:

```
Declare Sub ShellJob(sJob As String)

Const POS_ACTIVE% = 1
Const POS_COMMAND% = 33
Const POS_STYLE% = 31

If Mid$(sJob,POS_ACTIV,1) = "A" Then
   TaskId% = Shell(Mid$(sJob,POS_COMMAND%),Val(Mid$(sJob,POS_STYLE%,1))
Endif

End Sub
```

Even with the `Constant` declarations, the source code soon becomes difficult to read and even more difficult to modify, especially when you start adding date and time conversions. Visual Basic, however, has a special feature to handle storing complex data relative to one object: the user-defined type or structure.

Creating a Job Structure

A structure is a special variable type that the user defines in the global module using `Type` and `End Type`. This new type is really a grouping of standard variable types, like `Integer` and `String`. The job structure in the `Scheduler` utility is defined like this:

```
Type JobStructure
    Active As Integer
    Weekday As String
```

continues

```
    Time As Double
    HasRun As Integer
    LastRan As Double
    Style As Integer
    Path As String
    Filename As String
    Parameters As String
End Type
```

This code closely mimics how a job is displayed in the ListJob control. The difference is that much of a job's information is not stored as a string, but as variable types closer to how the data needs to be converted for Visual Basic functions. Active, typed as an integer, is a logical variable determining whether the job should be run. Time and Weekday are used to specify when the job should be started. Style is an integer, as required by the Shell function.

Notice that the job's path (directory), filename, and parameters are separate strings, and that there is an integer variable HasRun. As you will see later in this chapter, the separation of the full command string into three components simplifies modifying a job in the FormModifyJob form. HasRun allows you to maintain information about LastRan that you could not store as a date, such as whether the job has ever run, and whether its last run erred.

By passing a structure, the Shell subroutine becomes more readable:

```
Declare Sub ShellJob(Job As JobStructure)

If Job.Active Then
   TaskId% = Shell(Job.Path+Job.Filename+" "+Job.Parameters,Job.Style)
Endif

End Sub
```

Converting from String to Structure and Back Again

Because you cannot display the new type JobStructure as an item in the ListJob control, you will need a method to convert JobStructure to a string. There is no point in keeping this data elsewhere (such as an array of JobStructures) if you are already storing all the vital information about all the jobs in the ListJob control. Therefore, you will also need a method to convert a string back into a JobStructure. Because you are likely to do these conversions often, it is a good idea to construct them as user-defined functions that can be called from many points within the program. Here is how the first of these functions appears in the general area of the `FormJobList` form:

```
Function Job2String (Job As JobStructure, JobString As String)
    As Integer

    If Job.Active Then
        JobString = "A "
    Else
        JobString = "I "
    End If

    JobString = JobString + Rack$(Job.Weekday, 9) + " "
    JobString = JobString + Format$(Job.Time, "hh:mm AM/PM") + " "

    If Job.HasRun = -1 Then
        JobString = JobString + Format$(Job.LastRan, "mm/dd/yy") + " "
    ElseIf Job.HasRun = 0 Then
        JobString = JobString + Space$(9)
    Else
        JobString = JobString + Rack$("Error", 9)
    End If

    JobString = JobString + Format$(Job.Style, "#") + " "
    JobString = JobString + Job.Path + Job.Filename + " " +
        Job.Parameters

    Job2String = -1

    Exit Function

End Function
```

The `Rack` function is not native to Visual Basic; it is, however, a user-defined function to force a string to a specific length, like a torture rack. Because this function is broadly useful, I've placed it in a separate module named FUNCS.BAS, which follows.

```
Function Rack$ (Victim As String, Length As Integer)

    If Len(Victim) < Length Then
        Rack$ = Victim + Space$(Length - Len(Victim))
    Else
        Rack$ = Left$(Victim, Length)
    End If

End Function
```

The `Integer HasRun` stores additional information about the value of `LastRan`. A value of –1 flags that `LastRan` contains a valid date. A value of 0 indicates that the job has not yet been run, and 1 indicates that the last attempt to run the job failed.

`Job2String` converts all the data types in `JobStructure` to a string the user can read. This is also the same form in which jobs are saved to a disk file, which can then be loaded into the list box `ListJob` when the program starts. When it is time to run a job, the function `String2Job`, also in the general area of `FormJobList`, converts a job string to a job structure:

```
Function String2Job (JobString As String, Job As JobStructure)
    As Integer
    Dim Filepath As String
    Dim ParmSep As Integer
    Dim PathSep As Integer

    On Error GoTo ErrorBadJobString

    If Left$(JobString, 1) = "A" Then
        Job.Active = -1
    Else
        Job.Active = 0
    End If
    Job.Weekday = RTrim$(Mid$(JobString, 3, 9))
    Job.Time = TimeValue(Mid$(JobString, 13, 8))
    If Mid$(JobString, 22, 5) = "Error" Then
        Job.HasRun = 1
    ElseIf Mid$(JobString, 22, 8) = Space$(8) Then
        Job.HasRun = 0
    Else
        Job.HasRun = -1
        Job.LastRan = DateValue(Mid$(JobString, 22, 8))
    End If
    Job.Style = Val(Mid$(JobString, 31, 1))

    ParmSep = InStr(Mid$(JobString, 33), " ")
    If ParmSep = 0 Then
        Filepath = Mid$(JobString, 33)
        Job.Parameters = ""
    Else
        Filepath = Left$(Mid$(JobString, 33), ParmSep - 1)
        Job.Parameters = Mid$(JobString, 33 + ParmSep)
    End If

    PathSep = RInStr(Filepath, "\")
```

Chapter 6: Job Scheduler

```
    If PathSep = 0 Then
        Job.Path = ""
        Job.Filename = Filepath
    Else
        Job.Path = Left$(Filepath, PathSep)
        Job.Filename = Mid$(Filepath, PathSep + 1)
    End If

    String2Job = -1

    Exit Function

ErrorBadJobString:
    String2Job = 0
    Exit Function

End Function
```

The `String2Job` function contains an error handler. The functions `TimeValue` and `DateValue` could produce a run-time error, in which case the routine jumps to the error handler and `String2Job` returns 0 (FALSE) to indicate failure. If the functions execute normally, `String2Job` returns –1 (TRUE).

First, a job's parameters are separated from the job's file path (a fully qualified filename) by locating the first space. Then the file path is parsed into the directory and filename by finding the rightmost path (\) character.

The Visual Basic function `InStr` is used to find the first, or leftmost, occurrence of a substring in a string. Visual Basic, however, does not contain a rightmost version of this function, which you need in order to separate the filename from the rest of the file path string. `RInStr` is found in FUNCS.BAS. The user-defined function to accomplish this, `RInStr`, is found in FUNCS.BAS.

```
Function RInStr (SearchString As String, ForString As String)
    Dim Position As Integer

    For Position = Len(SearchString) - Len(ForString) + 1 To 1 Step -1
        If Mid$(SearchString, Position, Len(ForString)) = ForString Then
            RInStr = Position
            Exit Function
        End If
    Next

    RInStr = 0

End Function
```

Loading the List from a Disk File

The first routine that is called when you run the program is the `Form_Load` subroutine for the main form. In this routine, which is called only once in the Scheduler program, the `ListJob` list box is loaded with the contents of a disk file. This file, created by another routine of this utility, is exactly parallel to the `ListJob` list box. Therefore, you only have to read a record (line) from the disk file, add the record to the list box, read the next record, and so on, until the end of the disk file. The following is the `Form_Load` subroutine for the main form `FormJobList`:

```
Sub Form_Load ()
    Dim Windir As String * 128
    Dim Job As JobStructure

    FormAbout.Show 1

    PathLen% = GETWINDOWSDIRECTORY(Windir, 128)
    Filename$ = Left$(Windir, PathLen%) + "\DEFAULT.SCH"

    If Dir$(Filename$) <> "" Then
        Open Filename$ For Input Access Read Shared As 1
        Do While Not EOF(1)
            Input #1, JobItem$
            If Not String2Job(JobItem$, Job) Then
                MsgBox "Invalid Schedule File!"
                End
            End If
            Result% = Job2String(Job, JobItem$)
            ListJob.AddItem JobItem$
        Loop
        Close #1
    End If

End Sub
```

The first action is to display another form named `FormAbout` using the `Show` method. This form displays authorship, copyright, and a disclaimer. The form needs no further description; it is incidental to the utility. You should know, however, that the `Show` method is called with a parameter of 1. This makes `FormAbout` *modal,* meaning the user cannot perform actions on another form (except a child form, which does not occur in this case) until `FormAbout` has been hidden or unloaded.

Next is a call to `GETWINDOWSDIRECTORY`. This is a Windows kernel function. Visual Basic can call many functions that are contained in the DLLs (dynamic link libraries) that are the heart of Windows, provided that you declare the functions in the global module. The following is the declaration for `GETWINDOWSDIRECTORY`:

```
Declare Function GETWINDOWSDIRECTORY% Lib "KERNEL"
    (ByVal F As String, ByVal FLEN As Integer)
```

`GETWINDOWSDIRECTORY` returns the directory that contains Windows. You use this call because in the Windows 3.0 Program Manager executing a program by selecting its icon did not guarantee a starting (working) directory (this works properly in Windows 3.1). The current DOS path at program execution would be the path the users were in when they started Windows. There are several approaches to resolving this problem. The simplest approach is to keep data files in the Windows directory.

After you build a fully qualified file path (for example, C:\WINDOWS\DEFAULT.SCH), use the `Dir$` function to determine if the file exists. If so, open the job file and read each record into the `ListJob` list box. Before adding each item, however, the subroutine calls `String2Job`. This is an easy method of determining that the job file is valid, because `String2Job` returns 0 (`FALSE`) if it is unable to convert the date and time fields to serial numbers. If the conversion fails, the program alerts the user and exits.

Running a Job

The main screen provides the `CommandRun` button so that the user can easily test a job entry. This is especially useful for DOS-based jobs, whose execution is highly dependent on their associated PIF settings or the _DEFAULT.PIF settings. The most significant of these settings is whether background processing is enabled. These PIF settings in turn depend on the CPU (286/386) of the host machine.

Selecting the Run button causes the `CommandRun_Click` routine to invoke the `Shell()` function for the selected `ListJob` item:

```
Sub CommandRun_Click ()
    Dim Job As JobStructure

    If String2Job((ListJob.List(ListJob.ListIndex)), Job) Then

        Job.HasRun = -1
        Job.LastRan = Now

        On Error GoTo CommandRunError
```

continues

```
        TaskID% = Shell(Job.Path + Job.Filename + " " +
            Job.Parameters, Job.Style)
        On Error GoTo 0

        Result% = Job2String(Job, JobString$)
        FormJobList.ListJob.List(I%) = JobString$

    End If

    Exit Sub

CommandRunError:
    Job.HasRun = 1
    Resume Next

End Sub
```

The subroutine first converts the selected item to a Job structure. If successful, the Shell command is called. An error handler is provided in case Shell causes a run-time error (for example, the job file is not executable). Finally, the Job structure is translated back to a string and the list box is updated.

Deleting a Job from the List

To eliminate a job from the job list, the user selects the CommandDelete button, which calls a very simple subroutine:

```
Sub CommandDelete_Click ()

    ListJob.RemoveItem ListJob.ListIndex

End Sub
```

Saving the Job List

Because creating a job list can be time-consuming, the ability to save this list is important. In Visual Basic, it is also easy. Because you use this procedure at more than one location in the program, I've placed it in a separate subroutine in the general area of FormJobList.

```
Sub SaveJobList ()
    Dim Windir As String * 128

    'Build the job list filename
    PathLen% = GETWINDOWSDIRECTORY(Windir, 128)
    Filename$ = Left$(Windir, PathLen%) + "\DEFAULT.SCH"
```

```
    'Create/overwrite the file
    Open Filename$ For Output Access Write As #1

    'Dump the list to file
    For I% = 0 To FormJobList.ListJob.ListCount - 1
        Write #1, FormJobList.ListJob.List(I%)
    Next

    Close #1

End Sub
```

This subroutine is essentially the reverse of the code in `Form_Load`. A call to GETWINDOWSDIRECTORY returns the Windows path; a file is created, and each item in the `ListJob` list box control is written to the file.

Processing the Job List

The main purpose of this utility is to continually monitor the job list and to launch jobs when appropriate. Accomplishing this includes setting the function the `Timer` control calls at regular intervals and enabling the timer. Disabling the timer is also an important feature.

The `Timer` event is called by the `Timer` control at regular intervals.

```
Sub TimerJob_Timer ()
    Static Occurrence As Integer

    Occurrence = Occurrence + 1
    If Occurrence = 5 Then
        Occurrence = 0
        CheckJobList
    End If

End Sub
```

To improve readability, I've placed the code to process the job list in the subroutine `CheckJobList`. The `TimerJob_Timer` subroutine also includes a static variable. Statics retain their value between calls to a subroutine. Here, a static is used to lengthen the time between calls to `CheckJobList`. At the maximum interval setting for a timer—which is 65,535 milliseconds—the job list is checked about once a minute. By setting the interval to 60,000 milliseconds and running `CheckJobList` every fifth call to the `Timer` event, I've lengthened the time between checks to five minutes.

The routine `CheckJobList`, found in the general area of `FormJobList`, demonstrates several of the high-level date and time functions found in Visual Basic.

```
Sub CheckJobList ()
    Dim Job As JobStructure

    'Save now
    StartNow# = Now

    'Now let's check each list item to see if we
    '   should run it
    For I% = 0 To FormJobList.ListJob.ListCount - 1

        If Not String2Job((ListJob.List(I%)), Job) Then
            Job.Active = 0
        End If

        'Is it active and not errored
        If Job.Active And Job.HasRun <> 1 Then

            'Has it already run today
            If Not Job.HasRun Or Int(StartNow#) > Job.LastRan Then

                'Is is time or past time to run
                If (StartNow# - Int(StartNow#) >= Job.Time) Then

                    'Is it the right day to run
                    If Job.Weekday = "Daily" Or Job.Weekday = ↩
                        Format$(StartNow#, "dddd") Then
                        Filepath$ = Job.Path + Job.Filename
                        If Job.Parameters <> "" Then
                            Filepath$ = Filepath$ + " " + ↩
                                Job.Parameters
                        End If

                        Job.HasRun = -1
                        Job.LastRan = Now

                        'Run the task, this could error
                        On Error GoTo CheckJobListError
                        TaskID% = Shell(Filepath$, Job.Style)
                        On Error GoTo 0

                        Result% = Job2String(Job, JobString$)
                        FormJobList.ListJob.List(I%) = JobString$
```

Chapter 6: Job Scheduler

```
                SaveJobList
            End If
        End If
    End If
End If

    'Call doevents so we don't hog
    Dummy% = DoEvents()

  Next

  Exit Sub

CheckJobListError:
    Job.HasRun = 1
    Resume Next

End Sub
```

First, the value of Now is saved to the variable StartNow#. This ensures even handling of the jobs in the list by preventing them from executing out of order because a change in the value of Now suddenly qualifies them.

A loop allows each item in the list to be processed. First, a job item is converted to a Job structure. If the conversion fails (which is unlikely), the job is marked as inactive. Next, a series of nested If/Endif statements determines if the job is active (and not erred), has not already been run, is past time to run, and should be run today. If everything qualifies, the Shell() function is called, with error handling similar to that found in the RunCommand_Click procedure.

After the job has run, the updated job structure is converted back to a string, and the job list is updated and saved to disk file by calling the SaveJobList subroutine. Saving the job list to file ensures that the job will not be run twice if the utility is exited without the user saving the job list.

Because processing the job list could potentially be CPU-intensive, a call to DoEvents enables other programs to get in a word. Also, the user could exit the utility in a runaway situation.

The user needs a method to enable and disable the Timer. This is accomplished through the CommandStart control. This command button is unusual because it works as a toggle. When selected, it renames itself (by changing its caption), and it uses the caption to determine its current state.

```
Sub CommandStart_Click ()

    'Toggle for activating timer
    If CommandStart.Caption = "Stop" Then
        TimerJob.Enabled = 0
        CommandStart.Caption = "Start"
    Else
        CommandStart.Caption = "Stop"
        TimerJob.Enabled = -1
    End If
End Sub
```

This technique saves a command button and provides a fast method for the user to determine the current state of the `TimerJob` control.

Next, we address how the user adds jobs to the job list and modifies them.

Designing the *Modify Job* Form

The user must supply some basic information about each job: the file path of the job file, any parameters, the window style, the day and time to run the job, and whether the job is active. Figure 6.2 shows the Modify Job form named `FormModifyJob` in design mode, which collects this information.

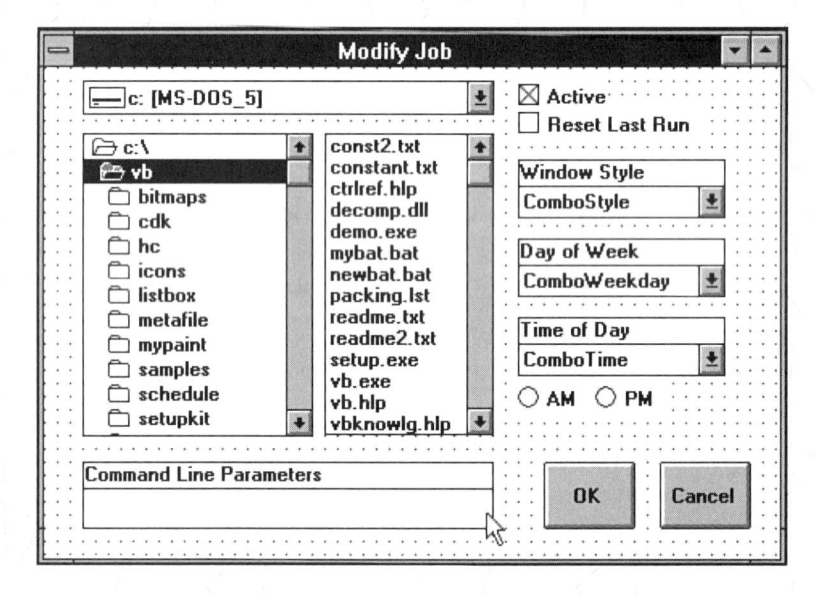

Figure 6.2. The Modify Job form.

Drawing the Controls

The drive list box, directory list box, and file list box (`DriveJob`, `DirJob`, and `FileJob`) enable the user to select any file on any drive. The `TextBox` control (`TextParameters`) enables the user to specify command-line parameters to the job. (Note: `TextBox` is the only control in the entire utility in which the user must type.) Two drop-down list boxes, `ComboWeekday` and `ComboTime`, help the user select a day and time for the job to run. The radio buttons, `OptionAM` and `OptionPM`, reduce the number of items in the `ComboTime` list box. The `CheckActive` check box maintains an active flag for the job. This allows the user to disable a job without deleting it from the job list. The `CheckReset` check box enables the user to reset the last ran field of the job. Finally, the familiar OK and Cancel buttons enable users to commit or discard their modifications.

Linking the *File, Directory,* and *Drive* Controls

It takes a minimum amount of code to link the file path controls. You do this through the `Change` subroutine provided with the `Drive` and `Directory` controls:

```
Sub DriveJob_Change ()
    DirJob.Path = CurDir$(DriveJob.Drive)
    FileJob.Path = DirJob.Path
End Sub

Sub DirJob_Change ()
    FileJob.Path = DirJob.Path
End Sub
```

Setting the path of one control now resets the path of its dependent controls. (Note: `DirJob` and `FileJob` have their paths reset in `DriveJob_Change`.) Manually setting the Directory control's path does not cause a call to `DirJob_Change`.

Populating the List Boxes

The Window Style, Day of Week, and Time of Day list boxes need to have items added during program execution. The most efficient place to put this code is in the subroutine that is called when `FormModifyJob` first loads: the `Form_Load` event.

```
Sub Form_Load ()
    ComboStyle.AddItem "1 Normal"
    ComboStyle.AddItem "2 Minimized"
    ComboStyle.AddItem "3 Maximized"
    ComboStyle.AddItem "4 Normal w/o Focus"
```

continues

```
    ComboStyle.AddItem "7 Minimized w/o Focus"

    ComboWeekday.AddItem "Daily"
    ComboWeekday.AddItem "Monday"

    ComboWeekday.AddItem "Sunday"

    ComboTime.AddItem "12:00"
    ComboTime.AddItem "12:30"
    ...
    ComboTime.AddItem "11:00"
    ComboTime.AddItem "11:30"
End Sub
```

Determining Whether a Job Was Modified

One shortcoming of Visual Basic is that there is no built-in method of determining how a form was exited. This is perhaps due to the event-driven nature of Windows. When showing a modal form, however, the parent often needs to know whether the user selected the OK or Cancel (or similar) Command Button Control. One method is to store the information in the child form's Tag property. For example:

```
Sub CommandOK_Click ()
    FormModifyJob.Tag = "OK"
    Hide
End Sub
```

If you apply similar logic to CommandCancel_Click, the calling procedure then reads FormModifyJob.Tag to determine if OK or Cancel were selected. There are two problems with this method:

- If the child form is unloaded rather than hidden, reading the FormModifyJob.Tag property reloads the form and always returns an empty string.

- When you modify the program later, you may forget this use of the form's Tag property and write conflicting code.

For these reasons, and to improve readability of the source code, it is better to use a global variable.

A global variable *has scope* (can be read and set) throughout the program. This provides an efficient method of sharing information between forms. You must declare a global variable in the global module.

```
Global ModifyList As Integer
```

Now, the OK and Cancel Command Control Buttons can set this integer (we'll treat it as a logical) and the parent form can determine what the user selected.

```
Sub CommandOK_Click ()
    ModifyList = -1
    Hide
End Sub

Sub CommandCancel_Click ()
    ModifyList = 0
    Hide
End Sub
```

Keeping the User from Unloading the Form

Visual Basic makes a distinction between *unloading* and *hiding* a form. Unloading a form causes all its contents to be reinitialized if the form is reloaded. This means other forms cannot read properties of the unloaded form. More specifically, an attempt to read an unloaded form's properties initializes the form, so generally such a call does not return useful information. To maintain data in a form, use the Hide method to exit the form and disallow the use of the Unload method—either through the form's Unload event or by setting the form's ControlBox property to FALSE, as done in FormModifyJob.

Adding a Job to the Job List

Most of the source code that addresses the controls in FormModifyJob actually resides in FormJobList. Two command buttons, CommandAdd and CommandModify, provide the interfacing between the two forms. The user selects CommandAdd to add a new job to the job list. The first portion of CommandAdd_Click resets many of the controls in FormModifyJob to defaults. This provides a more consistent interface for the user:

```
Sub CommandAdd_Click ()
    Dim Job As JobStructure

    'Set controls for FormModifyJob form to defaults
    FormModifyJob.ComboStyle.ListIndex = 0
    FormModifyJob.ComboWeekday.ListIndex = 0
    FormModifyJob.ComboTime.ListIndex = 0
    FormModifyJob.CheckActive.Value = 1
    FormModifyJob.CheckReset.Value = 0
    FormModifyJob.OptionAM.Value = -1
    FormModifyJob.FileJob.Pattern = "*.*"
    FormModifyJob.Show 1
```

continues

```
'If Canceled Exit Function
If Not ModifyList Then
    Exit Sub
End If

Result% = BuildJob(Job)

If Job2String(Job, JobItem$) Then
    ListJob.AddItem JobItem$
End If
```

The statement `FormModifyJob.Show 1` instructs Visual Basic that `FormModifyJob` is modal. This means that no code in any other form will be executed until `FormModifyJob` is hidden or unloaded. This disallows the possibility of the user attempting to modify or add another job while another modification is in progress.

After `FormModifyJob` is hidden (the user selected the OK or Cancel button), the global variable `ModifyList` is tested. If the user selects Cancel, the `CommandAdd_Click` subroutine is exited.

Next, the `BuildJob` user-defined function is called. This function creates a Job structure based on the settings of the controls in form `FormModifyJob`. Because the `CommandModify_Click` subroutine needs to build a job based on `FormModifyJob`, it's more efficient to put this code into a separate function.

Finally, the Job structure is converted to a string and the new string is added to the job list.

Modifying a Job in the Job List

The `CommandModify` button, when selected, must perform similarly to the `CommandAdd` button, except that the controls in `FormModifyJob` must be set to match the currently selected job:

```
Sub CommandModify_Click ()
    Dim Job As JobStructure

    'Parse list item into FormModifyJob controls
    If Not String2Job((ListJob.List(ListJob.ListIndex)), Job) Then
        Exit Sub
    End If

    If Job.Active Then
        FormModifyJob.CheckActive.Value = 1
```

```
    Else
        FormModifyJob.CheckActive.Value = 0
    End If

    FormModifyJob.CheckReset.Value = 0

    Result% = MatchItemLength(Format$(Job.Style, "0"), 1, _
        FormModifyJob.ComboStyle)
    Result% = MatchItem((Job.Weekday), FormModifyJob.ComboWeekday)
    Result% = MatchItem(Left$(Format$(Job.Time, "hh:mm AM/PM"), 5), _
        FormModifyJob.ComboTime)

    If Right$(Format$(Job.Time, "AM/PM"), 2) = "AM" Then
        FormModifyJob.OptionAM.Value = -1
    Else
        FormModifyJob.OptionPM.Value = -1
    End If

    FormModifyJob.DriveJob.Drive = Left$(Job.Path, 1)
    FormModifyJob.DirJob.Path = Left$(Job.Path, Len(Job.Path) - 1)
    FormModifyJob.FileJob.Pattern = "*.*"
    Result% = MatchItem(Job.Filename, FormModifyJob.FileJob)
    FormModifyJob.TextParameters.Text = Job.Parameters

    'Call the form
    FormModifyJob.Show 1

    'If Canceled exit this function
    If Not ModifyList Then
        Exit Sub
    End If

    Result% = BuildJob(Job)

    If Job2String(Job, JobItem$) Then
        ListJob.List(ListJob.ListIndex) = JobItem$
    End If

End Sub
```

This subroutine starts by converting the selected job in the job list to a Job structure and then setting properties in the FormModifyJob control to match. Of particular interest is the MatchItem function. There is no built-in method in Visual Basic for setting a list box's current item (ListIndex) based on a string match. `MatchItem` provides this functionality. Because you're likely to use this function in many Visual Basic programs, I've placed it in the FUNCS.BAS module.

```
Function MatchItem (ItemText As String, ListBox As Control) As Integer

    For I% = 0 To ListBox.ListCount - 1
        If ItemText = ListBox.List(I%) Then
            ListBox.ListIndex = I%
            MatchItem = -1
            Exit Function
        End If
    Next

    MatchItem = 0

End Function
```

`MatchItem` returns −1 (TRUE) if a match is found, and 0 if not. FUNCS.BAS also contains a similar function, `MatchItemLength`. This function behaves like `MatchItem` except that it considers only a specified number of characters from the left when matching the string. `MatchItemLength` is used for setting `ComboStyle`, because only the first character of this control is stored in the string version of a job.

Proofing the Application

Proofing an application means stabilizing it so that the program does not abort unexpectedly (crash), regardless of what the user does. Because Windows is event-driven, this can be quite difficult. But it also serves as an opportunity to make your utility appear more sophisticated. Disabling options so that the user does not crash the program also gives feedback to the user about the current state of the program.

Disabling Non-Sequiturs and Crashes

The first time the user runs the Scheduler program, there are no jobs in the `ListJob` list box. What would happen if the user selected the `CommandModify` control to modify a nonexistent job? If a programmer isn't careful, this could cause a run-time error when the program updates the "modified" job in the job list. The programmer could check for an empty list (and for no selected item in the list, because this is also possible in Windows), but a better solution is to disable `CommandModify` until a job is selected. The same also applies to the

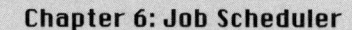

`CommandDelete` and `CommandRun` controls. Fortunately, this is easy to do. The technique is to set the initial state of the command buttons to be disabled at design time (set the `Enabled` property to `FALSE`), and to enable them when the user selects a list item. You can determine that a list item is selected using the `ListJob_Click` event.

```
Sub ListJob_Click ()
  CommandDelete.Enabled = -1
  CommandModify.Enabled = -1
  CommandRun.Enabled = -1
End Sub
```

The `CommandDelete` control is of special interest because deleting the current item from `ListJob` means that there is no currently selected job, so you need to disable the command buttons again. The following is the complete source code for this subroutine:

```
Sub CommandDelete_Click ()
    ListJob.RemoveItem ListJob.ListIndex
    CommandDelete.Enabled = 0
    CommandModify.Enabled = 0
    CommandRun.Enabled = 0
End Sub
```

Preventing Data Loss

In this utility, the user creates a list of jobs. This could take a great deal of time, so it is important that the user know that he has made unsaved changes to the job list. This is done in much the same way as for the `CommandRun`, `CommandDelete`, and `CommandModify` controls. First, disable the `CommandSave` control while the user is at the design screen. Next, add code to enable the control whenever the user makes a change to the list. To do this, add the following lines just prior to the end of `CommandAdd`, `CommandModify`, and `CommandRun`:

```
    NotSaved = -1
    CommandSave.Enabled = -1
```

`NotSaved` is a global variable declared in the global module similar to the way `ModifyList` was declared earlier in this chapter. After the user (or the program from `CheckJobList`) saves the job list, `CommandSave` is again disabled in the `SaveJobList` subroutine with the addition of the following lines:

```
    NotSaved = 0
    CommandSave.Enabled = 0
```

Finally, use the following code to warn users if they attempt to exit the program without saving changes:

```
Sub Form_Unload (Cancel As Integer)
    If NotSaved Then
        If MsgBox("Lose changes to the job list?", 1) = 2 Then
            Cancel = -1
        End If
    End If
End Sub
```

Preventing Program Conflicts

The `Timer` control has extra complications when compared to many of the other Visual Basic controls. One of these is that the `Timer` event can be called while the user is active elsewhere in the program. This means that the user could be modifying a job at the same time `TimerJob` is running it. To avoid this, disable all other controls except `CommandStart` while `TimerJob` is enabled. This also provides a quick reference to the user to the current state of the timer (it's difficult to miss all that gray). The following code shows how the complete source for `CommandStart` should read:

```
Sub CommandStart_Click ()

    'Toggle for activating timer/editing schedule list
    If CommandStart.Caption = "Stop" Then
        TimerJob.Enabled = 0
        ListJob.Enabled = -1
        CommandAdd.Enabled = -1
        If NotSaved Then
            CommandSave.Enabled = -1
        End If
        If ListJob.ListIndex <> -1 Then
            CommandDelete.Enabled = -1
            CommandModify.Enabled = -1
            CommandRun.Enabled = -1
        End If
        CommandStart.Caption = "Start"
    Else
        ListJob.Enabled = 0
        CommandAdd.Enabled = 0
        CommandSave.Enabled = 0
        CommandDelete.Enabled = 0
        CommandModify.Enabled = 0
```

```
        CommandRun.Enabled = 0
        CommandStart.Caption = "Stop"
        TimerJob.Enabled = -1
    End If
End Sub
```

Here the global variable NotSaved is used to determine if there are unsaved changes to the job list. Testing the property ListJob.ListIndex reveals if there is a currently selected item in the job list.

Modifications You Can Make

Sometimes the most difficult part about writing a utility is stopping. The following are some modifications you can make:

- Enable the user to set TimerJob's interval between calls to CheckJobList.
- Enable the user to save and load multiple job list files. Remember that CommandSave_Click and CheckJobList call SaveJobList.
- Include a method to easily load the Windows PIF Editor.
- Expand the intervals in which a user can schedule a job (for example, every 15 minutes or every 5 minutes). A method for the user to determine these intervals would be very helpful.
- Expand the days the job can be scheduled so that the user can schedule a job for a specific day of the month.

Chapter 6: Job Scheduler

7

SetTime

by Stephen Pruitt

Overview

The SetTime program serves two purposes. It is primarily a demonstration of programming techniques using Windows API calls for communications and private .INI files. It is also a useful utility to make sure your computer clock is accurate. You can use it to restore the system clock when it loses time, and to provide an accurate basis for setting all the other clocks in your house. SetTime works by dialing a special number at the U.S. Naval Observatory in Washington, D.C. This number provides a continuous series of ASCII messages with the current date and time. Each call takes only a few seconds, so the cost of the calls is minimal.

Windows APIs are functions that are part of the Windows system and can be called by any Windows program. All Windows programs use APIs extensively to control output display, keyboard and mouse input, printing, and so on. Languages such as Visual Basic provide a higher-level means of providing the aforementioned functions; ultimately, however, Visual Basic uses the basic API routines. The standard API functions provide many capabilities that can extend the power of Visual Basic even further. This program demonstrates two sets of such functions.

The communications API functions provide for opening and closing a selected communications (comm) port, setting communications parameters such as the baud rate and parity, and reading or writing data. You can perform simple communications functions without these functions by using basic file functions. This approach is severely limited: it does not enable you to set the comm parameters, and it provides limited error detection and handling. Using the API calls to perform these functions is not difficult, as the SetTime program demonstrates.

Private profile (.INI) files hold information for a program between executions. They use the same format as the WIN.INI file, but are dedicated to specific programs. Before the introduction of this capability, Windows programs often saved their optional information in the WIN.INI file. This slows down all processing of that file by all applications, including slowing the loading of Windows. This also causes problems when programs are to be uninstalled, because the appropriate sections in the common .INI file often remain, unnecessarily cluttering this critical resource. Many programs continue to follow this practice, although dedicated private files are becoming more common. Windows users who have had problems as a result of excessive use of the WIN.INI file prefer programs that use private files.

The profile file used by this program is named SETTIME.INI. It contains the current selections for the comm port and time zone, as well as descriptions of other supported time zones for the user's selection. The time zone entries all start with the difference between that zone and the Greenwich Mean Time (GMT) value supplied by the Observatory. GMT has been used as the standard time throughout the world for many years. It represents the local standard time in the town of Greenwich, England.

Before running this program, they must copy the SETTIME.INI file to your Windows directory. You can put the program file (SETTIME.EXE) in any directory you choose.

When users start this program, they see the selected communications port (COM1 to COM4) and time zone, as well as buttons labeled *Start*, *Set Options*, and *Quit* (see Figure 7.1). If the comm port or time zone is incorrect, the user can change them by pressing the Set Options button. After users change any values, they press OK to accept and save them.

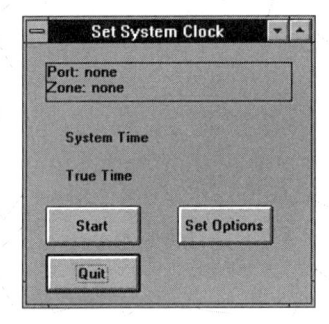

Figure 7.1. The initial SetTime screen.

Pressing the Start button on the main form tells the program to open the comm port, call the Observatory, set the time, hang up, and close the port. The box at the top of the form shows you the operation's progress, which helps you see what is happening so that you can troubleshoot and debug. When the operation is done, the box displays the old and new times so that you can see how much the time changed. Press the Quit button to end the program.

The phone number is hard-coded in the program. If your phone system requires you to dial 9 before dialing an outside number, or if you need to use pulse (rotary) dialing, you must change the program line that contains the phone number and recompile the program (you'll see how to do this later in the chapter).

Program Operation

I've listed the descriptions within each file in the order they appear in the Visual Basic Project Window. Because Visual Basic lists functions alphabetically, they are not in a logical sequence. This section of the chapter includes headings to help you locate specific parts of the program.

The SETTIME.BAS Module

This module starts with definitions of the various API calls the program uses. The programmer must define all API functions so that Visual Basic can use them. The names I used for the parameters are not necessarily used as variables later in the program. These definitions were taken from the WINAPI.TXT file (provided with Visual Basic), which includes all of the API and constant definitions in Visual Basic format. The names used for the parameters follow a special set of conventions: a lowercase prefix indicating the type of variable, followed by a descriptive name. (This naming convention is commonly used in C programming.) Prefix lp indicates a string, and a w or an n indicates integers.

You must enter all API definitions as a single line. You can declare the types of all variables and functions using the At... notation rather than the $, %, and & suffixes. This makes the definitions much easier to read. All parameters for API calls must be used with the ByVal option, except for very unusual cases. This option is needed to pass the values to the API routine in the proper format. You can specify the ByVal option in the definition or the call. You place ByVal in the definition to simplify coding and prevent errors, except for the unusual cases where it is not always used.

You can usually include all of the related APIs in categories such as COMM or PRIVATE .INI files, even if you do not initially plan to use all of them. This increases the file size and memory requirements slightly, but it makes ongoing modifications to the program much easier. This rule applies only if your program uses at least a few of the category's APIs.

The API definitions begin with Declare Function or Declare Procedure as appropriate. Procedures do not provide a return value. Next is the name of the function followed by the Lib entry, which indicates the file that contains the function. You then list the required parameters within parentheses with their data types. You must list these parameters in the proper order with the proper data types; otherwise, an error occurs when the function is called.

Communications APIs

The communications APIs are listed first. OpenComm() and CloseComm() are the communications equivalents of opening and closing a file. The parameters for OpenComm() are the port name (such as COM1) and the desired sizes of the input and output queues. The input queue holds received data until the program requests the data; the output queue holds data being sent by the program until the data has been transmitted.

The input queue must be large enough to hold the data that might accumulate between read commands, as well as a safety margin. The output queue must be larger than the largest message that will be sent in one command. In this program, the input queue is 256 bytes and the output queue is 128 bytes. The actual values are arbitrary, as long as they are greater than necessary. OpenComm() returns an ID number that is used in all other functions to identify the particular opened comm port on which the functions are to act. This ID is the only parameter CloseComm() uses.

WriteComm() and ReadComm() provide the ability to write or read data from the opened port. The first parameter for each is the ID. The parameters for WriteComm() are the ID number returned by OpenComm(), the string containing the data to be written, and the number of bytes to be written. The return value is the number of characters actually written. This is a negative number if an error occurred. The parameters for ReadComm() are the ID, the string to be filled with data, and the number of bytes to be read from the queue. The return value is the actual number of characters read. If an error occurred, the return value is the negative of the number of characters.

> Whereas all other Comm routines return the actual error code, ReadComm() and WriteComm() return character counts. The actual read or write error code is obtained by calling GetCommError(), which is defined later in this section. GetCommError() should be called after all read or write operations, regardless of the return code, to ensure that no errors are missed.

The GetCommState(), BuildCommDCB(), and SetCommState() routines go together. You use them to change the communications parameters of an open port. GetCommState() is called first. It fills a string with a *data control block* (DCB) that contains the options currently in use. It uses two parameters: the ID and a buffer to hold the current DCB. It returns zero (if successful) or a negative error code. The DCB is a complex structure that contains the communications parameters including the port, baud rate, parity, data bits, stop bits, and other information. `BuildCommDCB()` is used to alter the parameters in a DCB. The function's parameters are a string formatted like the DOS MODE command (COM*n*: *speed, parity, data bits, stop bits*) followed by the DCB to be updated with the new values. The return value is zero (if successful) or a negative error code. You can change these values directly in the DCB structure; however, this way is easier.

`SetCommState()` is then called to reset the port to use the modified options in a changed DCB. The DCB is the only parameter. The DCB is defined as a string because you won't be referencing any of the fields within the structure. The actual structure for reference is as follows:

```
Id As Integer            ' ID returned by OpenComm.
BaudRate As Long         ' Line speed.
ByteSize As Integer      ' Number of bits per byte
                         ' transmitted/received.
Parity As Integer        ' Even, odd, mark, space or none.
StopBits As Integer      ' Code representing 1, 1.5 or 2 stop bits.
RlsTimeout As Long       ' Maximum time in ms to wait for carrier
                         ' detect signal.
CtsTimeout As Long       ' Maximum time in ms to wait for clear to
                         ' send signal.
DsrTimeout As Long       ' Maximum time in ms to wait for data
                         ' set ready signal.
fBinary As Integer       ' Specifies binary or character mode.
fRtsDisable As Integer   ' Specifies whether RTS signal is disabled.
fParity As Integer       ' Specifies whether parity checking is
                         ' disabled.
fOutxCtsFlow As Integer  ' Specifies monitoring CTS for flow control.
fOutxDsrFlow As Integer  ' Specifies monitoring DSR for flow control.
fDummy As Integer        ' Reserved.
fDtrDisable As Integer   ' Specifies whether DTR signal is disabled.
fOutx As Integer         ' Specifies use of XON/XOFF flow control for
                         ' transmission.
fInx As Integer          ' Specifies use of XON/XOFF flow control for
                         ' reception.
fPeChar As Integer       ' Specifies replacement of characters
                         ' received with parity errors.
fNull As Integer         ' Specifies that null characters are
                         ' discarded.
fChEvt As Integer        ' Specifies that reception of EvtChar to be
                         ' flagged as event.
fDtrFlow As Integer      ' Specifies that DTR signal to be used for
                         ' flow control.
```

continues

```
    fRtsFlow As Integer     ' Specifies that RTS signal to be used for
                            ' flow control.
    fDummy2 As Integer      ' Reserved.
    XonChar As Integer      ' XON character to be used.
    XoffChar As Integer     ' XOFF character to be used.
    XonLim As Long          ' Minimum chars allowed in receive queue
                            ' before XON is sent.
    XoffLim As Long         ' Maximum chars allowed in receive queue
                            ' before XOFF is sent.
    PeChar As Integer       ' Replacement character for bytes with
                            ' parity errors.
    EofChar As Integer      ' Character used to signal end of data.
    EvtChar As Integer      ' Character used to signal an event.
    TxDelay As Long         ' Not used.
```

The GetCommError() function must be called after each WriteComm() or ReadComm() call. It returns the identification of any errors that may have occurred. FlushComm() clears either the read or write buffer; you use it if you don't care about further incoming data and want to prevent overrun errors that occur when the buffer is filled. The parameters are the ID and a string, which will be filled with additional information about any error that occurred. If successful, the return value is zero. If unsuccessful, the return value is a negative error code.

Private Profile (.INI) APIs

GetPrivateProfileInt() and GetPrivateProfileString() read an integer or string value from the .INI file. New or changed entries are only written as strings, using WritePrivateProfileString(). If an entry with the specified name is found in the file, the entry is updated; otherwise a new entry is added to the file. Integer values must be converted to string format to be written to the file. The parameters for GetPrivateProfileInt() are

- The application name (section name) defined in the .INI file
- The key name (entry name) of the particular entry desired
- The default value to be returned if the section or entry are not found
- The name of the .INI file

The file must be in the Windows directory, or you must specify the correct path. The return value is the integer value, or zero if the entry is negative or non-numeric. If you need to allow for negative numbers, the values should be read with GetPrivateProfileString() and converted to numbers with the Val() function.

The parameters for `GetPrivateProfileString()` are the application name and entry name, the string where the value is to be returned, the maximum number of characters to be returned (including a terminating null character), and the file name. The `ReturnedString` must be initialized, preferably to a series of null characters by coding `MyString$=string$(numchars,0)` before calling this function. The return value is the number of characters copied, excluding the terminating null.

You can get a list of all entries defined for the application by calling this function with a null value for the `KeyName`. To do this, change the function definition for `KeyName` to `KeyName as Any`. You must remove the `ByVal` from the `Declare` statement. The list of entries is retrieved by calling the function with a 0 for the `KeyName` parameter. Each entry in the resulting string ends with a null character, with one more null character ending the list. Your code must parse this compound string into separate values; it is not an array. If you use this technique, calls for specific entries must include the `ByVal` in the function calls.

Constants and Global Fields

The `IE_` constants are defined next. These constants define error codes that can be returned by comm APIs other than `ReadComm()` or `WriteComm()`. These definitions allow the values to be referenced by name within the program, which makes the program easier to understand and reduces the chance of a coding error. The comments after each entry describe the meaning of each error.

Program globals are fields used throughout this program. `OpenCom()` holds the integer returned by `OpenComm()`. This is used by all other comm API calls to identify the comm port being used by that function. `NewTime` holds the formatted time obtained from the U.S. Naval Observatory. `ComPort` contains the name of the selected port, as COM*n*. `TimeZone` holds the offset number for the selected time zone. It is used to convert GMT time to local time. `TimeDesc` holds the description of the selected time zone. `TimeIndex` holds the index number of the selected time zone. The first entry in the list is index zero.

The `Pgm_Status` field holds a value that indicates the current status of the comm port. The application code maintains this status indicator; the status is not used by any of the APIs. The field contains either 1 or 2 (`PGM_COM_OPEN` or `PGM_DIALED`) if the comm port is open, or 0 if the port is closed. It is used after errors to make sure the phone line is disconnected and the port is closed as necessary. The constant values are then defined.

The error flags that follow document the values returned by the `GetCommError()` function. (I did not use them in the error handling; they are present only for documentation.) You could change the code for the message box that reports communications errors to show the error description. Note that the computer system causes CE_BREAK at the other end of the phone line, asking for a pause in your data. The action for this case is strictly user-defined.

You can include the values of TRU and FALS if you need a global module for any other reasons. Their use makes any program much easier to read. You wouldn't create a global module just for these definitions, however.

The OPTFORM.FRM Module

This form gives the user the ability to change the selected comm port or time zone. It contains four radio buttons to select the comm port and a pull-down combo box to select the time zone. The form provides command buttons to return the user to the main form without saving changes, or to save the changes and then return to the main form.

The *Form_Load* Routine

When this form is loaded, it reads the information it needs from the .INI file. The AppName$ variable is set to match the file entry, FileName$ is set to the name of the .INI file, and nDefault and DefaultStr$ are the values returned if no matching entry is found. They are usually set to values that will never occur in the file, to allow the program to recognize a no-match condition.

`GetPrivateProfileInt()` is called looking for the MaxZones entry, and returns an integer value that is the highest number of the time zone descriptions in the file. They are numbered starting with 0.

The program then loops to read each of the time zone descriptions by calling `GetPrivateProfileString()` with entry names 'Zone' plus the number (for example, 'Zone1'). The AddItem procedure adds the returned values to the Combo1 combo box. Trailing null characters are stripped by using Left$(RetStr$, IZone%) to keep only the number of characters indicated by the API return code. Next, the radio button that corresponds to the selected comm port is marked by setting its Value property to TRU. The port selection was previously read from the .INI file when the main form was loaded. Finally, the combo box entry corresponding to the current time zone is selected to be displayed by setting the ListIndex property equal to TimeIndex%. The TimeIndex value was also read from the .INI file when the main form was loaded.

The values being read from the .INI file in this section could easily have been read when the main form was loaded, at the same time other values were read. I did not do that because the user rarely changes the comm port and time zone after the initial configuration—usually only when daylight saving time begins and ends. Reading the additional data would only slow the program unnecessarily. Instead of using a maximum-value entry and loop as described, I could have read the names of all entries in the section using the technique described in the SETTIME.BAS section. In this case, that would have added complexity to the code without any real value. That technique is best used when you cannot determine the names any easier way.

The *Command2* Routine (Quit Button)

The Command2 button quits this form without changing the .INI file or the selected values. Any selections the user made in the radio buttons or combo box are lost.

The *Command1* Routine (Done Button)

The Command1 button causes the updated values to be written to the .INI file and current selections stored in global variables to be changed. The AppName$ and FileName$ values are set here as a conservative programming technique. The values should already be correctly set from the Form_Load() procedure.

The NewPort$ variable is first set based on the radio button values. If this has not changed, this part of the .INI update is then bypassed for improved efficiency. Otherwise, the item name is set to ComPort and the new value is written to the file by calling WritePrivateProfileString(). If an error occurs, it is reported; however, execution continues.

The index of the selected combo box entry is then checked against the previous TimeIndex. If it has changed, it is converted to a string and written to the file as entry CurrZone with another call to WritePrivateProfileString(). The TimeZone field is then set to the GMT offset by extracting the value of the leading numeric digits with Val(Combo1.Text). TimeDesc is set to the current description, and TimeIndex is updated to the current index. The last instructions in this procedure update the option information displayed on the main form by changing the Caption value of the Label5 control on the SetTime form. This form is then unloaded.

Note that the entire .INI file is written to disk every time WritePrivateProfileString() is called. This can be time-consuming if a large number of entries in a large file are being updated.

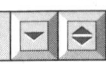

The return code from `WritePrivateProfileString()` is saved in a variable and then tested for errors as an aid in debugging. Because no descriptive error messages are being produced, the code could have been written as follows:

```
If Not WritePrivateProfileString(...) Then
        MsgBox ...
    End If
```

The SETTIME.FRM Module

This is the main form of the program. It contains a label box that displays the selected options or progress information. It also contains displays of the system and true time, and three command buttons. Using the first button, the user can load the OPTFORM.FRM form that is used to change the comm port or time zone. The user can click another button to begin the communications link, and can use the last button to end the program.

The program uses command buttons rather than menu entries because there are so few actions from which to choose. Buttons are also easier to use because they are larger than menu entries. This does not follow the recommended design for Windows applications. In a commercial program, there might be only one button to start the communications link. The other functions, plus additional features such as invocation of a help file, might be in menus.

The `Label5.Caption` property is used as a progress indicator throughout the program operation, displaying messages that keep the user informed by showing the latest activity. This helps the user understand any errors that may occur, and also assists during debugging.

The *Command1* Routine (Quit Button)

The `Command1` button ends the program. It calls `CleanUp()` to make sure the telephone line has been disconnected and the comm port has been closed. This is needed only in unusual cases after an error occurs, but it is helpful during debugging. The form is then unloaded and the program is terminated.

The *CleanUp()* Procedure

The `CleanUp()` procedure first checks the `Pgm_Status` for `PGM_DIALED`. If this is still set, the line has not been disconnected. It updates the `Label` box progress indicator and writes +++ to the modem by calling `WriteComm()`. This is defined in the Hayes AT command set to return the modem to command mode. The next characters sent to the modem by the computer are treated as AT commands rather than as data to be sent.

You then have to pause at least one second for this change in the modem mode to take effect. The program calculates a time two seconds later by extracting the current hours, minutes, and seconds from Time$, converting them to integers and adding 2 to the number of seconds. This results in a one- to two-second delay. The number of seconds and minutes is then adjusted to prevent illegal values greater than 60. (I did not check for the hours overflowing to 24, so if this routine is called at exactly one second before midnight, it will fail.)

The program then loops until one to two seconds have passed. The comm read buffer is flushed during each loop by calling the FlushComm() API function to prevent an error condition if the buffer is filled, because data is coming in continuously. DoEvents() is also called so that other Windows programs that may be running can continue to operate during this delay. You could not use a timer instead of the loop, because of the need to flush the buffer.

The Label box is then updated to show Hanging up ... and an ATH command written to the modem by calling WriteComm(). This instructs the modem to disconnect the phone line. An ATZ command is then written to the modem, which instructs the modem to return to its power-up default options. The reset is needed because this program sets several options that may not be the defaults. If the options are not reset, it could cause difficulties with other communications programs; they might be configured to assume that certain options are set. The comm port is then closed.

If the Pgm_Status field reflects PGM_COM_OPEN, the line has already been disconnected but the comm port was not closed successfully. When this is the case, another close is issued. Pgm_Status is reset to zero and the progress message is changed to Done....

The *Command2* Routine (Start Button)

The Command2 routine runs the communications process. The Pgm_Status is set to zero and three string variables are dimensioned and initialized as follows:

- ComByte is the area that data will be read into from the line.
- ComDCB is where the communications Data Control Block (DCB) will be held.
- ComStat is used in calls to GetCommError().

All three fields are set to a series of null characters with `String$(n,0)` statements. Many API functions require this string initialization, and it is good programming practice in all cases.

The progress indicator is set to `Opening Com port ...` to keep the user informed, and `DoEvents()` is called to give other programs an opportunity to run. The selected comm port is then opened, and any error is translated to text and reported. The `Pgm_Status` is updated to show that the port has been opened. The DCB is then initialized by calling `GetCommState()`. This sets the fields in that structure to the current values. The structure of the DCB is described along with the API definitions in the global SETTIME.BAS module. The structure is not used in this program.

`BuildCommDCB()` is then called to update the DCB image. It uses a string formatted exactly like the DOS MODE command: `COMn: speed, parity, data bits, stop bits`. This method of updating the DCB fields is easier and less error-prone than defining the actual structure and manipulating the individual fields directly. `SetCommState()` is then called to apply the changed DCB values to the communications link.

The `Label5` progress indicator is then set to `Dialing ....` The dial string contains the AT prefix to indicate that the string contains a modem command. It contains V1 to cause the modem to use character responses to commands, DT for dial tone, and the phone number. Change DT to DP if you must use rotary (pulse) dialing. You may need to insert a 9 or other prefix before the phone number if you are calling through a business phone system. The dashes are for readability; most modems ignore them. The string is then written to the comm port, and the `Pgm_Status` is updated. You can store the choice of DT or DP, and optional prefixes such as 9, in the .INI file and update them in the OPTFORM form if you want. I leave this as an exercise for the reader.

The code beginning at the `Next_Line` label reads data from the comm port until it finds the desired information. The `ComLine$` string is first cleared in case you come back to read another line of text. This field will be used to accumulate characters received until an end-of-line character is found. One byte at a time is read into `CVal$` by calling `ReadComm()`. `GetCommError()` is called to check for errors and to notify the user if needed. The communications process is terminated by branching to `Quit_Comm` if an error occurs. If a line feed or carriage return is read, the program branches to `Got_Line` to inspect the data received. Otherwise, the character is added to the accumulated line in `ComLine$`, and you return to `Read_Byte` to read another character from the line. This technique is used because lines of varying lengths can be read from the port.

Chapter 7: SetTime

In Got_Line(), the program analyzes the text that was received. Between full-time stamps, the U.S. Naval Observatory sends a line containing only an asterisk. If the program finds such a line, it goes back and reads another line. The same is done for lines that don't contain any characters, just in case you get an unusual error condition. Such empty strings would cause later code to abort the program.

The first response will be a status message from the modem such as CONNECT, BUSY, ERROR, NO DIALTONE, NO ANSWER, or NO CARRIER. If one of these is found, the progress message is updated. If any of the error responses is received, a message box is displayed and the line is disconnected and closed. The progress message is also updated, but this is replaced by other messages as the comm link is terminated. The ERROR message results from an invalid AT command. The others should be self-explanatory.

The program then checks for a five-digit number at the beginning of the message. If the program does not find the number, this is not a U.S. Naval Observatory time-stamp message, so the program goes back to read another line. This message could have been a modem status message (other than those recognized by the program), the result of line noise, or some other unforeseen message.

If the five-digit number is found, the program issues another DoEvents() call to let other programs have a chance at the system. During normal operation these are not critical, because the entire process is so quick. During debugging, or when an error has occurred, these prove to be critical.

The new hour is calculated in an involved compound calculation. First the two characters in the 11th and 12th bytes of the message are converted to numeric. This is the current hour in GMT. The program then adds 24 to prevent negative results, and it subtracts the GMT offset value from the selected time zone. Because the resulting value may be greater than 24, the program then uses Mod 24 to get a value from 0 through 23. This is the current hour in the selected time zone. This value is converted to a two-character string using the Format$ function.

A string containing the full current time as HH:MM:SS is then built. The current computer time is displayed on-screen along with the correct time, and the computer clock is reset.

The program then falls through to Quit_Comm, which calls the Clean_Up() procedure, which in turn disconnects the phone line and closes the comm port. The program also branches to this label after an error is detected during the communications procedure.

The *Command4* Routine (Change Options Button)

The `Command4` button loads `OptForm`, which enables the user to change the selected communications port or time zone. There is no `Command3` button. It was used during development for another function, but I removed it before the program was completed. I did not rename the `Command4` button because Visual Basic makes this clean-up process annoying. This also shows the benefit of renaming all objects to meaningful names when they are defined. That also makes the code easier to understand, which reduces coding errors.

The *Form_Load* Routine

The `Form_Load()` procedure reads some critical fields from the SETTIME.INI file. The section name in `AppName$` is set to `SetTime` and the file name in `FileName$` is set to SETTIME.INI. The entry name in `KeyName$` is set to `ComPort` to retrieve the selected communications port. The `RetStr$` buffer is initialized to 255 nulls to prevent possible problems with the data read by calling `GetPrivateProfileString()`. The returned string is then copied to the global `ComPort$` variable, using the `Left$` function with the number of bytes read from the `GetPrivateProfileString()` function return value. Note that Visual Basic would still consider the length of `RetStr$` to be 255.

The selected time zone and GMT offset are then read. The `KeyName$` parameter is set to `CurrZone`, and a call is issued to `GetPrivateProfileInt()`. This returns the selected zone index number. The `KeyName$` parameter is then set to `Zone`, followed by the index number. This is done by converting the integer value to a string in `KeyName$` with `Str$()`, then selecting all but the leading blank character with `Right$(KeyName$, Len(KeyName$) - 1)` and adding the `Zone` prefix. `RetStr$` is again initialized to 255 nulls, and `GetPrivateProfileString()` is called to read the selected zone description. The full description is then copied to `TimeDesc$` using the length returned by the function. `Val(TimeDesc$)` sets the GMT offset in `TimeZone%`. This takes advantage of the fact that the `Val()` function ignores the rest of the string after finding a non-numeric character.

The `Caption` property of `Label5` is then set to show the selected port and time zone. This box is used to display the selected options before the communications link is started, and contains progress messages after online operations have begun.

The `TimeStr()` function converts three integers representing hours, minutes, and seconds to a string in the form HH:MM:SS. `TimeStr()` is called during the disconnect process. This could have been written as inline code in that logic. I made it a separate routine because I thought it might be useful elsewhere in the program. Other techniques turned out to be better in the other cases, but I left this unchanged. This function uses `Format$(var,"00")` to convert each variable to a string that is certain to contain two numeric digits. This is necessary when comparing or setting `Time$`. Embedded blanks or one-digit values will cause inaccurate comparisons or program errors.

The SETTIME.INI File

This is a private .INI file that must be in the Windows directory. The API calls require that you supply the full path with the file name if the file is located anywhere else but in the Windows directory. Most programs require .INI files to be in the standard Windows directory. The format is similar to that of the WIN.INI or SYSTEM.INI files. You should always use private profile files instead of including entries in the system WIN.INI file. This speeds the loading of Windows and any operations using either the system or private files. It also greatly reduces the difficulty of uninstalling a program.

The first entry is the section name `[SetTime]`. Private profile files typically contain only one section, but can contain as many as desired. The section name is passed to the API functions as `AppName$`.

A series of comment lines then follow, which describe the file, and comments precede each entry. The API functions ignore any line beginning with a semicolon and treat it as a comment. Good programming practice dictates including a general description of the file, including the name of the application and descriptions of each entry. This prevents confusion when you try to identify one of many private .INI files in your Windows directory, or when you are customizing the file entries. File names are not always sufficient to identify these files, because users may have several similar applications.

The first entry is `ComPort=COM2`. This entry contains the selected comm port, and is read by calling `GetPrivateProfileString()` because it has a string value. The particular entry is selected by setting the `KeyName$` parameter to `ComPort`. The user can change the value through the `OPTFORM` form.

The next entries are `CurrZone` and `MaxZones`. `CurrZone` contains the index number of the selected time zone, and `MaxZones` contains the highest index number used. Both are integer values and are read by calling `GetPrivateProfileInt()` with the `KeyName$` parameter set to the appropriate entry name.

Chapter 7: SetTime

The individual time zone entries follow, beginning with Zone0 and continuing with Zone1, Zone2, and so on. The format of each entry is an integer GMT offset value, a dash, and the description of the time zone. Separate entries are required for daylight saving or standard time, because the program does not make that adjustment automatically. The GMT offset must be the first characters of the entry, without leading blanks, to allow the Val() function to extract the value properly.

Source Code for SetTime

The rest of the chapter shows all the code used to construct the SetTime program.

The SETTIME.BAS File

```
'   SETTIME
'   A utility to set the system clock and demonstrate use of
'   Communications and Private-INI API calls.
'
'   Copyright 1992 by Stephen Pruitt.
'   Comments can be sent via CompuServe to ID 70244,365
'
' Declare API Functions
'
' Communications API Functions
'
Declare Function OpenComm Lib "User" (ByVal lpComName
    As String, ByVal wInQueue As Integer, ByVal wOutQueue As Integer)
    As Integer
Declare Function CloseComm Lib "User" (ByVal nCid As Integer)
    As Integer
Declare Function WriteComm Lib "User" (ByVal nCid As Integer,
    ByVal lpBuf As String, ByVal nSize As Integer) As Integer
Declare Function ReadComm Lib "User" (ByVal nCid As Integer,
    ByVal lpBuf As String, ByVal nSize As Integer) As Integer
Declare Function GetCommState Lib "User" (ByVal nCid As
    Integer, ByVal lpDCB As Any) As Integer
Declare Function BuildCommDCB Lib "User" (ByVal lpDef As String,
    ByVal lpDCB As Any) As Integer
Declare Function SetCommState Lib "User" (ByVal lpDCB As Any)
    As Integer
```

Chapter 7: SetTime

```
Declare Function GetCommError Lib "User" (ByVal nCid As Integer,
    ByVal lpStat As Any) As Integer
Declare Function FlushComm Lib "User" (ByVal nCid As Integer,
    ByVal nQueue As Integer) As Integer

'
' Private Profile (INI) Functions
'
Declare Function GetPrivateProfileInt Lib "Kernel" (ByVal lpAppName
    As String, ByVal lpKeyName As String, ByVal nDefault As Integer,
    ByVal lpFileName As String) As Integer
Declare Function GetPrivateProfileString Lib "Kernel"
    (ByVal lpAppName As String, ByVal lpKeyName As String,
    ByVal lpDefault
    As String, ByVal lpReturnedString As String, ByVal nSize
    As Integer, ByVal lpFileName As String) As Integer
Declare Function WritePrivateProfileString Lib "Kernel" (ByVal
    lpAppName As String, ByVal lpKeyName As String, ByVal lpString
    As String, ByVal lplFileName As String) As Integer

' Comm Error Return Values
'
Global Const IE_BADID = (-1)         ' Invalid or unsupported ID.
Global Const IE_OPEN = (-2)          ' Device already open.
Global Const IE_NOPEN = (-3)         ' Device not open.
Global Const IE_MEMORY = (-4)        ' Unable to allocate queues.
Global Const IE_DEFAULT = (-5)       ' Error in default parameters.
Global Const IE_HARDWARE = (-10)     ' Hardware not present.
Global Const IE_BYTESIZE = (-11)     ' Illegal byte size.
Global Const IE_BAUDRATE = (-12)     ' Unsupported BaudRate.

'   Program Globals
Global OpenCom As Integer
Global NewTime As String
Global ComPort As String * 4
Global TimeZone As Integer
Global TimeDesc As String
Global TimeIndex As Integer

'   Program Status Codes
Global Pgm_Status As Integer
Global Const PGM_COM_OPEN = (1)
Global Const PGM_DIALED = (2)
```

continues

```
' Error Flags - for reference only, not used in code.
Global Const CE_RXOVER = &H1      ' Receive queue overflow.
Global Const CE_OVERRUN = &H2     ' Receive overrun error.
Global Const CE_RXPARITY = &H4    ' Receive parity error.
Global Const CE_FRAME = &H8       ' Receive framing error.
Global Const CE_BREAK = &H10      ' Break detected.
Global Const CE_CTSTO = &H20      ' CTS timeout.
Global Const CE_DSRTO = &H40      ' DSR timeout.
Global Const CE_RLSDTO = &H80     ' RLSD timeout.
Global Const CE_TXFULL = &H100    ' TX queue is full.
Global Const CE_PTO = &H200       ' LPTx timeout.
Global Const CE_IOE = &H400       ' LPTx I/O error.
Global Const CE_DNS = &H800       ' LPTx device not selected.
Global Const CE_OOP = &H1000      ' LPTx out-of-paper.
Global Const CE_MODE = &H8000     ' Requested mode unsupported.

' Booleans
Global Const TRU = -1
Global Const FALS = 0
```

The OPTFORM.FRM File

```
Sub Form_Load ()
    ' Read data from Private Profile File.
    '
    AppName$ = "SetTime"
    KeyName$ = "MaxZones"
    nDefault = 0
    DefaultStr$ = "0-none"
    Dim RetStr As String * 255
    nSize% = 255
    FileName$ = "SETTIME.INI"
    MaxZone% = GetPrivateProfileInt(AppName$, KeyName$, nDefault,
        FileName$)
    For ZoneNum% = 0 To MaxZone%
        KeyName$ = Str$(ZoneNum%)
        KeyName$ = "Zone" + Right$(KeyName$, Len(KeyName$) - 1)
        RetStr$ = String$(255, 0)
        lZone% = GetPrivateProfileString(AppName$, KeyName$,
            DefaultStr$, RetStr$, nSize%, FileName$)
        Combo1.AddItem Left$(RetStr$, lZone%)
    Next ZoneNum%

    Select Case ComPort$
    Case "COM1"
        Option1.Value = TRU
```

Chapter 7: SetTime

```
        Case "COM2"
            Option2.Value = TRU
        Case "COM3"
            Option3.Value = TRU
        Case "COM4"
            Option4.Value = TRU
        End Select

        Combo1.ListIndex = TimeIndex%

End Sub

Sub Command2_Click ()
    Unload OptForm
End Sub

Sub Command1_Click ()
    ' Prep for updating .INI file
    AppName$ = "SetTime"
    FileName$ = "SETTIME.INI"

    If Option1.Value = TRU Then NewPort$ = "COM1"
    If Option2.Value = TRU Then NewPort$ = "COM2"
    If Option3.Value = TRU Then NewPort$ = "COM3"
    If Option4.Value = TRU Then NewPort$ = "COM4"

    If NewPort$ <> ComPort$ Then
        ComPort$ = NewPort$
    '   Option changed, rewrite .INI file.
        KeyName$ = "ComPort"
        NewVal$ = NewPort$
        ResultCode% = WritePrivateProfileString(AppName$, KeyName$,
            NewVal$, FileName$)
        If ResultCode% = 0 Then
            MsgBox "Error updating INI file!", 16, "ERROR!"
        End If
    End If

    If TimeIndex% <> Combo1.ListIndex Then
        KeyName$ = "CurrZone"
        NewVal$ = Str$(Combo1.ListIndex)
        NewVal$ = Right$(NewVal$, Len(NewVal$) - 1)
        ResultCode% = WritePrivateProfileString(AppName$, KeyName$,
            NewVal$, FileName$)
        If ResultCode% = 0 Then
            MsgBox "Error updating INI file!", 16, "ERROR!"
```

continues

```
        End If

    End If

    TimeZone% = Val(Combo1.Text) 'Extract numeric prefix.
    TimeDesc$ = Combo1.Text
    TimeIndex% = Combo1.ListIndex
    SetTime.Label5.Caption = "Port: " + ComPort$ + Chr$(13) + "Zone: "
      + Combo1.Text
    Unload OptForm
End Sub
```

The SETTIME.FRM File

```
Sub Command1_Click ()
    CleanUp
    Unload SetTime
    End
End Sub

Sub CleanUp ()
    CR$ = Chr$(13) + Chr$(10)
    If Pgm_Status = PGM_DIALED Then
        Label5.Caption = "Return to command mode ..."
        Break$ = "+++"
        ModemOff% = WriteComm(OpenCom%, Break$, Len(Break$))

'       Wait a second; my modem requires a one-second delay.

        Hr% = Val(Left$(Time$, 2))
        Min% = Val(Mid$(Time$, 4, 2))
        Sec% = Val(Mid$(Time$, 7, 2))
        Sec% = Sec% + 2     'Between one and two seconds.
        If Sec% > 60 Then
           Sec% = Sec% - 60
           Min% = Min% + 1
           If Min% > 60 Then
             Min% = Min% - 60
             Hr% = Hr% + 1
           End If
        End If
        ntime$ = TimeStr$(Hr%, Min%, Sec%)   'Convert to string.
        nBuff% = 1
        Do While Time$ < ntime$
            Flush% = FlushComm(OpenCom%, nBuff%) 'Flush Rcv buffer.
```

Chapter 7: SetTime

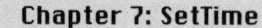

```
            nDo = DoEvents()        'Let other programs run.
        Loop

'       Hang up and reset modem to defaults.
        Label5.Caption = "Hanging up ..."
        Break$ = "ATH" + CR$      'Hang up.
        ModemOff% = WriteComm(OpenCom%, Break$, Len(Break$))
        Label5.Caption = "Resetting modem options ..."
        Break$ = "ATZ" + CR$      'Reset.
        ModemOff% = WriteComm(OpenCom%, Break$, Len(Break$))
        Label5.Caption = "Closing Com port .."
        If CloseComm(OpenCom%) < 0 Then
            MsgBox "Com port not closed", 16, "ERROR!"
        Else Pgm_Status = 0
        End If
    ElseIf Pgm_Status = PGM_COM_OPEN Then
        Label5.Caption = "Closing Com port ..."
        If CloseComm(OpenCom%) < 0 Then
            MsgBox "Com port not closed", 16, "ERROR!"
        Else Pgm_Status = 0
        End If
    End If
    Label5.Caption = "... Done ..."
End Sub

Sub Command2_Click ()

    Pgm_Status = 0
    Dim ComByte As String * 5
    Dim ComDCB As String * 50
    Dim ComStat As String * 20
    ComByte$ = String$(5, 0)
    ComDCB$ = String$(49, 0)
    ComStat$ = String$(20, 0)
    Label2.Caption = Time$
    CR$ = Chr$(13) + Chr$(10)
    Label5.Caption = "Opening Com port ..."
    n% = DoEvents()
    OpenCom% = OpenComm(ComPort$, 256, 128)
    If OpenCom% < 0 Then
        Select Case OpenCom%
            Case IE_BADID
                ComLine$ = "Invalid ID"
            Case IE_BAUDRATE
                ComLine$ = "Unsupported baud rate"
            Case IE_BYTESIZE
```

continues

Chapter 7: SetTime

```
                    ComLine$ = "Invalid size"
            Case IE_DEFAULT
                ComLine$ = "Error in defaultparameters"
            Case IE_HARDWARE
                ComLine$ = "Hardware not present"
            Case IE_MEMORY
                ComLine$ = "Unable to allocate queues"
            Case IE_NOPEN
                ComLine$ = "Device not open"
            Case IE_OPEN
                ComLine$ = "Device already open"
            Case Else
                ComLine$ = "Unknown error #" + Str$(OpenCom%)
            End Select
        MsgBox "Couldn't open Com Port" + CR$ + ComLine$, 16, "ERROR!"
        Exit Sub
    End If
    Pgm_Status = PGM_COM_OPEN

    'BuildCommDCB
    Mid$(ComDCB$, 1, 1) = Chr$(OpenCom%)
    GetState% = GetCommState(OpenCom%, ComDCB)
    If GetState% < 0 Then
        MsgBox "Error in GetCommState", 16, "ERROR!"
        CleanUp
        Exit Sub
    End If

'   Set to 1200-N-8-1.

    ComLine$ = ComPort$ + ":12,N,8,1"
    Build% = BuildCommDCB(ComLine$, ComDCB)
    If Build% < 0 Then
        MsgBox "Error " + Str$(Build%) + " in BuildCommDCB", 16, "ERROR!"
        CleanUp
        Exit Sub
    End If

    'SetCommState
    SetState% = SetCommState(ComDCB)
    If SetState% < 0 Then
        MsgBox "Error " + Str$(SetState%) + " in SetCommState", 16,
            "ERROR!"
        CleanUp
        Exit Sub
    End If
```

Chapter 7: SetTime

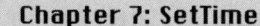

```
    ' Dial
    Label5.Caption = "Dialing ..."
    n% = DoEvents()
    DialString$ = "ATV1DT" + "1-202-653-0351" + CR$
    ModemWrite% = WriteComm(OpenCom%, DialString$, Len(DialString$))
    Pgm_Status = PGM_DIALED

Next_Line:
    Label2.Caption = Time$
    ComLine$ = ""
Read_Byte:
    ModemRead% = ReadComm(OpenCom%, ComByte$, 1)
    CVal$ = Left$(ComByte$, 1)
    ComErr% = GetCommError(OpenCom%, ComStat$)
    If ComErr% <> 0 Then
        If ComErr% = CE_DSRTO GoTo Read_Byte
        MsgBox "Comm Error " + Str$(ComErr%), 16, "ERROR!"
        GoTo Quit_Comm
    End If
    If ModemRead% = 0 GoTo Read_Byte
    If CVal$ = Chr$(10) GoTo Got_Line   'Strip LF
    If CVal$ = Chr$(13) GoTo Got_Line   'or CR.
    ComLine$ = ComLine$ + CVal$ 'Else add to buffer.
    GoTo Read_Byte 'Go read another.
Got_Line:
    If Left$(ComLine$, 1) = "*" Then GoTo Next_Line
    If Len(ComLine$) = 0 Then GoTo Next_Line
    If Left$(ComLine$, 7) = "CONNECT" Then
        Label5.Caption = "Answered, reading data"
    ElseIf Left$(ComLine$, 5) = "ERROR" Then
        Label5.Caption = "ERROR in AT Command"
        Msgbox "ERROR in AT Command",16,"ERROR"
        GoTo Quit_Comm
    ElseIf Left$(ComLine$, 11) = "NO DIALTONE" Then
        Label5.Caption = "No dialtone ... Try again"
        Msgbox "No dial tone",16,"ERROR"
        GoTo Quit_Comm
    ElseIf Left$(ComLine$,94) = "NO ANSWER" Then
        Label5.Caption = "No answer ... Try again"
        Msgbox "No Answer",16,"ERROR"
        GoTo Quit_Comm
    ElseIf Left$(ComLine$, 4) = "BUSY" Then
        Label5.Caption = "BUSY ... Try again"
        Msgbox "Line is Busy",16,"ERROR"
        GoTo Quit_Comm
```

continues

```
    ElseIf Left$(ComLine$, 10) = "NO CARRIER" Then
        Label5.Caption = "No Carrier"
        Msgbox "No Carrier",16,"ERROR"
        GoTo Quit_Comm
    End If

    If Val(Left$(ComLine$, 5)) < 10000 Then GoTo Next_Line    'bad data
    n% = DoEvents()
    Hr = (Val(Mid$(ComLine$, 11, 2)) + 24 - TimeZone%) Mod 24
    HH$ = Format$(Hr, "00")
    NewTime$ = HH$ + ":" + Mid$(ComLine$, 13, 2) + ":" +
        Mid$(ComLine$, 15, 2)
    Label2.Caption = Time$
    Label4.Caption = NewTime$
    Time$ = NewTime$

Quit_Comm:
    CleanUp
End Sub

Sub Command4_Click ()
    ' Set options.
    Load OptForm
    OptForm.Visible = TRU
 End Sub

Sub Form_Load ()
'    Read private profile file.
'
    AppName$ = "SetTime"
    FileName$ = "SETTIME.INI"
    KeyName$ = "ComPort"
    DefltStr$ = "none"
    Dim RetStr As String * 255
    RetStr$ = String$(255, 0)
    nSize% = 255
'    Get default Comm port.
'
    GetStr% = GetPrivateProfileString(AppName$, KeyName$, DefltStr$,
        RetStr$, nSize%, FileName$)
    ComPort$ = Left$(RetStr$, GetStr%)
'
'    Get default time zone.
    KeyName$ = "CurrZone"
    nDefault% = 0
    TimeIndex% = GetPrivateProfileInt(AppName$, KeyName$, nDefault%,
        FileName$)
```

```
    KeyName$ = Str$(TimeIndex%)
    KeyName$ = "Zone" + Right$(KeyName$, Len(KeyName$) - 1)
    RetStr$ = String$(255, 0)
    GetStr% = GetPrivateProfileString(AppName$, KeyName$, DefltStr$,
        RetStr$, nSize%, FileName$)
    TimeDesc$ = Left$(RetStr$, GetStr%)
    TimeZone% = Val(TimeDesc$)

    Label5.Caption = "Port: " + ComPort$ + Chr$(13) + "Zone: " + TimeDesc$

End Sub

Function TimeStr (Hr As Integer, Min As Integer, Sec As Integer) As String

'   Convert integers to strings.

    HH$ = Format$(Hr%, "00")
    MM$ = Format$(Min%, "00")
    SS$ = Format$(Sec%, "00")

'   Put it all together.

    TimeStr$ = HH$ + ":" + MM$ + ":" + SS$

End Function
```

The SETTIME.INI File

```
[SetTime]
;   Private Profile file for SETTIME.EXE
;     must be located in WINDOWS directory
;
;   ComPort is the current/default COM port COM1-COM4
ComPort=COM2
;
;
;   CurrZone is the index (0-MaxZones) of the current time zone
;   MaxZones is the highest time zone index number used
;
CurrZone=0
MaxZones=7
;
;   Zone0 - Zonen are the selectable time zones
;
```

continues

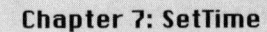

```
Zone0=4-Eastern Daylight Time
Zone1=5-Eastern Standard Time
Zone2=5-Central Daylight Time
Zone3=6-Central Standard Time
Zone4=6-Mountain Daylight Time
Zone5=7-Mountain Standard Time
Zone6=7-Pacific Daylight Time
Zone7=8-Pacific Standard Time
```

GroupWorker

by Jerry Miller, Ph.D.

8

Grpwrker

Overview

GroupWorker is a shareware utility that enables Windows users to create groups of applications that can be launched with a single mouse click. I originally wrote GroupWorker to serve my own needs when I work in Windows. Only later, as the concept and program evolved, did I think GroupWorker would become a shareware utility that could serve a shared need among other Windows users.

Windows contains rudimentary capacities to launch multiple applications by listing them on the `Win.ini` `'Load='` line or including them in the Program Manager's Startup Group, but these can be used only at start-up and can contain only one work group. During a typical day in Windows, I frequently used repeated sets of applications, each of which had to be started one at a time (for example, communication program, File Manager and Clock, or checkbook program, spreadsheet, and Calculator). I wanted to easily launch each of these groups as the application sets that they really were. When Microsoft released Visual Basic in 1991, I saw an opportunity to develop a program that would do this.

Program Operation

Although the user of GroupWorker first sees the MAIN.FRM shown in Figure 8.1, it was not the first form I developed for the program. The real order of module development is evident in the program's project window (see Figure 8.2).

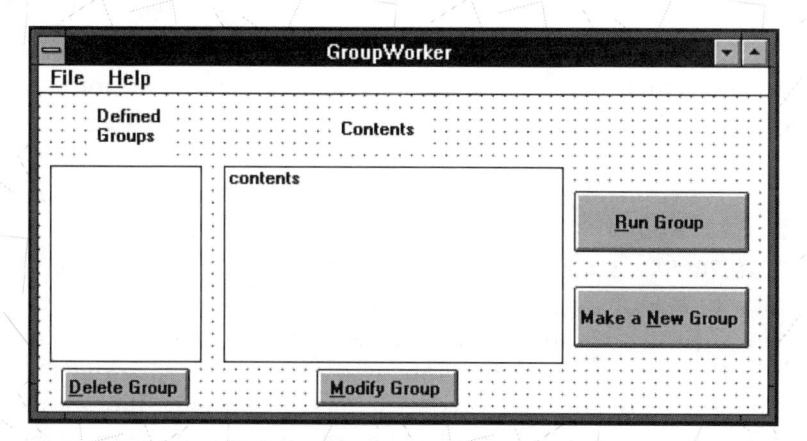

Figure 8.1. The main GroupWorker form.

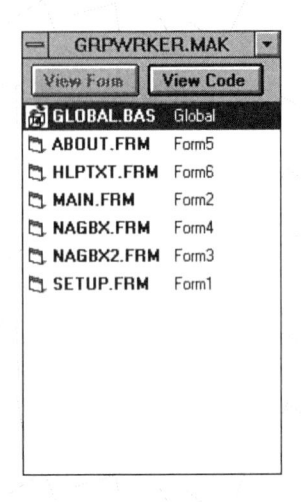

Figure 8.2. The GroupWorker project window.

I actually began developing the program with the definition of five global variables in the GLOBAL.BAS module. The variables are used to pass disk, file, and parameter information between forms and procedures:

```
Global.bas     Global
'This section contains all variables that will be passed between
'      forms and procedures.

Global defdir As String        'Default directory.
Global defdri As String        'Default drive.
Global modfile As String       'Name of group to modify.
Global fileindex As Integer    'Listbox size: -1=no filenames in listbox
Global winsize As Integer      'Window size for app startup: 1=Norm/2=Min
```

The first visible form I developed was the form through which the user could select programs to include in each group. Visually designing the form was a snap with Visual Basic.

The *Setup* Form

The SETUP.FRM contains standard Drive and Directory controls and two list boxes, all with identifying labels. The rightmost list box has its `Sorted` property set to `TRUE`, so file names are alphabetized as the user selects them. Below the Files list box are four option buttons and labels to designate the kinds of files to display in the list box. I did not add the `Norm` and `Min` option buttons until after the product's first release. They enable the user to designate whether the selected application should start in a normal state or a minimized state. The form also contains two command buttons (Done and Save Group) that allow the user to exit this form when done, or to save the group that has just been created. In order to prevent the user from distorting the form shape, the form properties `MaxButton` and `BorderStyle` are set to `FALSE` and `Fixed Single`, respectively.

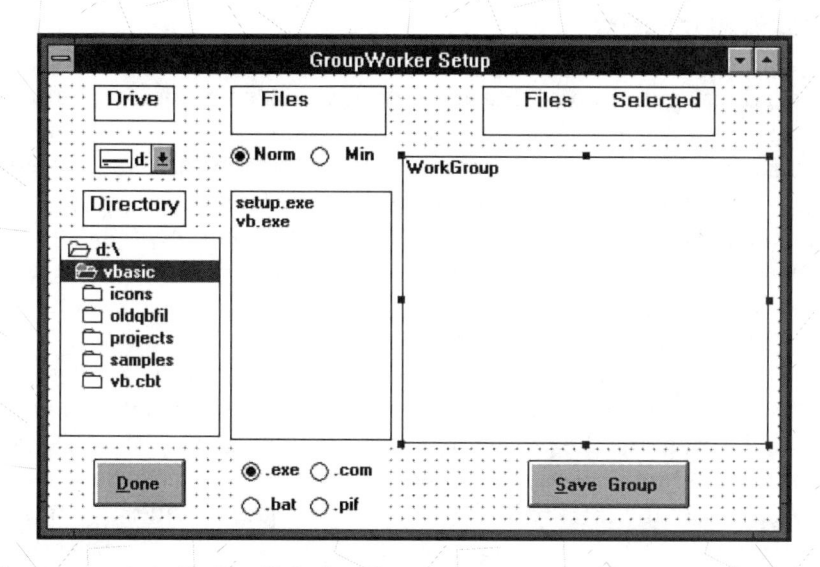

Figure 8.3. The GroupWorker Setup form.

The basic code in the SETUP.FRM is fairly straightforward. On loading (`Sub Form_Load()`), the application start size (`winsize`) is set to 1 for normal. Later, if the user selects the Max button, the `winsize` variable for that application is set to 2. The `Sub File1_DblClick()` procedure specifies that as the user double-clicks a file name, the file name is added using the `workgroup.additem filename$` command as either an uppercase (normal) or lowercase (minimized) name to the WorkGroup list box. The process for deleting unwanted files once in the WorkGroup list box is handled in the `Sub WorkGroup_DblClick()` procedure. After the user presses the **S**ave Group button, a prompt appears for the group name (`Sub Makegroup_Click()`). The program then appends a .GWP extension to the name entered so that it is unique and identifiable for future use. On successfully saving the workgroup into a simple ASCII sequential-line file (with the format `app=filename`), the `WorkGroup` list box is emptied in the `ClearList:` section.

The following is an example of a sample group file:

```
app=calc.exe
app=CLOCK.EXE
app=control.exe
app=NOTEPAD.EXE
```

Error Handling

Error handling is a very important feature of any program. The SETUP.FRM contains critical code for catching and redirecting all common user errors. Thus, note in the `Sub WorkGroup_DblClick()` procedure that if the user tries to delete a file before selecting one, the program passes control to the procedure-ending `noapp:` label and exits. If the user presses the **D**one button prior to saving a newly created group, a prompt offers the user another opportunity for saving it (`Sub Command1_Click()`). The `Sub Makegroup_click()` procedure, activated by pressing the **S**ave Group button, first makes sure that files were selected for saving. If `workgroup.listcount` equals 0, the program calls the `MsgBox` routine with a `type` value of 48 (`Display Warning Message Icon`), which states that `No Applications Have Been Selected`. Then, through the `noname:` section of the program, the procedure returns to the regular screen. If files are present, the program, in the `getgroupname` section, prompts the user to `Enter name of group:`. In the `checkforfile` section, the program verifies that this file name does not exist. If it does, the program displays an `OK to Overwrite?` message box with a type value of 52. The latter value was created by adding a value of 4 (which means to `Display Yes, No buttons`) with a value of 48 (`Display Warning Message icon`).

Processing the Groups

After completing the form that enables the user to create and save groups, I designed the MAIN.FRM to display these groups, and designated it as the `Startup` form through the Set Start**u**p Form selection in the **R**un menu. Again, visually designing this form was easy in Visual Basic. As the user double-clicks a group name, the .GWP file is opened and read, and the contents are added to the `contents` list box (`Sub File1_Click()`). The list box's `Sorted` property is set to `TRUE` so that files are again listed alphabetically. The four command buttons in Figure 8.1, all of which may be either mouse-activated or keyboard-activated, enable the user to

Delete an established group, again with critical error and safety messages (`Sub Command3_Click()`)

Modify a group, in which case the group selected will be passed through the global `modfile` variable to the SETUP.FRM (`Sub Command4_Click()`)

Make a new group, which simply hides this form and shows the SETUP.FRM (`Sub Command2_Click()`)

Run a group, in which case the group is opened and read, and each application runs via the `Shell()` command (`Sub Command1_Click()`)

Two important error-handling routines were also included in this procedure. The first shows a message box if no group was selected to be run. The second, more critical routine is that the `Runlist:` section indicates that if the program encounters an error in starting a program, control passes to the `badname:` section. The `badname:` section posts an `Application Error` message box before returning to the next application name to be run.

File and Help Menus

The File and Help menu items are part of the main form (MAIN.FRM). The File menu contains an About item that shows the ABOUT.FRM with two small text boxes, a Picture Box icon, and an OK command button (`Sub Aboutb_Click()`). The other item in the File menu is Exit (`Sub Exitb_Click()`), which terminates the program. The Help menu item is considerably more complicated. As the user clicks Help, control passes to the `Sub Helpb_Click()` procedure. The procedure first checks for the existence of the GRPWRKER.HLP file (included in the shareware package) and then posts an error message if the file is missing. Since the help compiler was not available when I wrote the GroupWorker program, I created GRPWRKER.HLP as a read-only ASCII file. If the file is found, the program loads the HELPTXT.FRM. I did a considerable amount of experimentation to get this particular form to display the help file correctly.

The final design of the HELPTXT.FRM is a specially designed picture box. Although it was easy enough to set the `BorderStyle` property to `Fixed Double` and the `MaxButton` property to `FALSE` (so that the user would not be able change the shape of the help display), much trial-and-error was involved in establishing other picture box properties. Thus, I finally found that a `Height` property of 17745 successfully loads the entire help file with no space left at the bottom of the box. The `VScroll` properties of `SmallChange` moves of 75 and `LargeChange` moves of 7000 give the most acceptable scroll rates. The `Vscroll Max` property of 14000 correctly scrolls the help file only to the point where the bottom of the text touches the bottom of the picture box.

Miscellaneous Program Notes

Some of the more interesting features of the MAIN.FRM occur during the initialization of the program (`Sub Form_Load()`), in activities unknown to the user. After storing the name of the default directory (`defdir`) for later use throughout the program, the code, using the Visual Basic `Command$` function, checks to see if a file name has been entered on the GroupWorker command line. If a file name is present, the program does not display the GroupWorker forms; otherwise, the program shows the MAIN.FRM and loads the SETUP.FRM for faster use later. The program then checks for the presence of the GRPWRKER.INI file that contains the user's shareware registration information (in a single-line ASCII file with the format `regnum=aaaa9999a`).

If the file is not present, control passes immediately to the first of two "nag screens" that prompt the user to register the program and create the GRPWRKER.INI file. If the file is already present, the program reads it for the registration information and checks the validity of the registration number. For the GroupWorker program, the registration number consists of the author's initials (`JM`) followed by the user's last initial, the sum of the ASCII decimal values of the user's first and last name initials, and then the user's first initial. Thus, if the user's name is Ghana Miller, the registration number would be `JMM212G` (a valid registration number that readers can enter at the program's registration prompt). The code in the `checkregnum:` section validates only the unique five rightmost elements of the registration number. If the registration number is invalid, control again passes to show the first of the two nag screens. If the number is valid, the program either launches any files that were in the group on the command line, again with error-handling code for bad file names (`On Error GoTo Badfile`), or displays the main program screen.

Closing Activities and Thoughts

After I completed the initial GroupWorker program code, I distributed copies to several beta testers for evaluation. All feedback for improvement was integrated, especially that related to the handling of any user errors that had occurred. I then wrote the documentation file, part of which I edited and used as the text for the GRPWRKER.HLP file. I also developed a sample group containing common Windows programs (such as CALC.EXE, CLOCK.EXE, CONTROL.EXE, and NOTEPAD.EXE) to include with the shareware package. Finally, the program elements (.EXE, .DOC, .WRI, and .HLP files, and the sample.GWP), were placed in a .ZIP file for uploading to bulletin boards around the country. The complete final shareware package, including all user documentation files, is on the disk that accompanies this book.

Visual Basic made the development of GroupWorker a relatively straightforward and fun programming project. It was easy to modify program code as it developed; it was also easy to immediately test the results. Hopefully, the project ended up serving not only my own daily Windows needs, but also those of the hundreds of people who downloaded and registered it.

Full Source Code for GroupWorker

The remainder of the chapter shows all the Visual Basic code in each of the GroupWorker forms.

GLOBAL.BAS—Global Declarations

```
'This section contains all variables that will be passed between
'       forms and procedures.

Global defdir As String           'Default directory.
Global defdri As String           'Default drive.
Global modfile As String          'Name of group to modify.
Global fileindex As Integer       'Listbox size: -1=no filenames
                                  'in list box.
Global winsize As Integer         'Window size for app startup:
                                  '1=Norm/2=Min
```

MAIN.FRM—*Form2* (Startup Form)

```
Sub Command2_Click ()

ClearLs:
    Do While contents.listcount
        contents.RemoveItem 0
    Loop

    form2.Hide
    form1.drive1.drive = defdri
    form1.dir1.path = defdir
    fileindex = -1
```

continues

```
    form1.Show

End Sub

Sub exitb_Click ()
    End
End Sub

Sub Aboutb_Click ()
    form5.Show 1

End Sub

Sub File1_Click ()

Clearlist:
    Do While contents.listcount
        contents.RemoveItem 0
    Loop


file1.path = defdir
   fname$ = file1.filename


openfile:
Open (defdir + "\" + fname$) For Input As #1
For x = 1 To 25
If EOF(1) Then GoTo fileclose
 Input #1, ap$
 l = Len(ap$)
 ap$ = Right$(ap$, l - 4)
 contents.AddItem ap$
 Next


fileclose:
Close #1

End Sub

Sub main ()

End Sub

Sub Form_Load ()
```

Chapter 8: GroupWorker

```
    defdir = CurDir$
    l = Len(defdir)
    If Right$(defdir, 1) = "\" Then defdir = Left$(defdir, l - 1)
    defdri = Left$(CurDir$, 2)
    fname$ = Command$
    If fname$ = "" Then GoTo regload Else GoTo checkregnum


regload:
    file1.path = defdir
    form2.Show
    Load form1
    form1.label2.caption = ("    Programs   " + Chr$(13) + "  Click to Add")
    form1.label4.caption = ("    Programs Selected" + Chr$(13) +
        "           Click to Delete")


checkregnum:
    checkname$ = Dir$(defdir + "\grpwrker.ini")
    If checkname$ = "" Then GoTo loadnagger

    Open (defdir + "\grpwrker.ini") For Input As #1
    Input #1, regnum$
    Close

    l = Len(regnum$)
    regnum$ = Right$(regnum$, 7)
    If Asc(Mid$(regnum$, 3, 1)) + Asc(Right$(regnum$, 1)) =
        Val(Mid$(regnum$, 4, 3)) Then GoTo gotcommand


loadnagger:
    form4.Show 1



If fname$ = "" Then GoTo endload


gotcommand:
If fname$ = "" Then GoTo endload

Open (defdir + "\" + fname$) For Input As #1

On Error GoTo badfile
For x = 1 To 25
    If EOF(1) Then GoTo filclose
```

continues

```
    Input #1, ap$
    l = Len(ap$)
    ap$ = Right$(ap$, l - 4)
    If Asc(ap$) > 90 Then state = 7 Else state = 1
    Y = Shell(ap$, state)
 Next

filclose:
Close
GoTo endload

badfile:
    msg$ = ("     The Program " + Chr$(13) + Chr$(10) + ap$ +
       Chr$(13) + Chr$(10) + "    Could Not Be Found!")
    MsgBox msg$, 48, "Application Error"
    Resume Next


End


endload:

    End Sub

Sub Command1_Click ()

    If file1.filename = "" Then MsgBox
       "You Must First Select a Group to Run", 0,
       "No Group Selected": GoTo norun


Runlist:

    On Error GoTo badname

    For x = 0 To contents.listcount - 1
    ap$ = contents.list(x)
    If Asc(ap$) > 90 Then state = 7 Else state = 1
    Y = Shell(ap$, state)
    Next

    GoTo norun

badname:    msg$ = ("     The Program " + Chr$(13) + Chr$(10) + ap$
    + Chr$(13) + Chr$(10) + "    Could Not Be Found!")
```

Chapter 8: GroupWorker

```
    MsgBox msg$, 48, "Application Error"
    Resume Next


norun:

End Sub

Sub Command3_Click ()
    delname$ = file1.filename

    If delname$ = "" Then MsgBox
    "You Must First Select a Group to Delete", 0,
    "No Group Selected": GoTo noname
    delresp = MsgBox("Press OK to Delete Group or Cancel to Abort", 1,
        "Delete File?")
    If delresp = 2 Then GoTo noname Else Kill delname$

Clearlst:
    Do While contents.listcount
        contents.RemoveItem 0
    Loop

noname:
    file1.Refresh


End Sub

Sub Command4_Click ()

'contents is on form2.
'workgroup is on form1.

    modfile = file1.filename
    If modfile = "" Then MsgBox
    "You Must First Select a Group to Modify",
    0, "No Group Selected": GoTo nofile


    Do While contents.listcount
        ap$ = contents.list(x) 'two new lines
        form1.workgroup.AddItem ap$
            contents.RemoveItem 0
    Loop
```

continues

```
        form2.Hide
        form1.drive1.drive = defdri
        form1.dir1.path = defdir
        form1.Show

nofile:

End Sub

Sub Helpb_Click ()

    helpfile$ = (defdir + "\grpwrker.hlp")
    checkname$ = Dir$(helpfile$)
    If checkname$ = "" Then GoTo nohfile Else form6.Show
    GoTo gotit

nohfile:
    MsgBox "Help File is Missing", 48, "GroupWorker"

gotit:

End Sub
```

SETUP.FRM—*Form1*

```
Sub Dir1_Change ()
    ChDir dir1.path
    file1.path = dir1.path


End Sub

Sub Drive1_Change ()
    dir1.path = drive1.drive
    ChDrive drive1.drive
End Sub
 Sub rbutton_Click ()
    ChDrive drive1.drive
    ChDir file1.path
    X = Shell(file1.filename, 1)
End Sub

Sub makegroup_click ()
```

Chapter 8: GroupWorker

```
    If workgroup.listcount > 0 GoTo getgroupname
    MsgBox "No Applications Have Been Selected", 48, ""
    GoTo noname

getgroupname:
    If modfile = "" Then modfile = "Group1"
    msg$ = "                          Enter name of group:"
    filespec$ = InputBox$(msg$, "Save New Group", modfile)
    If filespec$ = "" Then GoTo noname

    p = InStr(1, filespec$, ".")
    l = Len(filespec$)
    If p - 1 > 8 Then filespec$ = Left$(filespec$, 8)
    If p = 0 Then filespec$ = filespec$ + ".gwp" Else filespec$ =
        Left$(filespec$, p - 1) + ".gwp"
    filespec$ = (defdir + "\" + filespec$)


checkforfile:
    checkname$ = Dir$(filespec$)
    If checkname$ = "" Then GoTo savefile
    overwr = MsgBox("OK to Overwrite?", 52, "File Exists!")
    If overwr = 7 Then GoTo getgroupname


savefile:
    Open filespec$ For Output As #1
    For X = 0 To workgroup.listcount - 1
        Print #1, "app="; workgroup.list(X)
    Next
    Close


ClearList:
    Do While workgroup.listcount
        workgroup.RemoveItem 0
    Loop

noname:
   Close

   modfile = ""
End Sub


Sub Command1_Click ()
```

continues

```
        If workgroup.listcount = 0 Then GoTo saved
        notsaved = MsgBox("Save Work Group Now?", 52, "Group Not Saved!")
        If notsaved = 6 Then Call makegroup_click

saved:
    Do While workgroup.listcount
        workgroup.RemoveItem 0
    Loop


    ChDrive defdri
    form2.file1.path = defdir
    form2.file1.Refresh
    form1.Hide
    form2.Show

End Sub

Sub Option4_Click ()
     file1.pattern = "*.pif"
End Sub

Sub change ()

End Sub

Sub exebut_Click ()
    file1.pattern = "*.exe"
End Sub

Sub combut_Click ()
    file1.pattern = "*.com"
End Sub

Sub batbut_Click ()
    file1.pattern = "*.bat"
End Sub

Sub pifbut_Click ()
    file1.pattern = "*.pif"
End Sub

Sub main ()

End Sub
```

Chapter 8: GroupWorker

```
Sub Form_Load ()
   form1.drive1.drive = defdri
   form1.dir1.path = defdir
   winsize = 1
End Sub

Sub form2_file1_pathchange ()

End Sub

Sub Command2_Click ()

    If fileindex = -1 GoTo noapp
    workgroup.RemoveItem fileindex

noapp:

End Sub

Sub WorkGroup_DblClick ()

    If workgroup.listindex = -1 GoTo noap
    X = workgroup.listindex
    workgroup.RemoveItem X noap:


End Sub

Sub Option1_Click ()
    file1.pattern = "*.exe"
End Sub

Sub Option2_Click ()
    file1.pattern = "*.bat"
End Sub

Sub Option3_Click ()
    file1.pattern = "*.com"
End Sub

Sub File1_DblClick ()

    filename$ = file1.path

    If Right$(filename$, 1) <> "\" Then
    filename$ = filename$ + "\" + file1.filename
```

continues

```
        Else filename$ = filename$ + file1.filename
        End If

        If winsize = 2 Then filename$ = LCase$(filename$) Else filename$
            = UCase$(filename$)

        workgroup.AddItem filename$


End Sub

Sub Option5_Click ()
    winsize = 1
End Sub

Sub Option6_Click ()
    winsize = 2
End Sub
```

ABOUT.FRM—*Form5*

```
Sub Form_Load ()
    text1.text = "        GroupWorker Ver 1.2" + "          " +
        "  Copyright 1991 Miller Software"
    text2.text = "                   1113 Lutz" +
        "                        Ann Arbor, Michigan 48103" +
        "                    CIS: 75016,2406"
End Sub

Sub Command1_Click ()
    Unload form5
End Sub
```

HELPTXT.FRM—*Form6*

```
Sub exitb_Click ()
    Unload form6
End Sub

Sub Picture1_GotFocus ()
    On Error GoTo closeit

    helpfile$ = (defdir + "\grpwrker.hlp")

    Open helpfile$ For Input As #1
```

Chapter 8: GroupWorker

```
    Do Until EOF(1)
        Line Input #1, helpline$
        picture1.Print helpline$
    Loop

closeit:
    Close
    Exit Sub

End Sub

Sub VScroll1_Change ()
    picture1.Top = -VScroll1.Value
End Sub
```

NAGBX.FRM—*Form4*

```
Sub Form_GotFocus ()
    Print
    Print "                        Group Worker":
    Print "                           is a "
    Print "                       Shareware Product":
    Print "                              of":
    Print "                         Miller Software": Print
    Print "    It can be permanently registered for just $10"
    Print "                             AND"
    Print "    You will never have to see this message again!"
End Sub

Sub reglater_Click ()
    Unload form4
    form3.Show 1
End Sub

Sub regnow_Click ()
    nl$ = Chr$(13)

regentry:
    regnum$ = InputBox$(nl$ + nl$ + "      Thank you for
    choosing to register your copy of GroupWorker." + nl$ +
    nl$ + nl$ + "        Please enter your Registration Number
    in the box below.", "Thanks for Registering")
    If regnum$ = "" Then GoTo outreg
    If Len(regnum$) <> 7 Then MsgBox "      Registration
    number is invalid. Please try your entry again.", 0,
    "Invalid Registration Number": GoTo regentry
```

continues

```
    If Asc(Mid$(regnum$, 3, 1)) + Asc(Right$(regnum$, 1))
      = Val(Mid$(regnum$, 4, 3)) Then
        MsgBox "          Thanks for Registering. This
            message is going away forever.", 0,
            "Valid Registration Number": GoTo regsave
    Else
        MsgBox "         Registration number is invalid. Please
            try your entry again.", 0, "Invalid Registration Number":
            GoTo regentry
    End If

regsave:
    Open (defdir + "\grpwrker.ini") For Output As #1
        Print #1, "regnum="; regnum$
    Close


outreg:
    Unload form4

End Sub
```

NAGBOX2.FRM—*Form3*

```
Sub Command1_Click ()
    Unload form3
End Sub

Sub Form_GotFocus ()
    Print
    Print "                    REMEMBER:"
    Print
    Print "          THE FUTURE OF SHAREWARE"
    Print
    Print "                    DEPENDS ON":
    Print
    Print "                  --> YOU! <-- "

End Sub

Sub NAGB_Click ()
    Unload form3
End Sub
```

VBClock

by Sarah Holland

9

Chapter 9: VBClock

Overview

VBClock is a utility written in Visual Basic that can display the date, time, day of the week, free system resources, and free memory; it also has a simple alarm feature (see Figure 9.1). VBClock works only with Windows 3.1.

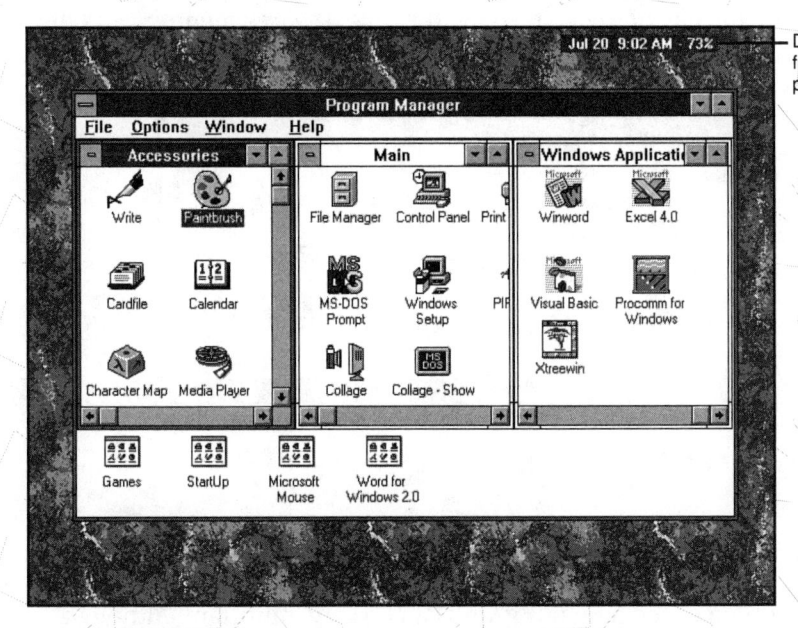

Figure 9.1. VBClock shows the date, time, and free resource percentage.

I wrote VBClock because I wanted to display the time and the free system resources. Although I could find programs that could do one or the other, I couldn't find anything that did both. After finding much Visual Basic programming material on CompuServe, I decided to write my own. I hope you learn as much from reading this program as I did from writing it.

Options

You should set VBClock to run automatically when the user starts Windows. In the upper-right corner of the screen, VBClock displays a form that includes the date, time, and free system resources. To change the display, either double-click the form with the left mouse button or click once with the right mouse button. The VBClock Options dialog box displays, from which the user chooses

- The options that appear on the clock
- The font and font size in which the information appears
- The colors in which the information appears

(See Figure 9.2.) You can also set an alarm. The options that may appear on the clock are the day of week, the date, the time, the free memory, and the free system resources.

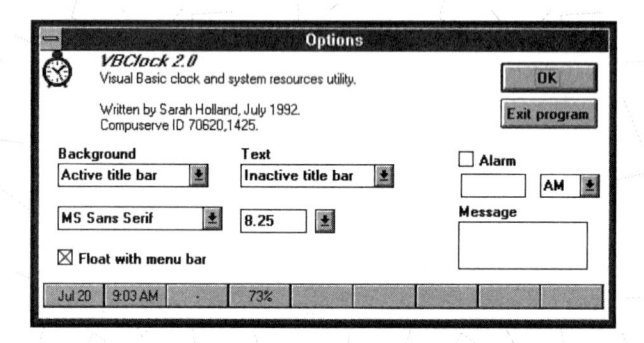

Figure 9.2. The VBClock Options dialog box.

In Windows, there is a limited amount of space available for resources (controls, menu items, forms, and documents). Free system resources is a measure of the amount of space remaining, and can be very important. Although Windows 3.1 added more space for resources, running several applications at the same time is still a problem. I find that under Windows 3.1, my system can run three big applications (with caution). Under Windows 3.0, however, I can run only two big applications. If your free system resources drop to much under 20 percent, you are more likely to experience crashes and other trouble with Windows. The limited memory available for system resources is a major problem with Windows. Having said that, of course, I realize that my first computer didn't have anywhere near the total amount of memory that Windows allots for system resources.

VBClock provides examples of how to:

- Keep a window on top
- Use a private .INI file
- Calculate free system resources and free memory

Chapter 9: VBClock

- Move a form without a title bar
- Use a pop-up menu
- Place a form on-screen in a position relative to another program
- Use a picture control as a fake button
- Use API calls
- Program using less memory

Program Operation

The following section does not give a line-by-line description of VBClock. Rather, it explains the most interesting and most useful points of this program.

Fundamental Concepts

Visual Basic insulates the programmer from most of the technical aspects of Windows. However, to do more advanced operations with Visual Basic, you need to be at least somewhat familiar with the internal workings of Windows.

Windows identifies each window by a handle to that window. In Visual Basic, hWnd gives the handle of the current form as an integer number. API functions need to know the handle of a window to address it.

You must declare the API function in the declarations section before you can use the function in your program. If you use API calls, you have to be very careful. Passing incorrect values can crash your system or give some very strange error messages. Often, problems are the result of the programmer using the wrong type of variable, such as giving a variable-length string to a function that expects a fixed-length string. In general, if it is possible to do something in both Visual Basic and the API, use Visual Basic.

The following is a list of the API calls VBClock uses:

> GetPrivateProfileInt(), GetPrivateProfileString(), WritePrivateProfileString(), and GetWindowsDirectory() are used in reading and writing the private .INI file.
>
> GetFreeSystemResources() and GetFreeSpace() are used to get display information.

`MessageBeep()` is used to call the appropriate sound for the message box.

`GetWindowRect()`, `WindowFromPoint()`, and `GetWindowText()` are used to determine where to put the clock on-screen.

`GetMenu()`, `GetSubMenu()`, and `TrackPopupMenu()` are used to show the pop-up menu bar.

Keeping VBClock on Top

The Clock form stays on top of any windows placed over it so that the information is always available. This is done through the following API call:

```
On_top% = SetWindowPos(FRM_Clock.hWnd, -1, 0, 0, 0, 0,
    &H2 Or &H1 Or &H40 Or &H10)
```

To set it back to a normal window, use the following call:

```
Normal% = SetWindowPos(FRM_Clock.hWnd, -2, 0, 0, 0, 0,
    &H2 Or &H1 Or &H40 Or &H10)
```

You need to execute these statements only once.

Floating VBClock with the Active Title Bar

You can place the Clock form to stay where you move it, or it can "float" on the right side of the active title bar. This is especially handy with title bars that do not extend all the way across the screen, such as on the Visual Basic design screen. It will, however, float only with an active window that has some part of itself on the coordinates (15, 15)—in other words, if the window is down any further than the control box of a maximized window, it will not float with that active window. I use these coordinates because they work best with the programs I run. You may want to change them.

The following routine in `DisplayInfo()` does the actual floating:

```
If IsFloat Then
    Wnd = WindowFromPoint(15, 15)
    If (Wnd > 0) And (Wnd <> FRM_Clock.hWnd) Then
        GetWindowRect Wnd, MyRect
        a% = GetWindowText(Wnd, WndName, 255)
```

```
        If (MyRect.Left = 0) And (MyRect.Top = 0) And
            (Left$(WndName, 14) = "Norton Desktop") Then
            MyRect.Right = MyRect.Right + 4
            MyRect.Top = -4
        End If
        FRM_Clock.Left = Pixels_To_Twips(MyRect.Right) -
            (FRM_Clock.Width + 700)
        FRM_Clock.Top = Pixels_To_Twips(MyRect.Top) + 75
    End If
End If
```

The subroutine `DisplayInfo()` is called every time the `Timer` event is executed. If the Clock form is set to float, it checks to see what the handle of the windows under the coordinates (15, 15) is. If there is a window there, and if that window isn't the clock window, it gets the coordinates and the name of that window. The coordinates of the window are obtained by the API call `GetWindowRect()`, which returns the coordinates in the variable `MyRect`, of type `RECT`. The coordinates are `MyRect.Left`, `MyRect.Right`, `MyRect.Top`, and `MyRect.Bottom`.

The next line is necessary because of Norton Desktop, which has a peculiarity in the placement of its title bar. All programs I have checked have their upper-left coordinates at (–4, –4) when maximized. Norton Desktop, however, has its upper-left coordinates at (0, 0). If you don't allow for that, the Clock form is incorrectly placed on-screen. Therefore, the program adjusts the coordinates to allow for that difference of 4. The program then sets the left and top coordinates of the Clock form, which is placed in the right corner of the title bar.

Storing Display Options

The global array `DispInfo` corresponds with a table in the private .INI file. There are nine entries in this .INI file—one for each item you can possibly place in the VBClock window. If you look at this Display section of the .INI file, you will see that each of the nine entries has a value associated with it. These values, which range from one to eight, have the following meanings:

1   Month and Date (for example, `Sep 3`)

2   Time (for example, `10:03 AM`)

3   Abbreviated day of the week (for example, `Thu`)

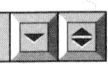

4   Full name for the day of the week (for example, Thursday)

5   Dash (-), for readability

6   Blank

7   Percentage of free resources (for example, 60%)

8   Amount of free resources (for example, 8787 KB)

Each element in the global array DispInfo holds a value that, when passed to function GetInfo(), produces the desired display option. For example, if DispInfo(1) equals 4 (full name for the day of the week), GetInfo(DispInfo(1)) equals *Tuesday* (presuming it is Tuesday).

The global constant NumTypes contains the number of possible display options, and the global constant MaxItems contains the number of possible options that can be displayed. To change how many items can be displayed on the clock, you only need to change the MaxItems constant.

Working with the VBCLOCK.INI File

The initialization file is the VBCLOCK.INI file. You should store all .INI files in the Windows directory. Therefore, you have to find the directory from which Windows runs. Don't assume that Windows is in C:\WINDOWS; it is possible that it is in a different directory. Use the following block of code to locate the Windows directory and set up the path/file name:

```
uh% = GetWindowsDirectory(TempStr, TempLen)
IniFile$ = TrimZeroTerm(TempStr)
If Right$(IniFile$, 1) <> "\" Then IniFile$ = IniFile$ + "\"
IniFile$ = IniFile$ + "VBCLOCK.INI"
```

The function GetWindowsDirectory() has two parameters passed to it: TempStr and TempLen. TempStr is a fixed-length string variable of length TempLen. The variable uh% contains a value indicating whether the function succeeded. The variable TempStr will then contain the Windows directory as a null-terminated string, which you can convert to a normal string with the function TrimZeroTerm() (which is found in the Cardfile program distributed with Visual Basic). Next, append a backslash (if it's not already there) and the name of the initialization file.

Next, you read from the initialization file. There are two ways to read: `GetPrivateProfileInt()` and `GetPrivateProfileString()`. These functions return an integer value and a string value as follows:

```
value% = GetPrivateProfileInt(section name, topic name, default value,
    initialization file name)
errorcode% = GetPrivateProfileString(section name, topic name,
    default value, string variable, length of string variable,
    initialization file name)
```

Each item is given a section name and a topic name. The topic name is each value's identifier, and the section name enables you to group them. The default value is the value that is assigned if there is no initialization file, or if the topic is not in the initialization file. The string variable and length of the string variable work just the same as in the `GetWindowsDirectory()` function. For example:

```
IsFloat = GetPrivateProfileInt("Position", "Floating", TRU, IniFile$)
uh% = GetPrivateProfileString("Typeface", "Font", "MS Sans Serif",
    TempStr, TempLen, IniFile$)
DispFont = TrimZeroTerm(TempStr)
```

When you write to the initialization file, you can use only `WritePrivateProfileString()`. You have to convert all integer values into string values with either `Str$()` or `Format$()`. Because `Str$()` inserts a leading space and `Format$()` does not, this program uses `Format$()`.

As you can see, the syntax for the initialization file write statement is very simple:

```
errorcode% = WritePrivateProfileString(section name, topic name,
    string value, initialization file name)
```

Choosing Fonts and Colors

Most systems running Windows 3.1 have the MS Sans Serif font installed. If this font is not available, however, VBClock defaults to the first screen font.

Visual Basic provides in the CONSTANT.TXT file constants for the desktop colors in the CONSTANT.TXT file. The VBClock default colors are `ACTIVE_TITLE_BAR` and `INACTIVE_TITLE_BAR`. These are the same colors that you select through the Control Panel for the desktop.

The `Form_Load()` procedure in `FRM_Opts` sets the index of the list boxes to the font or color in use. If the font or color cannot be found, defaults are set.

Moving the Form Without a Title Bar

The variable `AllowFormToMove` is set to `TRU` when the `Form_MouseDown()` event is executed, and the current mouse position is recorded. If `AllowFormToMove` is `TRU` when `Form_MouseMove()` is executed, the form is moved to its new position. When the `Form_MouseUp()` event is executed, `AllowFormToMove` is set to `FALS`.

Timer and Alarm Internals

The timer control in VBClock is set to activate every 500 milliseconds, or twice a second. You can, however, reset this interval according to your own preference. Every time this event occurs, VBClock redisplays the information on-screen. It also resets the colors, just in case any of the Windows desktop colors have been changed. It then checks to see if an alarm is set to go off.

Because there are only 16 timer controls available in Windows, use them carefully. At most, use one per program, and then only if necessary.

Each time the timer event occurs, the program checks to see if there is an alarm set; if so, the program checks to see if the time for the alarm has come yet. If it is time, a message box is placed on-screen. `MessageBeep()`, an API call, is called with the same numeric expression that `MsgBox()` is called with, and makes the appropriate sound as set in the Control Panel:

```
MessageBeep (48)
MsgBox AlarmMessage, 48, "Alarm"
```

The alarm is stored in the .INI file; this ensures that you don't have to reenter the alarm if you exit and restart Windows. When VBClock starts, it reads the `IsAlarm` variable in the .INI file. Then, if `IsAlarm` is true, it reads the `AlarmTime` variable. If that time has not passed, VBClock reads `AlarmMessage`. If the time has passed, it resets `IsAlarm`.

Manipulating the Pop-up Menu

You can easily customize the clock display. To change anything, double-click the Clock form, click a button at the bottom of the form, and then choose which display option you want from a pop-up menu.

You design the menus in the Menu Design Window, and then call them with the API call `TrackPopupMenu()`. You don't have to do anything special to the menu in the design process, other than making sure that it is visible when `TrackPopupMenu()` is called. Unfortunately, that means the menu can't be on either FRM_Clock or FRM_Opts, because neither has any space for a visible menu. Therefore, the form FRM_Disp was created solely to put the menu on.

When FRM_Disp is loaded, it creates NumTypes menu entries. Each time the user displays the menu, the current menu items are set to the current time, date, or free memory. Then, when the user selects one of the menu items, FRM_Disp sets the global variable DispItem to the selected item.

The following code shows the pop-up menu:

```
hMenu = GetMenu(FRM_Disp.hWnd)
hSubMenu = GetSubMenu(hMenu, 0)
j% = TrackPopupMenu(hSubMenu, 0, PopUpX, PopUpY, 0, FRM_Disp.hWnd, 0)
```

PopUpX and PopUpY are the coordinates at which the menu appears, and j% indicates whether the operation succeeded.

After this last command has been executed, the global variable DispItem indicates the selected item.

Conserving Memory

One of the reasons this program is so useful is that it enables you to keep an eye on how much of the system resources remain, and how much memory the currently running programs are using. This is often necessary because many applications use so much memory.

Programmers should strive to make their programs take up as little room in memory as possible. One of the most effective ways of doing this is by minimizing the use of controls. In VBClock, this is done in two different ways. One is by printing to the form instead of using label controls, and the other is by using one picture box to fake several button controls.

The only problem that arises is that "faked controls" are not redrawn if the screen is overwritten when AutoRedraw is set to FALS. In that case, Form_Paint() should contain the code necessary to redraw those faked controls. This is only necessary in FRM_Opts, because FRM_Clock has AutoRedraw set to TRU. AutoRedraw should be FALS due to the amount of memory consumed by it.

There are other ways to reduce memory use. For example, the picture of the clock on the Options form is copied from the Icon property assigned to the Clock form, and is assigned to the FRM_Opts.Picture rather than to a picture control. It will then be displayed on the top left corner of the form, and no extra control is needed.

Using integer variables uses less memory and speeds up operations.

Printing on a Form Versus Using a Label

A label control has 30 properties, 11 events, and 6 methods. You can change its font, position, visibility, and size on demand. All these properties and abilities take up memory and consume resources. If you want to display only one piece of nonchanging information, you don't need a label—you can just print the text on the form.

The subroutine PrintLabel() prints text above the specified control.

Using the Picture Box as a Button Bar

To reduce the number of controls, the picture box control pDisp is made to look as if it has MaxItems number of button controls on it. These buttons are drawn by the procedure ShowBar(), which draws lines on the picture box to approximate a button control.

The program first finds out how wide each faked button is by calculating pStep in Form_Load():

```
pStep = Int(pDisp.ScaleWidth / MaxItems) - 1
```

The procedure ShowBar() takes as parameters the area on the button bar to be redrawn. If only one button needs to be redrawn, Ind equals the number of the button to be redrawn:

```
ShowBar Ind * pStep, Ind * (pStep + 1) - 1
```

A value of 1 is subtracted from the last parameter; otherwise the button to the right would also be redrawn. For example, if the width of each button is 100, ShowBar 100, 199 would draw one button.

Each loop of ShowBar() draws one faked button. ShowBar() draws a box around the fake button, and draws two highlighting lines and two shadowed lines. ShowBar() then centers and prints the current display option:

```
For X% = st% To fin% Step PStep
    pDisp.DrawWidth = 2
    pDisp.Line (X% - PStep, 0)-(X%, pDisp.ScaleHeight - 8),
        Forecolor, B
    pDisp.DrawWidth = 1
    pDisp.Line (X% - PStep + 9, 9)-(X% - PStep + 9,
        pDisp.ScaleHeight - 25), WHITE
    pDisp.Line (X% - PStep + 9, 9)-(X% - 9, 9), WHITE
    pDisp.Line (X% - PStep + 9, pDisp.ScaleHeight - 25)-(X% - 9,
        pDisp.ScaleHeight - 25), BUTTON_SHADOW
    pDisp.Line (X% - 5, 9)-(X% - 5, pDisp.ScaleHeight - 25),
        BUTTON_SHADOW
    Info$ = LTrim$(RTrim$(GetInfo(DispInfo(X% / PStep))))
    pDisp.CurrentX = (X% - (PStep / 2)) - pDisp.TextWidth(Info$) / 2
    pDisp.CurrentY = cY
    pDisp.Print Info$
Next X%
```

When pDisp executes the MouseDown() event, highlighting and shadowed lines are drawn on the faked button to make it look as if the button has been pressed.

Because all line coordinates were derived from trial and error, it may be possible to draw more pleasing lines than in these routines.

Ideas for Further Work

You will find that modifying the program is one of the best ways to learn about it. The following is a list of some modifications you can make to VBClock (remember to make a backup first!):

- Ring on the hour.
- If any alarm is active, put a little bell or clock picture on the clock.
- Make VBClock a better scheduler.
- Sound an alert if system resources drop below a certain percentage.
- Put user-defined text on the VBClock mini-window, such as `Gone to lunch`.
- Show times for different time zones.
- Try to reduce memory usage further.
- Load everything at the beginning to speed things up.

General Rules for Well-Behaved Programs

Here are some rules of thumb for writing well-behaved Windows programs. Feel free to add your own or change these!

- Make the program easy to delete if users want it off their systems.
- Write your own .INI file instead of using WIN.INI.
- Don't make the program dependent on finding a particular font.
- Change the cursor to an hourglass if the routine takes time.
- Use `MessageBeep` when you are using `MsgBox()`.
- Center forms on-screen.
- Use the least amount of memory possible.
- Reduce .EXE size by saving and loading text before making the executable file.

Source Code for VBClock

The remainder of the chapter shows all the Visual Basic code in each of the VBClock forms.

The Global Listing File

```
Type POINTAPI
  X As Integer
  Y As Integer
End Type

Type RECT
    Left As Integer
    Top As Integer
    Right As Integer
    Bottom As Integer
End Type

Declare Function GetPrivateProfileInt Lib "Kernel"
    (ByVal lpApplicationName As String, ByVal lpKeyName As String,
    ByVal nDefault As Integer,
    ByVal lpFileName As String) As Integer
Declare Function WritePrivateProfileString Lib "Kernel" (ByVal
    lpApplicationName As String, ByVal lpKeyName As String,
    ByVal lpString As Any, ByVal lplFileName As String) As Integer
Declare Function GetPrivateProfileString Lib "Kernel" (ByVal
    lpApplicationName As String, ByVal lpKeyName As String, ByVal
    lpDefault As String, ByVal lpReturnedString As String,
    ByVal nSize As Integer, ByVal lpFileName As String) As Integer
Declare Function GetWindowsDirectory Lib "Kernel" (ByVal lpBuffer
    As String, ByVal nSize As Integer) As Integer
Declare Function GetWindowText Lib "User" (ByVal hWnd As Integer,
    ByVal lpString As String, ByVal aint As Integer) As Integer
Declare Function SetWindowPos Lib "User" (ByVal hWnd As Integer,
    ByVal hWndInsertAfter As Integer, ByVal X As Integer,
    ByVal Y As Integer, ByVal cx As Integer, ByVal cy As Integer,
    ByVal wFlags As Integer) As Integer
Declare Function GetFreeSystemResources Lib "User"
    (ByVal wType As Integer) As Integer
Declare Function GetFreeSpace Lib "Kernel" (ByVal wFlags As Integer)
    As Long
Declare Sub MessageBeep Lib "User" (ByVal wType As Integer)
Declare Function GetActiveWindow Lib "User" () As Integer
Declare Sub GetWindowRect Lib "User" (ByVal hWnd As Integer,
    MyRect As RECT)
Declare Function WindowFromPoint Lib "User" (ByVal Y As Integer,
    ByVal X As Integer) As Integer
Declare Function GetMenu Lib "User" (ByVal hWnd As Integer) As Integer
Declare Function GetSubMenu Lib "User" (ByVal hMenu As Integer,
    ByVal nPos As Integer) As Integer
```

continues

```
Declare Function TrackPopupMenu Lib "User" (ByVal hMenu As Integer,
    ByVal wFlags As Integer, ByVal X As Integer, ByVal Y As Integer,
    ByVal nReserved As Integer, ByVal hWnd As Integer,
    ByVal lpReserved As Long) As Integer

Global DispItem As Integer
Global Bcolor As Long
Global FColor As Long
Global IsFloat As Integer
Global IsAlarm As Integer
Global AlarmTime As Double
Global AlarmMessage As String
Global DispFont As String
Global DispFontSize As Single
Global pStep As Integer
Global Scale_Pixel As Integer
Global Scale_Twip As Integer
Global Const NumTypes = 8
Global Const MaxItems = 9
Global DispInfo(1 To MaxItems)   As Integer

Global Const TRU = -1
Global Const FALS = 0

Global Const SHIFT_MASK = 1
Global Const CTRL_MASK = 2
Global Const ALT_MASK = 4
Global Const LEFT_BUTTON = 1
Global Const RIGHT_BUTTON = 2
Global Const MIDDLE_BUTTON = 4
Global Const BLACK = &H0&
Global Const RED = &HFF&
Global Const GREEN = &HFF00&
Global Const YELLOW = &HFFFF&
Global Const BLUE = &HFF0000
Global Const MAGENTA = &HFF00FF
Global Const CYAN = &HFFFF00
Global Const WHITE = &HFFFFFF

Global Const DESKTOP = &H80000001                        ' Desktop.
Global Const ACTIVE_TITLE_BAR = &H80000002               ' Active window caption.
Global Const INACTIVE_TITLE_BAR = &H80000003             ' Inactive window caption.
Global Const MENU_BAR = &H80000004                       ' Menu background.
Global Const WINDOW_BACKGROUND = &H80000005              ' Window background.
Global Const WINDOW_FRAME = &H80000006                   ' Window frame.
Global Const MENU_TEXT = &H80000007                      ' Text in menus.
```

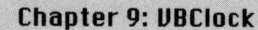

```
Global Const WINDOW_TEXT = &H80000008         ' Text in windows.
Global Const TITLE_BAR_TEXT = &H80000009      ' Text in caption, size
                                              ' box, scroll-bar arrow.
Global Const ACTIVE_BORDER = &H8000000A       ' Active window border.
Global Const INACTIVE_BORDER = &H8000000B     ' Inactive window border.
Global Const APPLICATION_WORKSPACE = &H8000000C  ' Background color of
                                              ' multiple document
                                              ' interface (MDI)
                                              ' applications.
Global Const HIGHLIGHT = &H8000000D           ' Selected item in
                                              ' a control.
Global Const HIGHLIGHT_TEXT = &H8000000E      ' Text of item selected
                                              ' in a control.
Global Const BUTTON_FACE = &H8000000F         ' Face shading on
                                              ' command buttons.
Global Const BUTTON_SHADOW = &H80000010       ' Edge shading on
                                              ' command buttons.
Global Const GRAY_TEXT = &H80000011           ' Grayed (disabled) text.
                                              ' This color is set to
                                              ' 0 if the current display
                                              ' driver does not support
                                              ' a solid gray color.
Global Const BUTTON_TEXT = &H80000012         ' Text on push buttons.

Global Const DEFAULT = 0                      ' 0 - Default
Global Const ARROW = 1                        ' 1 - Arrow
Global Const CROSSHAIR = 2                    ' 2 - Cross
Global Const IBEAM = 3                        ' 3 - I-Beam
Global Const ICON_POINTER = 4                 ' 4 - Icon
Global Const SIZE_POINTER = 5                 ' 5 - Size
Global Const SIZE_NE_SW = 6                   ' 6 - Size NE SW
Global Const SIZE_N_S = 7                     ' 7 - Size N S
Global Const SIZE_NW_SE = 8                   ' 8 - Size NW SE
Global Const SIZE_W_E = 9                     ' 9 - Size W E
Global Const UP_ARROW = 10                    ' 10 - Up Arrow
Global Const HOURGLASS = 11                   ' 11 - Hourglass
Global Const NO_DROP = 12                     ' 12 - No drop
```

FRM_Clock.FRM

```
DefInt A-Z
Dim IniFile$
Dim MyRect As RECT
Dim AllowFormToMove
Dim MStartX
```

continues

Chapter 9: VBClock

```
Dim MStartY
Dim WndName As String * 255
Dim Wnd As Integer
Rem Normal% = SetWindowPos(Form1.hWnd, -2, 0, 0, 0, 0, wFlags)

Sub Form_Load ()
    Const TempLen = 250
    Dim TempStr As String * TempLen

    On_top% = SetWindowPos(FRM_Clock.hWnd, -1, 0, 0, 0, 0,
        &H2 Or &H1 Or &H40 Or &H10)
    sm% = FRM_Clock.scalemode
    FRM_Clock.scalemode = 1
    Scale_Twip = FRM_Clock.ScaleWidth
    FRM_Clock.scalemode = 3
    Scale_Pixel = FRM_Clock.ScaleWidth
    FRM_Clock.scalemode = sm%

    ' Get windows directory for .INI file.
    uh% = GetWindowsDirectory(TempStr, TempLen)
    IniFile$ = TrimZeroTerm(TempStr)
    If Right$(IniFile$, 1) <> "\" Then IniFile$ = IniFile$ + "\"
    IniFile$ = IniFile$ + "VBCLOCK.INI"

    ' Get and set position from .INI file.
    FRM_Clock.Top = GetPrivateProfileInt("Position", "Top",
        Int(Screen.Height * .003), IniFile$)
    FRM_Clock.Left = GetPrivateProfileInt("Position", "Left",
        Int(Screen.Width * .71), IniFile$)
    IsFloat = GetPrivateProfileInt("Position", "Floating", TRU,
        IniFile$)
    If IsFloat And (FRM_Clock.Left <= Pixels_To_Twips(15)) And
        (FRM_Clock.Top <= Pixels_To_Twips(15))
        Then FRM_Clock.Left = Pixels_To_Twips(20)

    ' Get and set colors from .INI file
    uh% = GetPrivateProfileString("Color", "Background",
        Format$(ACTIVE_TITLE_BAR), TempStr, TempLen, IniFile$)
    bColor = Val(TempStr)
    uh% = GetPrivateProfileString("Color", "Foreground",
        Format$(INACTIVE_TITLE_BAR), TempStr, TempLen, IniFile$)
    fColor = Val(TempStr)

    ' Get and set typeface.
    uh% = GetPrivateProfileString("Typeface", "Font",
        "MS Sans Serif", TempStr, TempLen, IniFile$)
    DispFont = TrimZeroTerm(TempStr)
```

Chapter 9: VBClock

```
    uh% = GetPrivateProfileString("Typeface", "Fontsize",
        "8.25", TempStr, TempLen, IniFile$)
    DispFontSize = Val(TempStr)

    ' Get and set display.
    DispInfo(1) = GetPrivateProfileInt("Display", "Info1", 1, IniFile$)
    DispInfo(2) = GetPrivateProfileInt("Display", "Info2", 2, IniFile$)
    DispInfo(3) = GetPrivateProfileInt("Display", "Info3", 5, IniFile$)
    DispInfo(4) = GetPrivateProfileInt("Display", "Info4", 7, IniFile$)
    For X% = 5 To MaxItems
        nm$ = "Info" + Format$(X%)
        DispInfo(X%) = GetPrivateProfileInt("Display", nm$, 6,
            IniFile$)
    Next X%


    ' Get and set alarm.
    IsAlarm = FALS
    uh% = GetPrivateProfileString("Alarm", "Time", "0",
        TempStr, TempLen, IniFile$)
    AlarmTime = Val(TempStr)
    If AlarmTime > Now Then
        IsAlarm = TRU
        uh% = GetPrivateProfileString("Alarm", "Message", "",
            TempStr, TempLen, IniFile$)
        AlarmMessage = TrimZeroTerm(TempStr)
    End If

    SetForm
    DisplayInfo
End Sub

Sub Form_MouseDown (Button As Integer, Shift As Integer, X As Single,
    Y As Single)
    If (Button And LEFT_BUTTON) > 0 Then
        AllowFormToMove = TRU
        MStartX = X
        MStartY = Y
        MousePointer = SIZE_POINTER
    End If
End Sub

Sub Form_MouseMove (Button As Integer, Shift As Integer, X As Single,
    Y As Single)
```

continues

```
    If AllowFormToMove Then Move FRM_Clock.Left + (X - MStartX), _
        FRM_Clock.Top + (Y - MStartY)
End Sub

Sub Form_MouseUp (Button As Integer, Shift As Integer, X As Single, _
    Y As Single)
    RButt = (Button And RIGHT_BUTTON) > 0
    LButt = (Button And LEFT_BUTTON) > 0
    Ctrl = (Shift And CTRL_MASK) > 0

    If LButt Then
        AllowFormToMove = FALS
        MousePointer = DEFAULT
    ElseIf RButt Then
        Select Case Ctrl
            Case FALS
                ShowOptions
            Case TRU
                End
        End Select
    End If
End Sub

Sub Form_DblClick ()
    ShowOptions
End Sub

Sub Form_Unload (Cancel As Integer)
    WriteProfile
End Sub

Sub Timer1_Timer ()
    DisplayInfo
    If IsAlarm Then
        If AlarmTime <= Now Then
            MessageBeep (48)
            If AlarmMessage = "" Then AlarmMessage = "It's that time!"
            MsgBox AlarmMessage, 48, "Alarm"
            IsAlarm = FALS
            FRM_Opts.CHK_Alarm.Value = 0
        End If
    End If
End Sub
```

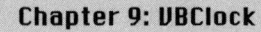

```
Sub DisplayInfo ()
    If IsFloat Then
        Wnd = WindowFromPoint(15, 15)
        If (Wnd > 0) And (Wnd <> FRM_Clock.hWnd) Then
            GetWindowRect Wnd, MyRect
            a% = GetWindowText(Wnd, WndName, 255)
            If (MyRect.Left = 0) And (MyRect.Top = 0) And
                (Left$(WndName, 14) = "Norton Desktop") Then
                MyRect.Right = MyRect.Right + 4
                MyRect.Top = -4
            End If
            FRM_Clock.Left = Pixels_To_Twips(MyRect.Right) -
                (FRM_Clock.Width + 700)
            FRM_Clock.Top = Pixels_To_Twips(MyRect.Top) + 75
        End If
    End If

    msg$ = ""
    For X% = 1 To MaxItems
        msg$ = msg$ + GetInfo(DispInfo(X%))
    Next X%
    msg$ = RTrim$(msg$)

    Backcolor = bColor
    ForeColor = fColor
    FRM_Clock.CurrentX = ((FRM_Clock.Width - TextWidth(msg$)) / 2)
    FRM_Clock.CurrentY = ((FRM_Clock.Height - TextHeight(msg$)) / 2)
    FRM_Clock.Print msg$
End Sub

Sub WriteProfile ()
    uh = WritePrivateProfileString("Color", "Background",
        Format$(bColor), IniFile$)
    uh = WritePrivateProfileString("Color", "Foreground",
        Format$(fColor), IniFile$)
    uh = WritePrivateProfileString("Typeface", "Font", DispFont,
        IniFile$)
    uh = WritePrivateProfileString("Typeface", "Fontsize",
        Format$(DispFontSize), IniFile$)

    uh = WritePrivateProfileString("Position", "Floating",
        Format$(IsFloat), IniFile$)
```

continues

```
  If Not IsFloat Then
    uh = WritePrivateProfileString("Position", "Top", 
        Format$(FRM_Clock.Top), IniFile$)
    uh = WritePrivateProfileString("Position", "Left", 
        Format$(FRM_Clock.Left), IniFile$)
  End If

  If IsAlarm Then
    uh = WritePrivateProfileString("Alarm", "Time", AlarmTime), 
        IniFile$)
    uh = WritePrivateProfileString("Alarm", "Message", AlarmMessage, 
        IniFile$)
  End If

  For X% = 1 To MaxItems
    nm$ = "Info" + Format$(X%)
    uh = WritePrivateProfileString("Display", nm$, 
        Format$(DispInfo(X%)), IniFile$)
  Next X%
End Sub

Sub ShowOptions ()
    Timer1.Enabled = FALS
    FRM_Opts.Show 1
    Timer1.Enabled = TRU
    SetForm
    WriteProfile
    DisplayInfo
End Sub

Sub SetForm ()
    FRM_Clock.FontName = DispFont
    FRM_Clock.FontSize = DispFontSize
    FRM_Clock.FontBold = TRU

    msg$ = ""
    For X% = 1 To MaxItems
        msg$ = msg$ + GetInfo(DispInfo(X%))
    Next X%
    msg$ = RTrim$(msg$)

    FRM_Clock.Width = TextWidth(msg$) * 1.05
    FRM_Clock.Height = TextHeight(msg$) * 1.15
End Sub
```

FRM_Disp.FRM

```
Sub Form_Load ()
    For x% = 2 To NumTypes
        Load mDisp(x%)
    Next x%
End Sub

Sub mdHead_Click ()
    For x% = 1 To NumTypes
        mDisp(x%).Caption = GetInfo(x%)
    Next x%
End Sub

Sub mDisp_Click (Index As Integer)
    DispItem = Index
End Sub
```

FRM_Opts.FRM

```
Dim Color$(0 To 20)
Dim Col(0 To 20) As Long
Dim PStep As Integer
Dim cY as Integer

Sub Form_Load ()
    Screen.MousePointer = HOURGLASS
    Move (Screen.Width - Width) / 2, (Screen.Height - Height) / 3
    pDisp.Backcolor = BUTTON_FACE
    pDisp.Forecolor = BUTTON_TEXT

    ' Set up color combo boxes.
    Color$(0) = "Black": Color$(1) = "Blue": Color$(2) = "Green"
    Color$(3) = "Cyan": Color$(4) = "Red": Color$(5) = "Magenta"
    Color$(6) = "Yellow": Color$(7) = "White": Color$(8) = "Gray"
    Color$(9) = "Light Blue": Color$(10) = "Light Green": Color$(11) = "Light Cyan"
    Color$(12) = "Light Red": Color$(13) = "Light Magenta": Color$(14) = "Light Yellow"
    Color$(15) = "Bright White"
    Color$(16) = "Desktop": Color$(17) = "Active title bar"
    Color$(18) = "Inactive title bar": Color$(19) = "Menu bar"
    Color$(20) = "Menu bar text"
```

```
For X% = 0 To 15
    Col(X%) = QBColor(X%)
Next
Col(16) = DESKTOP
Col(17) = ACTIVE_TITLE_BAR
Col(18) = INACTIVE_TITLE_Bar
Col(19) = MENU_BAR
Col(20) = MENU_BAR_TEXT
Do While CMB_Back.ListCount > 0
    CMB_Back.RemoveItem 0
    CMB_Fore.RemoveItem 0
Loop
For X% = 0 To 20
    CMB_Back.AddItem Color$(X%)
    CMB_Fore.AddItem Color$(X%)
Next X%
CMB_Back.ListIndex = 16
CMB_Fore.ListIndex = 17
For X% = 20 To 0 Step -1
    If BColor = Col(X%) Then CMB_Back.ListIndex = X%
    If FColor = Col(X%) Then CMB_Fore.ListIndex = X%
Next X%

' Set up AM/PM combo box.
Do While CMB_AMPM.ListCount > 0
    CMB_AMPM.RemoveItem 0
Loop
CMB_AMPM.AddItem "AM"
CMB_AMPM.AddItem "PM"
CMB_AMPM.ListIndex = Abs(Time$ > "12:00:00")

' Set up font size box.
Do While CMB_Size.ListCount > 0
    CMB_Size.RemoveItem 0
Loop
CMB_Size.AddItem "6"
CMB_Size.AddItem "7"
CMB_Size.AddItem "8.25"
CMB_Size.AddItem "9.75"
CMB_Size.AddItem "12"
CMB_Size.AddItem "13.5"
CMB_Size.AddItem "18"
CMB_Size.AddItem "24"
For X% = 0 To Screen.Fontcount - 1
    If CMB_Size.List(X%) = Format$(DispFontSize) ↵
        Then CMB_Size.ListIndex = X%
```

Chapter 9: VBClock

```
    Next X%
    If CMB_Size.ListIndex = -1 Then CMB_Size.Text =
        Format$(DispFontSize)

    ' Set up font name combo box.
    Do While CMB_Font.ListCount > 0
        CMB_Font.RemoveItem 0
    Loop
    For X% = 0 To Screen.Fontcount - 1
        CMB_Font.AddItem Screen.Fonts(X%)
    Next X%
    CMB_Font.ListIndex = 1
    For X% = 0 To Screen.Fontcount - 1
        If CMB_Font.List(X%) = DispFont Then CMB_Font.ListIndex = X%
    Next X%

    If IsAlarm Then
        at$ = Format$(AlarmTime, "hh:mm AM/PM")
        TXT_Alarm.Text = Left$(at$, Len(at$) - 3)
        TXT_Message.Text = AlarmMessage
        CHK_Alarm.Value = 1
        CMB_AMPM.ListIndex = Abs(Format$(AlarmTime, "h:mm") > "12:00")
    End If
    If IsFloat Then CHK_Float.Value = 1

    PStep = Int(pDisp.ScaleWidth / MaxItems) - 1
    pDisp.Fillcolor = pDisp.Backcolor
    pDisp.FillStyle = 0
    pDisp.FontSize = 7
    pDisp.FontBold = FALS
    cY = pDisp.ScaleHeight / 2 - pDisp.TextHeight("A") / 2

    Screen.MousePointer = DEFAULT
End Sub

Sub Form_Paint ()
    fs = FRM_Opts.FontSize
    fb% = FontBold
    fi% = FontItalic
    FontBold = TRU
    PrintLabel "Background", CMB_Back
    PrintLabel "Text", CMB_Fore
    PrintLabel "Message", TXT_Message

    FontSize = 9.75
    FontBold = TRU
```

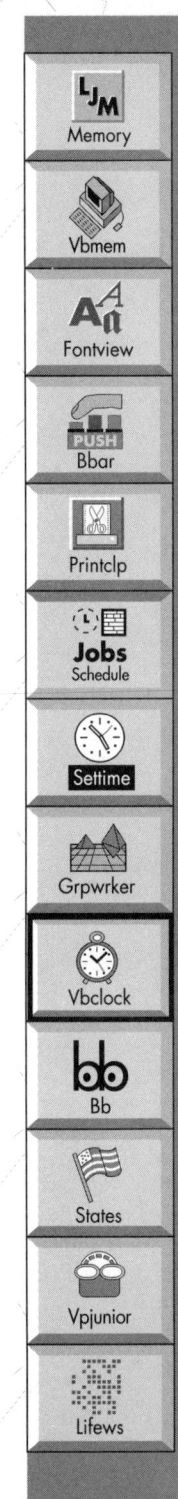

continues

```
        FontItalic = TRU
        CurrentX = 750
        CurrentY = 5
        Print "VBClock 2.0"
        FontSize = 8.25
        FontBold = FALS
        FontItalic = FALS
        CurrentX = 800
        Print "Visual Basic clock and system resources utility."
        Print
        CurrentX = 800
        Print "Written by Sarah Holland, July 1992."
        CurrentX = 800
        Print "Compuserve ID 70620,1425."
        FontSize = fs
        FontBold = fb%
        FontItalic = fi%
        ShowBar PStep, Int(pDisp.ScaleWidth)
End Sub

Sub BUT_OK_Click ()
    BColor = Col(CMB_Back.ListIndex)
    FColor = Col(CMB_Fore.ListIndex)
    DispFont = CMB_Font.List(CMB_Font.ListIndex)
    DispFontSize = Val(CMB_Size.Text)
    If DispFontSize < 2 Then DispFontSize = 2

    If CHK_Alarm.Value = 1 Then IsAlarm = TRU
    If (TXT_Alarm.Text = "") Or (Val(TXT_Alarm.Text) = 0) Then   IsAlarm
        = FALS
    If IsAlarm Then
        AlarmTime = INT(Now) + TimeValue(TXT_Alarm.Text +
            CMB_AMPM.List(CMB_AMPM.ListIndex))
        AlarmMessage = TXT_Message.Text
    Else
        FRM_Opts.CHK_Alarm.Value = 0
    End If

    FRM_Opts.Hide
End Sub
Sub BUT_Exit_Click ()
    Unload FRM_Clock
```

Chapter 9: VBClock

```vb
        Unload FRM_Opts
        End
End Sub

Sub pDisp_MouseDown (Button As Integer, Shift As Integer, x As Single,
    Y As Single)
    Ind = Int(x / pStep + 1)
    j% = Ind * pStep
    pDisp.Line (j% - pStep + 9, 9)-(j% - pStep + 9, pDisp.ScaleHeight -
        25), BUTTON_SHADOW
    pDisp.Line (j% - pStep + 9, 9)-(j% - 9, 9), BUTTON_SHADOW
    pDisp.Line (j% - pStep + 9, pDisp.ScaleHeight - 23)-(j% -
        5, pDisp.ScaleHeight - 23), BUTTON_FACE
    pDisp.Line (j% - 9, 9)-(j% - 9, pDisp.ScaleHeight - 25), BUTTON_FACE
End Sub

Sub pDisp_MouseUp (Button As Integer, Shift As Integer, X As Single,
    Y As Single)
    Dim hMenu As Integer
    Dim hSubMenu As Integer
    Dim hWnd As Integer

    If Ind <> Int(x / pStep + 1) Then
        ShowBar Ind * pStep, Ind * (pStep + 1) - 1
        Exit Sub
    End If
    Ind = Int(x / pStep + 1)

    PopUpX = Twips_To_Pixels((Ind - 1) * (PStep + 25) + FRM_Opts.Left
        + pDisp.Left)
    PopUpY = Twips_To_Pixels(FRM_Opts.Top + pDisp.Top -
        (TextHeight("A") * NumTypes))
    hMenu = GetMenu(FRM_Disp.hWnd)
    hSubMenu = GetSubMenu(hMenu, 0)
    j% = TrackPopupMenu(hSubMenu, 0, PopUpX, PopUpY,
        0, FRM_Disp.hWnd, 0)
    DispInfo(Ind) = DispItem
    Unload FRM_Disp
    ShowBar Ind * PStep, Ind * (PStep + 1) - 1
End Sub

Sub CHK_Alarm_Click ()
    IsAlarm = CHK_Alarm.Value
End Sub
```

continues

```
Sub CHK_Float_Click ()
    IsFloat = CHK_Float.Value
End Sub

Sub TXT_Alarm_Change ()
    CHK_Alarm.Value = 1
End Sub

Sub ShowBar (st%, fin%)
    For X% = st% To fin% Step PStep
        pDisp.DrawWidth = 2
        pDisp.Line (X% - PStep, 0)-(X%, pDisp.ScaleHeight - 8),
            Forecolor, B
        pDisp.DrawWidth = 1
        pDisp.Line (X% - PStep + 9, 9)-(X% - PStep + 9,
            pDisp.ScaleHeight - 25), WHITE
        pDisp.Line (X% - PStep + 9, 9)-(X% - 9, 9), WHITE
        pDisp.Line (X% - PStep + 9, pDisp.ScaleHeight - 25)-(X% - 9,
            pDisp.ScaleHeight - 25), BUTTON_SHADOW
        pDisp.Line (X% - 5, 9)-(X% - 5, pDisp.ScaleHeight - 25),
            BUTTON_SHADOW
        Info$ = LTrim$(RTrim$(GetInfo(DispInfo(X% / PStep))))
        pDisp.CurrentX = (X% - (PStep / 2)) - pDisp.TextWidth(Info$)
            / 2
        pDisp.CurrentY = cY
        pDisp.Print Info$
    Next X%
End Sub

Sub PrintLabel (Text As String, Ctl As Control)
    CurrentX = Ctl.Left
    CurrentY = Ctl.Top - 225
    Print Text
End Sub
```

VBCLOCK.BAS

```
Static Function Signed (XNum&)  As Integer
    If XNum& > 32767 Then
        Signed = XNum& - 65536
    Else
        Signed = XNum&
    End If
End Function
```

Chapter 9: VBClock

```vb
Function TrimZeroTerm$ (s$)
    Dim temp As String
    Dim nullspot As Integer

    temp = String$(1, 0)
    nullspot = InStr(s$, temp)
    If nullspot = 0 Then
        TrimZeroTerm = s$
      Else
        TrimZeroTerm = Left$(s$, nullspot - 1)
    End If
End Function

Function GetInfo (InfType As Integer) As String
    Select Case InfType
        Case 1
            GetInfo = " " + Format$(Now, "MMM d") + " "
        Case 2
            GetInfo = " " + Format$(Now, "h:mm AM/PM") + " "
        Case 3
            GetInfo = " " + Format$(Now, "ddd") + " "
        Case 4
            GetInfo = " " + Format$(Now, "dddd") + " "
        Case 5
            GetInfo = "-"
        Case 6
            GetInfo = ""
        Case 7
            GetInfo = " " + Format$(GetFreeSystemResources%(0) /
                100, "00%") + " "
        Case 8
            GetInfo = " " + Format$(GetFreeSpace(0) \ 1024) +
                " KB" + " "
    End Select
End Function

Function Pixels_To_Twips (ByVal N&) As Long
  Pixels_To_Twips = Scale_Twip / Scale_Pixel * N&
End Function

Function Twips_To_Pixels (ByVal N&) As Long
  Twips_To_Pixels = Scale_Pixel / Scale_Twip * N&
End Function
```

… Chapter 9: VBClock

Blink Blank!

by Max Burgstahler

10

Chapter 10: Blink Blank!

Overview

Blink Blank! is a screensaver with a new twist: it's useful. Instead of filling your screen with airborne kitchen appliances, Blink Blank! actually puts your PC to work while you are gone. When you invoke Blink Blank!, you can display a message on your PC while you are away.

Through a series of intuitive menus, you can build and store up to 99 messages. When it's time to go to a meeting (or whatever), simply bring up Blink Blank! and choose a message to display with a couple of mouse clicks. Here's the fun part: if someone wants to leave a message for you while you are away, all they have to do is press the spacebar on your PC and start typing. Blink Blank! holds up to five messages (of any length) and displays them when you return. You can even print your messages, and they are automatically time-stamped!

Of course, after watching all those other fancy exploding screensavers, you might want some colorful effects. Not to worry. Blink Blank! enables you to customize the appearance of your screen by choosing the background and foreground colors, as well as the font for the message.

Custom Messages

At the top of the main screen, Blink Blank! provides a text box into which you can type a custom message up to 30 characters long (see Figure 10.1). Your custom message should be one that you may never use again, and one that you do not wish to add to your Miscellaneous Messages list box.

If you start Blink Blank! with any command-line argument, it immediately begins flashing that command-line parameter as a message when invoked. A use for this feature might be to set up a Blink Blank! group item in which you have several Blink Blank! icons. Each icon could have a different name and command line representing four or five of your most common messages. Clicking the appropriate icon would then allow you to bypass the main screen for commonly used messages.

To use the Custom Message feature from the main screen, type a message in this text box and either press Enter or click the Use Custom button.

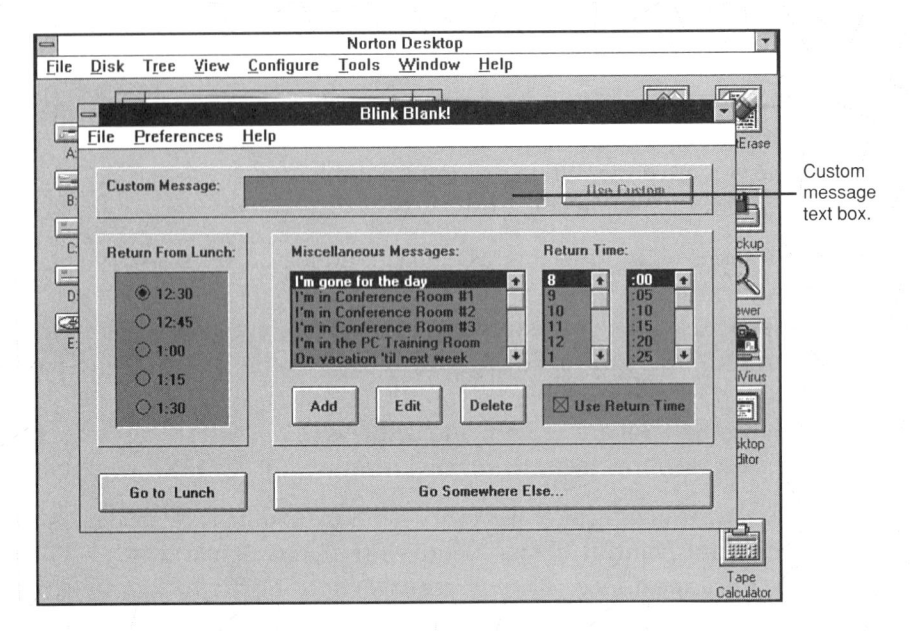

Figure 10.1. The main Blink Blank! window.

Miscellaneous Messages

Blink Blank! enables you to store up to 99 commonly used messages in the Miscellaneous Messages list box. An Add button enables you to add any messages you like up to 30 characters long. The box displays the messages in alphabetical order. You can edit any message by highlighting it and clicking the Edit button. Clicking the Delete button deletes the highlighted message.

In conjunction with a miscellaneous message, you can specify a time when you will return. You do this by selecting hours and minutes from the Return Time list boxes. You can choose to omit the return time by deselecting the Use Return Time check box below the Return Time list boxes.

To use the miscellaneous messages feature from the main screen, click the desired message and return time and then click Go Somewhere Else.... Alternatively, you can choose the return time and double-click the desired message.

Lunch Messages

Blink Blank! allows you to display the five most common times you return from lunch on the main window as radio buttons.

To change the five lunch times, select Lunch from the Preferences menu. The Lunch Messages dialog box appears (see Figure 10.2), asking you to choose the five times. It also provides you with an instant preview of how the options will appear on the main screen. To the right of the example radio buttons is another set of radio buttons that you can use to select the default lunch time. To use the Lunch Messages feature from the main screen, click the appropriate return time and click the Go to Lunch button.

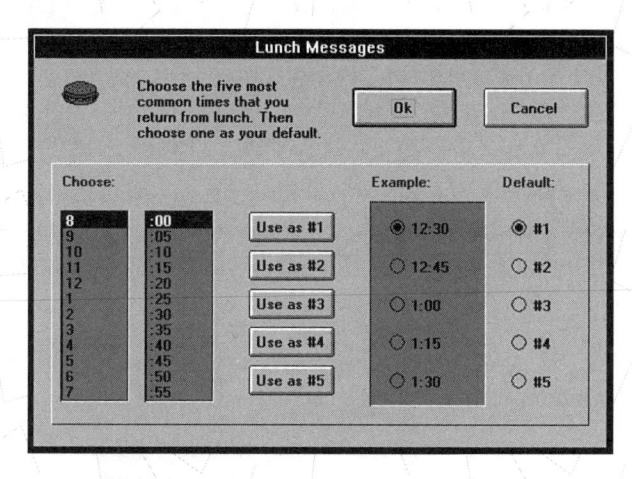

Figure 10.2. The Lunch Messages dialog box.

Leaving a Message

While Blink Blank! is flashing its message, your office visitors can leave a note by pressing the spacebar and typing their message. The dialog box that appears indicates to your visitor the number of messages that can be left. Blink Blank! holds up to five messages for you.

Your office visitors no longer have to search your desk for a blank piece of paper and a pen. You can actually save paper with this program (as long as you don't print the messages).

When your visitors finish their messages, they can either press Enter or click OK. Blink Blank! then returns to flashing your screensaver message.

Retrieving Messages

When you return to your office, you will want to check for messages. When you enter your password, Blink Blank! checks your mailbox for messages. (See the next section for more information on passwords.) Blink Blank! automatically displays your messages and asks if you want to print any or all of the messages you received.

When you are finished viewing and printing, click the Done button.

Using a Password

Blink Blank! uses a password to restrict entry to your PC while it is flashing the selected message. When you return to your office, press the Esc key and then type your password into the dialog box presented. The password is displayed as asterisks as you type it—this is to prevent someone from looking over your shoulder and stealing your password as it appears on the screen.

The first time you use Blink Blank!, the default password is *password*. To set the password, choose Password from the Preferences menu. The password must be at least three characters and not more than eight. You cannot enter spaces for a password.

> The password is not case-sensitive; in other words, *password* = *Password* = *PASSWORD*.
>
> The password is encrypted and stored in BB.INI. It is important that the password entry not be tampered with. If you change the password and forget what you changed it to, you could lock yourself out of your PC.

Setting Display Options

Blink Blank! enables you to control how the flashing message displays on your PC screen. By choosing Display from the Preferences menu, you can set the foreground color, background color, and font (see Figure 10.3). The sample display in the Preview box (in the upper-right corner of the Display Options dialog box) indicates your selections.

The Display Options dialog box also gives you the choice of whether to minimize Blink Blank! after you type your password. This is convenient if you want to keep Blink Blank! as an open icon on your desktop. When you return to your office and enter your password, Blink Blank! automatically shrinks to an icon. To turn this feature on or off, select or deselect the *Minimize after message* check box in the Display Options dialog box.

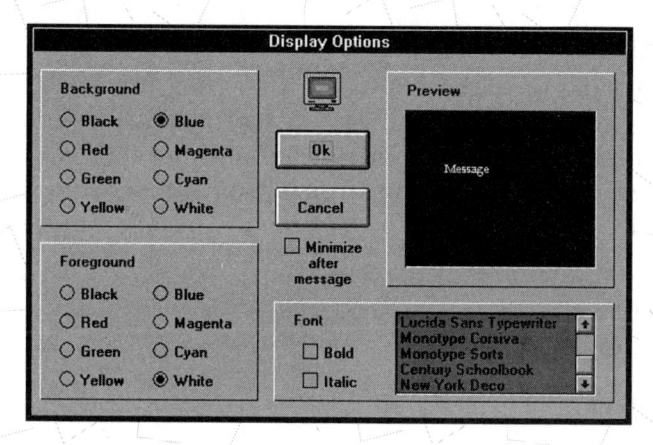

Figure 10.3. The Display Options dialog box.

Program Operation

Before getting into the nuts and bolts of the Blink Blank! program, I would like to quickly discuss a few key elements of the code: Windows API functions, Hungarian notation, and the gang screen.

Windows API Functions

The GLOBAL.BAS module lists all the Windows API functions that Blink Blank! uses. One invaluable aid for using Windows API functions is the Microsoft Windows Programmers Reference. Don't leave DOS character mode without it!

Blink Blank! uses GetPrivateProfileString() and SetPrivateProfileString() to read and manipulate BB.INI. I chose to use the private .INI file because I did not want to mess with anyone's WIN.INI file.

You will also notice I have used the SetSysModalWindow() function. This allows Blink Blank! to prevent bringing up the Windows Task List (and breaching security) while the screen is blanked. This function is quite particular about its usage. I found myself resorting to the "three-fingered salute" quite a few times while exploring this function!

Another very useful function is WinHelp(). This function is used in any program that invokes the Windows WinHelp engine. A full explanation of how to create and use WinHelp files is included with the Professional Toolkit for Visual Basic. Finally, I have used the ShowCursor() function to show and hide the cursor.

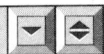

Hungarian Notation

I'm not sure if this is real, honest-to-goodness Hungarian notation, but it's good enough for me. This is my own system of naming the various controls. This convention becomes quite invaluable once your code grows beyond two or three forms with a few controls. Take my word for it—devise and use a system to identify control types by their name. The following system is what I use:

   lb = List Box

   cb = Check Box

   tb = Text Box

   pb = Push Button

   rb = Radio Button

   mi = Menu Item

   frm = Form

These prefixes are used for identifiers throughout the program.

Gang Screen

Some people call them *doo-dads*—whatever you call them, they are fun to program! Doo-dads are secret messages within an application that are activated by a special key combination. Many Windows 3.1 About dialog boxes have hidden messages that are displayed when you double-click the box's icon while pressing the Shift and Control keys. While coding Blink Blank!, I had several of my friends give the program a test drive. They gave me numerous suggestions for features and feature improvements, so I decided that they deserved some credit. Here's a challenge: Find the "secret screen" that rolls off some of the beta testing credits. Hint: Look in the vicinity of the About box.

Now, let's take a look at all the source code used to construct the Blink Blank! program.

The Global Module

The global module contains the following declaration sections:

File constants—Store the names of the .INI (initialization) files and .HLP (help) files.

Declare functions—Declare the Windows API functions.

Color constants—Declares color display constants to make the code more readable.

Boolean constants—Define TRU, FALS, and so on.

WinHelp() Constants—All the constants that the WinHelp() function will ever use. This version of Blink Blank! uses only a portion of the functionality available with WinHelp(). (How else can I entice you to register and get the latest and greatest version when it's available?)

MousePointer constants—Let you alter the shape of the cursor

Miscellaneous constants—Anything that won't fit anywhere else!

Variables—Various global variables. Some purists will argue that I use too many global variables. So sue me.

Forms

The remainder of the source code explanation summarizes the declarations and events for each of the Blink Blank! forms.

frmAbout

Declarations
WasteTime()—This function does just that—it wastes time. I needed this to control the speed at which my gang screen scrolls across the screen.

Events
Form_Load()—Centers the form, inserts the copyright symbol (which can't be entered from the keyboard), and gets the name and registration from the global pool.

Form_Paint()—Sets up three-dimensional effects.

pbAboutOK_Click()—Unloads the About box.

Picture1_Click()—Shhhhh!

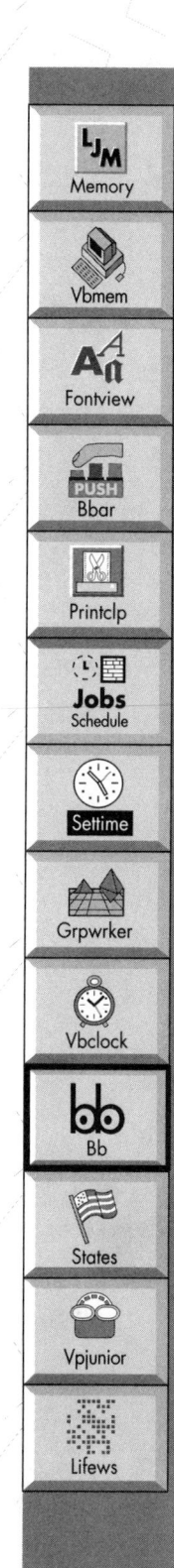

frmBB

Declarations

`Decrypt()`—Decrypts the password. (The version of Blink Blank! that comes with this book does not include decryption.)

`Encrypt()`—Encrypts the password. (The version of Blink Bank! that comes with this book does not include encryption.)

`ValidateRegistration()`—Accepts a registration number and returns an integer that can be interpreted as a Boolean (`TRU`/`FALS`) value. This version of Blink Blank! accepts a certain registration number, which is revealed somewhere in this chapter. I hope this results in your seeing a registration reminder at least a few times! The commercial version has full registration number validation.

Events

`miExit_Click()`—Exits Blink Blank!. I made Alt-F4 the exit keystroke because Alt-F4 is a key combination commonly used to exit other Windows applications).

`miAbout_Click()`—Invokes the About box.

`Form_Load()`—This event does quite a bit, and I've tried to comment it fairly thoroughly. Because this is the main form, quite a bit happens when it is loaded. First, the .INI file is read. The `GetPrivateProfileString()` routine enables you to assign a default value to a variable if the corresponding key is not found in the .INI file. After this is accomplished, the appropriate lunch button is set, messages are read and inserted in the message list box, the return time list boxes are populated, the form is centered on-screen, and the registration is validated. Finally, the command line is checked for the presence of a string. If a string is found, Blink Blank! immediately begins flashing the text of the command-line string.

`miSetDisplay_Click()`—Invokes the Set Display screen. Notice that I changed the cursor to an hourglass so that the user knows the wait is intentional and the program is not bombing.

`miSetPassword_Click()`—Invokes the Set Password screen. First I set the global variable `GOKToShowPass` to `TRU`. This tells the password entry screen to show the password while the user sets it. (The password is obscured when the user types it to gain entry to the PC.) Once the password is set and recorded in the global variable `GMasterPassword`, `GOKToShowPass` is reset to `FALS`.

Chapter 10: Blink Blank!

`Form_Paint`—This module is responsible for adding three-dimensional effects to the Blink Blank! program. It also makes sure that the lunch options are the most current, and sets the proper default lunch item.

`pbUseCustom_Click()`—Invokes the blanking routine with a custom message. First, `MessageType` is set to 1 to show that this is a custom message. After the screen is blanked, `pbUseCustom_Click()` checks to see if the `MinimizeOnPassword` variable is set. This feature allows Blink Blank! to automatically minimize after the password is entered. It is set on the Display Options screen. If that option is enabled, `WindowState` is set to 1 (minimized).

`pbGoToLunch_Click()`—This is the same as `pbUseCustom_Click()`, with a different `MessageType`.

`pbGoSomeWhereElse_Click()`—This is the same as `pbUseCustom_Click()`, with a different `MessageType`.

`tbCustomMessage_Change()`—This event causes the `pbUseCustom` button to be enabled only if there is text in the Custom Message text box. This makes sense if you think about it: Why let the user select that button if there is no text to display?

`pbAdd_Click()`—Invoke the `GetNewMessage` dialog box for the purpose of adding a new message. First, change the title bar caption, then show the form.

`pbEdit_Click()`—Invoke the `GetNewMessages` dialog box for the purpose of editing a selected message. First, check to see if anything is selected to edit. If not, set the appropriate warning message and call the Warning dialog box. Otherwise, change the title bar caption and call the dialog box.

`pbDelete_Click()`—It is not necessary to invoke any dialog box here as with the `Add` and `Edit` functions. Simply make sure that something was selected; if so, delete it.

`miSetLunch_Click()`—Invokes the Set Lunch Options dialog box. Here again, the cursor is set to an hourglass to indicate that something is going on.

`Form_Unload()`—First, encrypt the password. (The version of Blink Blank! that comes with this book does not encrypt.) Next, using `WritePrivateProfileString()`, update the .INI file with currently selected defaults. Before updating any messages, however, check the global variable `MessagesChanged` to see if any have changed. If none have changed, why take the time to write them to the .INI file? The last few lines of the `Form_Unload()` event close down the WinHelp engine if it happens to still be running. Because WinHelp is a separate program, this step is necessary to ensure that Blink Blank! Help is not still running after Blink Blank! is exited.

`miIndex_Click()`—Invokes the Blink Blank! help system.

`lbMiscWhere_DblClick()`—Often in Windows programs, the programmer allows for more than one way to accomplish a task (for example, selecting an item and clicking an OK button is the same as double-clicking the item). This code enables the user to double-click a miscellaneous message in the list and immediately launch the blanking screen.

`tbCustomMessage_KeyPress()`—Ensures that custom messages are no longer than MAXMESASGELEN (30 in this case) characters long. If users try to enter another character, they hear an annoying little beep. Notice that you must allow for the backspace character as the 31st keystroke.

frmBlank

Declarations
`GetMessage()`—Construct the appropriate message for display on-screen, depending on the value of MessageType.

Events
`Form_Load()`—Loads the blanking screen. This event clears out the password field, sets the appropriate background colors, calls `GetMessage()` to construct the appropriate message, sets the font size, hides the cursor, and sets the current window as system modal (this prevents bringing up the Task List).

`Form_Resize()`—Randomizes the timer.

`Form_KeyPress()`—Checks for keystrokes while screen is flashing. If a press of the spacebar is detected, this event shows the EnterMessage dialog box. Notice that I use a combination of resetting the timer, manipulating the cursor, and setting the new windows as system modal. Although this combination works, I cannot fully explain why. System modal windows are a strange animal. Someday I will figure out how I finally got this to work properly. The second function this event handles is to show any messages accumulated while you were away.

`Timer1_Timer()`—This one looks complicated, but it's not that bad. Blink Blank! simulates a flashing message by alternately turning all foreground and background colors the same, and then randomly picking a set of three adjacent text boxes on the `frmBlank` form. Once the random number is picked, the appropriate text boxes are populated with the messages and the foreground color is turned on. This timer repeats the process every two seconds.

frmDisplay

Declarations
None

Events

`Form_Load()`—Centers the screen, sets the sample screen attributes to their proper values, updates the color radio buttons from the global pool, sets the font attributes from the global pool, sets the *minimize on password* option, and loads the font list from the system font list. Finally, this event resets the cursor to the default shape, because we turned it into an hourglass coming into this routine.

`Form_Paint()`—Manages the three-dimensional effects.

`pbCancel_Click()`—Unloads the form.

`pbOK_Click()`—Sets the global color variables according to the current attributes of the sample text and then unloads the form.

`pbOK_KeyPress()`—Because the OK button is the default, you can pick up any keystrokes directed at the form here. If the Escape key (ASCII 27) is detected, invoke the `pbCancel_Click()` event.

`cbBold_Click()`—Indicates that the font attributes have changed in preparation for this form's timer to change the sample text. (See the code for this form's timer.)

`cbItalic_Click()`—Indicates that the font attributes have changed in preparation for this form's timer to change the sample text. (See the code for this form's timer.)

`rbBackBlack_Click()`—Makes the corresponding change to the sample text.

`rbBackBlue_Click()`—Makes the corresponding change to the sample text.

`rbBackCyan_Click()`—Makes the corresponding change to the sample text.

`rbBackGreen_Click()`—Makes the corresponding change to the sample text.

`rbBackMagenta_Click()`—Makes the corresponding change to the sample text.

`rbBackRed_Click()`—Makes the corresponding change to the sample text.

`rbBackYellow_Click()`—Makes the corresponding change to the sample text.

`rbBackWhite_Click()`—Makes the corresponding change to the sample text.

`rbForeBlack_Click()`—Makes the corresponding change to the sample text.

`rbForeBlue_Click()`—Makes the corresponding change to the sample text.

`rbForeCyan_Click()`—Makes the corresponding change to the sample text.

`rbForeGreen_Click()`—Makes the corresponding change to the sample text.

`rbForeMagenta_Click()`—Makes the corresponding change to the sample text.

`rbForeRed_Click()`—Makes the corresponding change to the sample text.

`rbForeYellow_Click()`—Makes the corresponding change to the sample text.

`rbForeWhite_Click()`—Makes the corresponding change to the sample text.

`lbFontList_Click()`—Makes the corresponding change to the sample text.

`Timer1_Timer()`—Checks to see if font attributes have changed. If so, go get the `cbBold` and `cbItalic` check box values and update the sample text.

frmEnterMessage

Declarations
`FileMessage()`—Attaches a date/time stamp to the message being filed in your mailbox. Looks for an open mail slot and files the message.

Events
`Form_Load()`—Centers the form on-screen, updates the number of available message slots, and sets the windows as system modal. System modality is necessary because this window pops up over another system modal window.

`Form_Paint()`—Manages the three-dimensional effects.

`tbMailMessage_Change()`—Prevents the user from pressing the Enter key before any text is entered in this text box.

`pbOk_Click()`—Files the new message using `FileMessage()`, turns on the flag to indicate that there is mail, and unloads the form.

`pbCancel_Click()`—Unloads the form.

frmGetNewMessage

Declarations
None

Events
Form_Load()—Centers the form.

Form_Paint()—Manages the three-dimensional effects.

tbNewMessage_Change()—Enables the Enter key only if there is text in tbNewMessage.

tbNewMessage_KeyPress()—Ensures that new messages are no longer than MAXMESASGELEN (30 in this case) characters long. If users try to enter another character, they hear an annoying little beep. Notice that you must allow for the backspace character as the 31st keystroke.

pbCancel_Click()—Unloads the form.

pbOk_Click()—First, checks to see if the message consists of all spaces using the AllSpaces() function. If the message is all spaces, call the Warning dialog box, then determine if this is adding a new entry or changing an existing entry. Process the new entry accordingly, turn on the MessagesChanged flag, and unload the form.

frmLunchMessages

Declarations
None

Events
Form_Load()—Populates the hours and minutes list boxes, as well as the radio buttons. Centers the form on-screen. Selects the proper default radio button representing the time at which one would return from lunch most often. Resets the cursor to the default shape.

Form_Paint()—Manages three-dimensional effects.

pbCancel_Click()—Unloads the form.

pbOk_Click()—Resets the lunch options in the global pool. Sets the default lunch in the global pool. Unloads the form.

`pbOk_KeyPress()`—Because the OK button is the default, you can pick up any keystrokes directed at the form here. If the Escape key (ASCII 27) is detected, invoke the `pbCancel_Click()` event.

`pbUseAs1_Click()`—Updates the first radio button caption with the current selection from the hours and minutes list boxes.

`pbUseAs2_Click()`—Updates the second radio button caption with the current selection from the hours and minutes list boxes.

`pbUseAs3_Click()`—Updates the third radio button caption with the current selection from the hours and minutes list boxes.

`pbUseAs4_Click()`—Updates the fourth radio button caption with the current selection from the hours and minutes list boxes.

`pbUseAs5_Click()`—Updates the fifth radio button caption with the current selection from the hours and minutes list boxes.

`rbUse1_Click()`—This ensures that both sets of radio buttons match on the form. Because the example set is merely for informational use, this is not crucial.

`rbUse2_Click()`—This ensures that both sets of radio buttons match on the form. Because the example set is merely for informational use, this is not crucial.

`rbUse3_Click()`—This ensures that both sets of radio buttons match on the form. Because the example set is merely for informational use, this is not crucial.

`rbUse4_Click()`—This ensures that both sets of radio buttons match on the form. Because the example set is merely for informational use, this is not crucial.

`rbUse5_Click()`—This ensures that both sets of radio buttons match on the form. Because the example set is merely for informational use, this is not crucial.

frmMessages

Declarations
None

Events

`Form_Load()`—Centers the form on-screen, displays the messages, and sets the window as system modal.

`Form_Paint()`—Manages the three-dimensional effects.

`pbDoneMessages_Click()`—Resets all messages along with the mail flag and unloads the form.

`pbPrintMessages_Click()`—This prints your messages. The printed form and the messages are time-stamped. First, the function checks to see if any Print check boxes were checked. If not, it calls the Warning form with the appropriate message. Next, the function sets the cursor to the hourglass—probably not a bad idea anytime the user begins to print under Windows. Next, `pbPrintMessages_Click()` prints each checked message using the `PrintString()` function. It then time-stamps the printed output and unloads the form.

frmPassword

Declarations
None

Events

`Form_Load()`—Sets temporary password-holding fields to null, centers the form on-screen, and sets the window as system modal.

`Form_Paint()`—Manages the three-dimensional effects.

`tbPassword_Change()`—Enables the Enter key if there is text in `tbPassword`.

`tbPassword_KeyPress()`—This code is used only when the keyboard is being used to gain access. Note the check for `OKToShowPass`, which is an indicator of how the dialog box is being used at this point. Notice that keystrokes are turned into asterisks if it is not acceptable to show the password. Note also that you must check for the Backspace key to remove the last character entered from the variable `password`. Also, checking the length of the string entered so far prevents the code from stripping off characters that do not exist!

`pbCancel_Click()`—Unloads the form.

`pbOk_Click()`—Checks for spaces and displays warnings as appropriate. Then the event checks the length to make sure it is not less than three characters or greater than eight. Finally, it picks up the password from the right place (depending on whether is OK to show the password), changes it to lowercase (the password is not case-sensitive), and unloads the form.

frmWarning

Declarations
None

Events
Form_Load()—Centers the form on-screen, sets the window as system modal, and picks up the proper warning message.

Form_Paint()—Manages the three-dimensional effects.

pbOk_Click()—Unloads the form.

frmPrintReg

Declarations
None

Events
Form_Load()—Centers the form.

Form_Paint()—Manages the three-dimensional effects.

tbQuantity_Change()—Recalculates the price every time the quantity changes.

pbCancel_Click()—Unloads the form.

pbPrintReg_Click()—Uses PrintString() to print the registration form based on information gathered from the user.

frmRegistration

Declarations
None

Events
Form_Load()—Centers the form on-screen. Gets the user's name and registration number from the global pool.

Chapter 10: Blink Blank!

`Form_Paint()`—Manages the three-dimensional effects.

`Form_Unload()`—Sets the global name and registration number variables in the global pool to the values entered. Unloads the form.

`pbContinue_Click()`—Unloads the form.

`pbRegister_Click()`—Shows the registration form for the user to register.

The MODULE1.BAS Routines

MODULE1.BAS contains an assortment of routines used by other pieces of the Blink Blank! program:

`AllSpaces()`—Returns `TRU` if `StringIn` is all spaces; otherwise it returns `FALS`.

`BorderBox()`—Creates the illusion of a recessed control by drawing lines around the control to simulate a shadow.

`BorderBoxRaised()`—Creates the illusion of a raised control by drawing lines around the control to simulate a shadow.

`ConvertColorIn()`—Converts the character string form of a color to its numeric representation. Used to convert color values stored in BB.INI.

`ConvertColorOut()`—Converts the numeric form of a color to its character representation. Used to convert color values stored in BB.INI.

`GetWord()`—Used with `PrintString()` to ensure that nothing is printed off the edge of the page.

`HideCursor()`—Uses the Windows API function `ShowCursor()` to hide the cursor.

`PrintString()`—Prints a string and uses `GetWord()` so that nothing is printed off the edge of the page.

Now that you have seen each of the routines that make up the Blink Blank! application, consider some ways to make it an even more interesting screensaver. How about adding the ability to display graphics files that move around the screen? Or how about having it draw random lines or other geometric images? Regardless of whether you modify the Blink Blank! code, be sure to track down the hidden doo-dad!

Chapter 10: Blink Blank!

Name the States

by Dan Lewczyk

11

Chapter 11: Name the States

Overview

Name the States is a Visual Basic program that teaches the names, locations, and capitals of the 50 states.

The program provides two levels of difficulty. The easier level tests the user on the location of states. The more difficult level asks for state capitals as well. Figure 11.1 shows a map of the United States with the state in question colored in blue. The user selects the name of the state from the list shown in Figure 11.1.

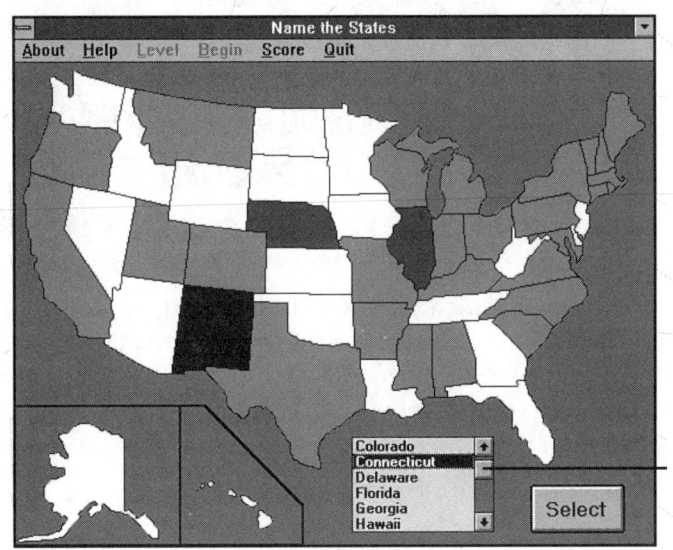

Figure 11.1. Selecting the name of the highlighted state.

When the user guesses a state correctly, it is colored green (in these black-and-white figures, colors appear as shades of gray). If the answer is wrong, the correct answer is shown and the state is colored red (see Figure 11.2).

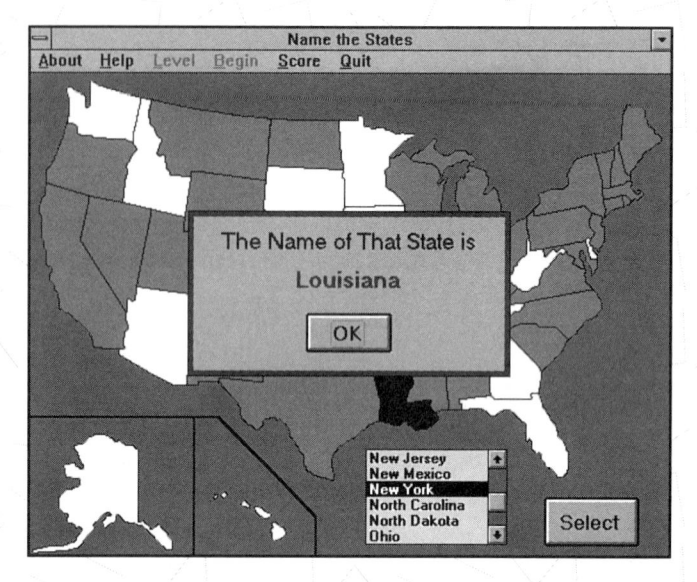

Figure 11.2. The correct state name is shown when the user guesses an incorrect name.

When using the more difficult level, the user must correctly answer the name of the state and its capital before the state is colored green. A new state is then selected, and the process continues until all the states have been chosen. A score is then displayed showing how well the user has done. To obtain help, select the **Help** option from the menu bar. To exit the program at any time, select the **Quit** option from the menu bar.

Program Operation

Name the States is made up of 10 forms and a global code module. Most of the forms are for informational purposes and consist of some text and an OK button to get them off-screen when the user is done with them (see Table 11.1).

Table 11.1. The Name the States forms and their purposes.

Form Name	Purpose
Main_Form	Main program form
About_Form	Shows program information
Help_Form	Shows program help
Instructions	Gives instructions at the beginning

Chapter 11: Name the States

Form Name	Purpose
Score1	Shows score when using level one
Score2	Shows score when using level two
Wrong_State	Shows correct state when answer is wrong
Wrong_Cap	Shows correct capital when answer is wrong
Quit_Form	Allows option to quit or continue program
Cap_Form	Capital selection

Almost all the working code is associated with the main form of the program, Main_Form. This form controls the program flow, enables the user to set the level of difficulty, and starts and ends the program.

The last form of the program is Cap_Form. This form allows users to choose a capital for the selected state when they set the higher difficulty level.

Windows API

Name the States relies on a Windows API call to do most of the work. This function is ExtFloodFill() and its purpose is to change the color of an area surrounded by a border of a different color. This function is used to change the color of each state to blue as the program selects it, and then change it to green or red depending on whether the user gave the correct answer or answers.

ExtFloodFill() is declared in the GLOBAL.BAS module:

```
Declare Function ExtFloodFill Lib "Gdi" (ByVal hdc As Integer,
    ByVal X As Integer, ByVal Y As Integer, ByVal crColor As Long,
    ByVal wFillType As Integer) As Integer
```

The following is a list of the parameters for the ExtFloodFill routine:

hdc	Handle of the form
X	X coordinate of the point to fill from
Y	Y coordinate of the point to fill from
crColor	32-bit color value specifying either the boundary color or the color to replace, depending on the next value

wFillType	FLOODFILLBORDER (0)—Fills an area surrounded by one color
	or
	FLOODFILLSURFACE (1)—Fills an area by replacing one color

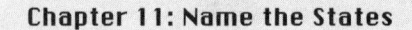

The two `wFillType` constants are defined in the GLOBAL.BAS module. The one used in Name the States is `FLOODFILLSURFACE`, which causes the function to replace one enclosed color with another. (The other is `FLOODFILLBORDER`, which is equal to 0.) When I prepared the map, I had to enclose each state by a boundary to prevent the color change from "leaking" out of one state and into another.

GLOBAL.BAS Declarations

The following is a list of other constants defined in the GLOBAL.BAS file:

TRU, FALS	For true/false Boolean values
RED, BLUE, GREEN	Fill colors
CORRECT, INCORRECT, NOT_USED	Status indicators
NUMBER_STATES	Set to 50

A `Type` variable is created to hold information for each state. The following is a list of the elements:

Name	Name of state
X_Position	X coordinate of fill point
Y_Position	Y coordinate of fill point
Capital	Name of capital
State_Status	Either NOT_USED, CORRECT, or INCORRECT
Capital_Status	Either CORRECT or INCORRECT

`X_Position` and `Y_Position` for each state were determined from a paint program like Paintbrush. After loading the map, I selected a point in each state to serve as the origin for the fill routine. The X and Y pixel coordinates for each point were noted. Two states, Michigan and Hawaii, require more than one area to be filled when their color is changed. These points were noted, and the program needed special consideration to account for this.

Chapter 11: Name the States

Procedural Operation

The main form of the program controls program flow. The map bitmap, USA.BMP, is loaded into the `Picture` property of the form. `Autoredraw` is set to `TRU`. `FillStyle` is set to `Solid` so that the user can see the fill. `ScaleMode` is set to `Pixel` to correspond to the pixel coordinates of the points for the fill origins for each state.

When the program first runs, an array of type `State_Data` is dimensioned to hold the data for each state:

```
Dim State(50) As State_data
```

Then the `Form_Load()` procedure of `Main_Form` is executed. The first statement

```
Move (Screen.Width - Width)\2, (Screen.Height - Height)\2
```

centers the form on-screen. This line of code is used in all the `Form_Load()` procedures of all the forms. The next line

```
Randomize
```

ensures that the random number generator returns a different sequence of numbers each time the program is run. This makes certain that the states are chosen in a different order each time.

The next few lines of code

```
State_List.Visible = FALS
Choose.Visible = FALS
```

hide the two controls on the form until they are needed. The next line

```
Score.Enabled = FALS
```

disables the **Score** option on the menu bar until there is a score to keep. The next few lines

```
Lev_One.Checked = TRU
Lev_Two.Checked = FALS
Game_Level = 1
```

put a check mark next to **One** in the **Level** menu and set the game level to easy (1), which is the default.

The `Initialize()` procedure is called next. This procedure loads the `State` array with the data for the program. The name, capital, and the X and Y fill point for each state are entered into elements 1 through 50 of the array. The following `For` loop:

```
For I = 1 To NUMBER_STATES
    State_List.AddItem State(I).Name
    Cap_Form.Capital_List.AddItem State(I).Capital
    State(I).State_Status = NOT_USED
    State(I).Capital_Status = NOT_USED
Next I
```

does several things. First, it loads the state names into the `State_List` list box on `Main_Form`. It then loads the capital names into the `Capital_List` list box on `Cap_Form`. Next, each state's `State_Status` and `Capital_Status` variables are set to `NOT_USED`. These variables are used to track whether a state has been picked yet. If the state has been picked, the variables are used to track whether the user answered correctly or incorrectly. In the difficult level, `State_Status` and `Capital_Status` track whether the capital was guessed right.

The program now waits for some input from the user. The menu bar controls all the action. If the user selects About or Help, the appropriate form appears. These forms are displayed until the user clicks the OK button, and then they are hidden. The user selects **Quit** to end the program. Selecting Level allows the user to set the difficulty level by clicking on **One** or **Two**. Remember that the program starts with a default level of 1, with the **One** selection checked. If the user selects **Two**, then **One** is unchecked, **Two** is checked, and `Game_Level` is set to 2 with this block of code:

```
Sub Lev_Two Click()
    Lev_Two.Checked = TRU
    Lev_One.Checked = FALS
    Game_Level = 2
End Sub
```

The program really gets started when the user selects **Begin**:

```
Sub Start_Click ()
    Start.Enabled = FALS
    Level.Enabled = FALS
    Score.Enabled = TRU
```

These lines disable **Begin** and **Level** on the menu bar and enable the **Score** option. Next, the `Instructions` form appears and waits for the user to click the OK button:

```
Instructions.Show (1)
```

Then the following lines show the list box and the `Select` button on the form, and set the variable `Number_States_Left` to 50:

Chapter 11: Name the States

```
State_List.Visible = TRU
Choose.Visible = TRU
Number_States_Left = NUMBER_STATES
```

The procedure `Select_State()` is then called to start the main part of the program:

```
Sub Select_State ()
    Do
        Selected = Int(NUMBER_STATES * Rnd +1)
    Loop Until State(Selected).State_Status = NOT_USED
```

This `Do` loop randomly selects a number from 1 to 50. It then checks to see if the `State_Status` for that array element is `NOT_USED`, signifying that state has not yet been picked. If the state has been picked before, a new number is generated and the new state is checked.

The next line

```
Main_Form.FillColor = BLUE
```

sets the color of the form's `FillColor` to blue to color the state of interest with the next command:

```
Fill State(Selected).X_Position, State(Selected).Y_Position
```

This line calls the procedure `Fill`, using the X and Y pixel coordinates of the state of interest as parameters.

The `Fill()` routine is defined as follows:

```
Sub Fill (X As Integer, Y As Integer)
    R = ExtFloodFill(Main_Form.hdc, X, Y,
        Main_Form.Point(X, Y), FLOODFILLSURFACE)
End Sub
```

`Fill()` calls `ExtFloodFill()`, the Windows API function declared in the GLOBAL.BAS module of the program. `ExtFllodFill()` changes the color of the area inside the boundaries for the state. The `Main_Form.Point` parameter gives the color to be changed.

After the selected state is colored blue, a check needs to be made for a couple of occurrences. If the selected state is Hawaii or Michigan, more than one area needs to be filled. The array index for Hawaii is 11, and the index for Michigan is 22. If either of these two numbers was selected, the program fills the additional areas by using extra `Fill()` calls:

Chapter 11: Name the States

```
If Selected = 11 Then
    Fill 199, 365
    Fill 185, 358
    Fill 168, 351
    Fill 161, 351
End If

If Selected = 22 Then
    Fill 347, 69
End If
```

The program now waits for the user to make a selection by either double-clicking the state name in the list box:

```
Sub State_List_DblClick ()
    Choose_Click
End Sub
```

or by selecting the state name and clicking the Select button.

The number of remaining states is then decreased by 1, and a correct answer is set by default for the state's capital:

```
Sub Choose_Click ()
    Number_States_left = Number_States_Left -1
    Is_Capital_Right = TRU
```

The next section of code checks whether the selected state name was correct or incorrect:

```
If State_List.Text = State(Selected).Name Then
```

If the answer was correct, a couple of flags are set and the total number of correct states is increased by one:

```
        State(Selected).State_Status = CORRECT
        Is_State_Right = TRU
        Number_States_Right = Number_States_Right + 1
```

If the answer was incorrect, set the flags to FALS and increase the total number of incorrect states by one:

```
        State(Selected).State_Status = INCORRECT
        Is_State_Right = FALS
        Number_States_Wrong = Number_States_Wrong + 1
```

Chapter 11: Name the States

The program now sets up the text on the Wrong_State form to show the user the correct answer:

```
Wrong_State.State_Name.Caption = State(Selected).Name
Wrong_State.Refresh
Wrong_State.Show (1)
```

    End If

The program now checks to see if the user set the harder difficulty level; if so, the program asks the user for the capital's name:

```
If Game_Level = 2 Then

    Capital_Test
```

Next, using logic that is similar to the logic used with the state's name answer, a check is made to see if the capital's name answer is right or wrong, and the appropriate action is taken:

```
If Capital_Chosen = State(Selected).Capital Then
    Number_Capitals_Right = Number_Capitals_Right + 1
    State(Selected).Capital_Status = CORRECT
Else
    Is_Capital_Right = FALS
    Number_Capitals_Wrong = Number_Capitals_Wrong + 1
    State(Selected).Capital_Status = INCORRECT
    Wrong_Cap.Cap_Name.Caption = State(Selected).Capital
    Wrong_Cap.Label1.Caption = "The Capital of " +
        State(Selected).Name + " is"
    Wrong_Cap.Refresh
    Wrong_Cap.Show (1)
End If
```

The correct fill color for the state is selected depending on the answers given by the user. If correct, the color is set to green; if incorrect, the color is set to red:

```
If Is_State_Right = TRU and Is_Capital_Right = TRU Then
    Main_Form.FillColor + GREEN
Else
    Main_Form.FillColor = RED
End If
```

The state is now filled in with the chosen color. Once again, Hawaii and Michigan receive special consideration.

The program now checks to see if there are any states left to pick:

```
If Number_States_Left > 0 Then
```

If there are states left, the program selects a new state and starts over again:

```
    Select_State
```

If there aren't any states left, the program hides the list box and the Select button, displays the final score, and waits for the user to exit. Two different score forms can be shown, depending on the level used. `Score1` shows the number of states correctly and incorrectly chosen. `Score2` shows score information for both states and capitals. The different score forms are also shown if the user selects Score in the menu bar.

Comments and Suggestions

Name the States is a simple program that accomplishes a useful task. The most tedious part of creating it was fixing up the map picture to ensure that the color changes would remain contained in the one state of interest. Everything else was basic programing.

The following list describes a few ideas for improvement:

- Keep a record of high scores for each level or user. A data file would need to be read in and written back to the disk.

- Add a timer to keep track of elapsed time, and incorporate this into the scoring system. This would be triggered when the user selects the Begin option.

- Allow for retesting the incorrect answers. You could accomplish this by having the program check the `State_Status` and `Capital_Status` variables of each state for an `INCORRECT` status.

- This same principle of operation could be applied to other maps, such as countries on continents, counties in a state, and so on. All that you need is a picture of the map that you could fix up to work in the program.

ViewPoint Jr.

by Barry Seymour

Chapter 12: ViewPoint Jr.

Overview

Recently I took a consulting job where we had to write a tutorial/guided tour program for a Windows application in Visual Basic. Our approach to emulating the behavior of the program was to load bitmap files from disk for many of the operations to be demonstrated. This meant we had to do much graphics work—you know, bitmap slinging, pixel pushing, whatever you like to call it. In a matter of hours, we were inundated with scores of separate .BMP files to manage and view.

I didn't mind drawing a lot of pictures, but after a while I forgot which file was named what, and who it was for. When naming bitmaps for topics and steps, a file name like RTB145A.BMP may be programatically correct, but it's no help when I'm looking for a screen shot of the File Open dialog box, for example. Using Paintbrush was no help because I had to perform a laborious File Open for each file I wanted to view—not a pleasant prospect when you have to wade through 50 files in the current directory.

But wait! It got better. Because Visual Basic can read .RLE (run length encoded) files just like it can read .BMP files, we decided to convert all our bitmaps to .RLE (.RLE files are smaller than .BMP files, because they're coded to take up less space). Now we had *two* file extensions to worry about, followed by .DIB files, icon files, and even a Windows metafile or two.

The nature of the project made it evident to me that Visual Basic could read these file formats. I also desperately needed a graphics file viewer. Thus, I developed ViewPoint Jr. in Visual Basic.

ViewPoint Jr. has a simple appearance. It consists of two windows: the `Controller` and the `Viewer`. The `Controller` is a standard File Open type box; unlike a dialog box, however, it is open all the time. In fact, the `Controller` is the main interface for the program. The `Viewer` is an empty form that does nothing but display the currently selected picture (see Figure 12.1).

Using the directory list box, the user can select the desired drive and directory to view. Then, using the file list box, the user can view each graphics file in the list box with a single mouse click, or by pressing the up arrow and down arrow keys. No clumsy File Open—just point and look.

You can also edit graphics files with ViewPoint Jr. by specifying the name of your favorite graphics editor program (Paintbrush is the default). Then, double-click the file name of your choice, or highlight the file name and press the Enter key, and the graphics editor is launched with the picture loaded.

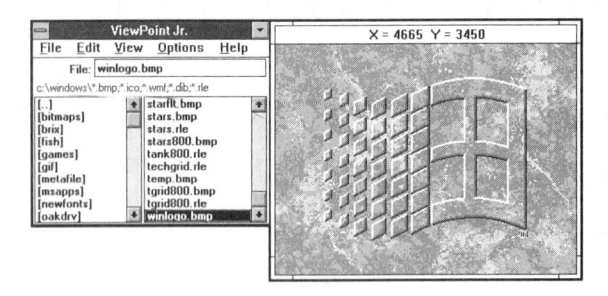

Figure 12.1. ViewPoint Jr. enables you to view a variety of graphics file formats.

Because ViewPoint Jr. can also view the .ICO file format, the user can specify an icon editor as well, which is launched when an .ICO file is selected. An additional feature allows the user to type a path or filespec (see Figure 12.2).

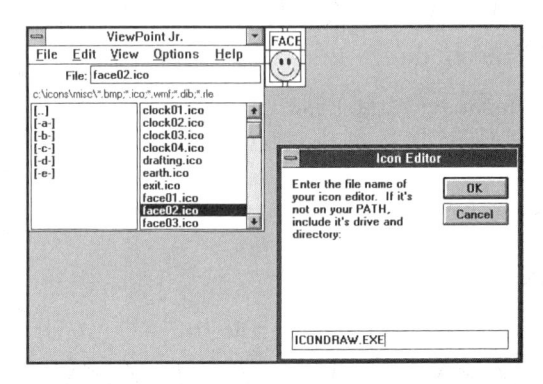

Figure 12.2. ViewPoint Jr. enables you to specify your own icon editor.

Program Operation

Surprisingly, the hardest part about writing ViewPoint Jr. wasn't the picture-handling functions. Visual Basic's LoadPicture() function performs that quite nicely, reading .BMP, .DIB, .RLE, .ICO, and even .WMF files with the same LoadPicture() statement. The complicated part was creating the static dialog box to handle file manipulation.

To keep things simple for the user and to conserve screen space, I chose to use an older style dialog box with the combination drive and directory listing. This

Chapter 12: ViewPoint Jr.

required using a few API calls and much error checking in the code. The result, however, was a quick and compact `Controller`.

The heart of the system is the API call `SendMessage()`. The program uses a regular list box rather than Visual Basic's directory list box, and `SendMessage()` is used to quickly clear the list box and fill it with the currently visible directories and drives. You can use `GetFocus()` to obtain the handle of the list box to which you send messages. This sort of arrangement works much faster than the drive/directory control combination in standard Visual Basic.

The API calls `OpenFile()` and `lclose()` can help you determine if a file exists, or if a drive is available. `IsWindow()` and `GetActivewindow()` are used when Paintbrush is the graphics editor, so control can return directly to ViewPoint Jr. when that program ends. `GetWindowsDirectory()` is used to determine where the initialization file VPJUNIOR.INI should be located, and the API calls `GetPrivateProfileString()` and `WritePrivateProfileString()` are used to read and write data to that file.

Roll Up Your Sleeves...

For starters, create the `Controller` (CONTROL.FRM) with the controls in Table 12.1.

Table 12.1. Controls used to create the Controller form.

Control	Property	Value(s)
Form	FormName	Controller
	BorderStyle	0
	MaxButton	FALSE
Text Box	CtlName	txtCurrentFile
List Box	CtlName	lstDirectories
File List Box	CtlName	filFiles
	Pattern	*.BMP;*.WMF;*.ICO;*.RLE;*.DIB
Label	CtlName	lblPattern
	FontBold	FALSE

The `Controller` is basically a file open dialog box that won't go away. A single click on a file name views the file; a double-click launches the editor.

You also need to create a menu structure for the form, as shown in Table 12.2.

Table 12.2. Menu structure for the Controller form.

Caption	Name
File	FileMain
Open	FileOpen
New	FileNew
Reset	FileReset
Exit	FileExit
Edit	EditMain
Copy	EditCopy
View	ViewMain
Max Viewer	ViewMax
Clipboard	ViewClipBoard
Home Windows	ViewHome
Fetch Viewer	ViewFetch
Options	OptMain
Graphics Editor...	OptGraphEd
Icon Editor...	OptIconEditor
Help	HelpMain
File Menu	HelpSub(0)
Edit Menu	HelpSub(1)
View Menu	HelpSub(2)
Options Menu	HelpSub(3)
About ViewPoint Jr.	HelpSub(4)

When the Form Loads, the Cradle Will Rock

ViewPoint Jr. does several things when it first loads; these housekeeping and system evaluation functions are handled in the Controller's Form_Load() procedure. There are some API calls to get the current file name and the

Windows directory, global variables are initialized, and menu items are enabled or disabled according to the circumstances.

At the beginning of the routine, you use the function WinDir$() to obtain the name of the Windows directory where you'll be placing your .INI file:

```
Sub Form_Load ()
    Load Viewer

    'GET THE .INI FILE NAME...
    'Start by getting the Windows directory.
    WindowsDir$ = WinDir$()
    'Add a backslash if the Windows directory is the root (!).
    If Right$(WindowsDir$, 1) <> "\" Then WindowsDir$ = WindowsDir$ _
        + "\"
    'Add the .INI file name to the Windows path.
    INIFileName = WindowsDir$ + "VPJUNIOR.INI"
```

Thus, the global variable INIFileName is set. Armed with this information, you'll read and write information in that file later. For now, set up default file-handling variables:

```
    FullFileName = ""
    CurrentPattern = filFiles.Pattern
    DefaultPattern = CurrentPattern 'This doesn't change.
    lstDirectoriesFlag = 0  ' Update Drive/Subdirectory list box.
    txtCurrentFileFlag = 0  ' Limit text length.
    If CurrentPath <> "" Then
    If Right$(CurrentPath, 1) = "\" Then
        CurrentPath = Left$(CurrentPath, (Len(CurrentPath) - 1))
        If Right$(CurrentPath, 1) = ":" Then CurrentPath = CurrentPath _
            + "\"
    End If
    filFiles.Path = CurrentPath
    End If
    If CurrentPath = "" Then CurrentPath = filFiles.Path

    filFiles.Pattern = CurrentPattern
    txtCurrentfile.Text = filFiles.Pattern
    TheDrive = Left$(filFiles.Path, 2)

    Temp$ = LCase$(filFiles.Path)
    If Len(Temp$) = 3 Then ' Root directory.
        lblPattern.Caption = Temp$ + CurrentPattern
    Else
        lblPattern.Caption = Temp$ + "\" + CurrentPattern
    End If
```

Next, set up the menus on the form to reflect the fact that no files are being viewed yet. Then position both the `Controller` and the `Viewer`.

```
Controller.FileOpen.Enabled = 0
Controller.FileRename.Enabled = 0
Controller.FileCopy.Enabled = 0
Controller.EditCopy.Enabled = 0
Controller.FileMove.Enabled = 0
Controller.FileDelete.Enabled = 0

'Position the controller.
Controller.Left = 15 ' This is in twips!
Controller.Top = 15
Controller.WindowState = 0

'Position the Viewer...
Viewer.Left = Controller.Left + Controller.Width
Viewer.Top = Controller.Top
Viewer.WindowState = 0
SavedCaption = "ViewPoint Jr." ' Save the generic caption.
```

Remember where you obtained the name of the .INI file? Now read it and assign global variables based on its contents. (The user-defined function `StringFromINI()` is a *wrapper,* a function wrapped around another function to make the interior function's use easier. The wrapper insulates you from some of the details involved in using `GetPrivateProfileString()`—more on that later.)

```
'Read .INI file, set windowstate and show both...
Select Case Val(StringFromINI("Options", "WindowState", "0", _
    INIFileName))
    Case 0 'Normal
        ViewMax.Caption = "Restore &Viewer"
    Case 1 'Maximized
        ViewMax.Caption = "Max &Viewer"
End Select
ViewMax_Click
Controller.Show

GraphicsEditor = StringFromINI("Editors", "Graphics", _
    "PBRUSH.EXE", INIFileName)
IconEditor = StringFromINI("Editors", "Icon", "IconDraw.EXE", _
    INIFileName)
ConfirmActions = Val(StringFromINI("Options", "Confirm Actions", _
    "TRU", INIFileName))
```

Chapter 12: ViewPoint Jr.

When you first set focus to the directory list box, its `GotFocus` event forces `lstDirectories` to update itself:

```
lstDirectories.SetFocus    ' See lstDirectories_GotFocus.
X% = DoEvents()
filFiles.SetFocus
If filFiles.ListCount > 0 Then filFiles.ListIndex =
    0 Else txtCurrentfile.SetFocus

'Set other global variables.
TABB = Chr$(9)
QUOTE = Chr$(34)
LF = Chr$(13) + Chr$(10)
End Sub
```

API Calls Used in ViewPoint Jr.

Many API calls involve returning strings that contain information from Windows. These strings are terminated with a null character (in Visual Basic language, `Chr$(0)`) that needs to be trimmed off before the strings can be used. This is one of the reasons I use wrappers. Most notable of the wrappers I use here is `WinDir()`, a wrapper for `GetWindowsDirectory()`. When you look at `WinDir()`, you'll see why I prefer to use it:

```
Function WinDir () As String
    Temp$ = Space$(255)
    StringLen% = GetWindowsDirectory(Temp$, 255)
    WinDir = Left$(Temp$, StringLen%)
End Function
```

There's much happening in this small bit of code. First, the string `Temp$` is initialized to prepare it for the data the API call will return. Then the string variable and an integer representing the length of that string are passed to Windows. `GetWindowsDirectory()` returns the length of the string that is the Windows directory, so if your Windows directory is C:\WINDOWS, the function returns 10. Using the `Left$()` function to strip off the 10 leftmost characters neatly handles the problem of both the trailing null character and the 245 empty spaces at the end of `Temp$()`.

The same thing happens in the `StringFromINI()` wrapper function, which takes a few more parameters but does the same thing in obtaining a value from VPJUNIOR.INI:

```
Function StringFromINI (SectionName As String, KeyName As String,
    Default As String, FileName As String) As String

    MaxStringLen% = 255 'Set string length.
    ReturnedStr$ = Space$(MaxStringLen%) ' Init the receiving string.
    StringLen% = GetPrivateProfileString(SectionName, KeyName,
        Default, ReturnedStr$, MaxStringLen%, FileName)
    StringFromINI = Left$(ReturnedStr$, StringLen%)
End Function
```

`StringFromINI()` reads from Windows' .INI files, which contain information in the following format:

```
[Section Name]
KeyName=DataString
```

This functionality makes it quick and easy to store information in a text file on a disk, which you can read at load time to initialize any variables that you want to control program operations. The parameter `Default` establishes the value to be returned if there isn't any corresponding section or key name in the .INI file queried.

The wrapper `StringToINI()` isn't actually required because it takes the same parameters as its API counterpart `WritePrivateProfileString()`, which is included only for consistency's sake. `StringToINI()` enables you to write information to that same disk file for future use, if required.

SendMessage and the Directory List Box

`SendMessage()` is used to send a message to the `lstDirectories` control, telling it to fill itself with a list of all the currently visible drives and directories. First, here is the definition of the function and related constants:

```
Declare Function SendMessage Lib "User" (ByVal hWnd As Integer,
    ByVal wMsg As Integer, ByVal wParam As Integer, lParam As Any)
    As Long

Global Const WM_USER = &H400
Global Const LB_RESETCONTENT = (WM_USER + 5)

Global Const LB_DIR = (WM_USER + 14)
```

`hWnd` is the handle of the Window to receive the message, `wMsg` is the message sent, `wParam` and `lParam` are parameters, and the result of the function is a long integer. Note that the function declaration itself must all be on one line. The constant `WM_USER` is a base constant to which values are added to get the desired constants for this function. If `LB_DIR` is sent as the message, the list box adds the names of all currently visible drives and directories. If `LB_RESETCONTENT` is sent as the message, the list box clears itself. This method of clearing a list box is faster than using a `Do` loop in Visual Basic.

As you may know, you need to have the handle of a Window if you're going to send a message to it. This is where the API call `GetFocus()` comes in; the code sets the focus to the control and uses `GetFocus()` to get its handle. Then you can use `SendMessage()`.

The command to fill a list box with drive names and directory names is as follows:

```
X& = SendMessage(ListHandle, LB_DIR, &HC010, ByVal s$)
```

The command to clear a list box is as follows:

```
Y& = SendMessage(ListHandle, LB_RESETCONTENT, 0, ByVal "")
```

This methodology is used in the `DblClick` event of `lstDirectories` and at program startup. This is what enables the user to change among drives and directories.

The `lstDirectories_DblClick()` routine evaluates the new directory that was double-clicked in the list box and changes it as required:

```
Sub lstDirectories_DblClick ()
'    This sub responds to the user request to change drive or directory.

 If lstDirectories.ListIndex > -1 Then ' no directory is selected...

   'Get the current selection.
    NewItem$ = lstDirectories.List(lstDirectories.ListIndex)
'Save the old path in case of error.
    OldPath$ = filFiles.Path
' User selected a drive.
    If Left$(NewItem$, 2) = "[-" And Len(NewItem$) = 5 Then
        If Right$(NewItem$, 2) = "-]" Then
            NewDriveLtr$ = Mid$(NewItem$, 3, 1)
            ChangeDrive NewDriveLtr$, ErrState%
            If Controller.filFiles.ListIndex = -1 ↵
                And Controller.filFiles.Listcount > 0 Then
                Controller.filFiles.ListIndex = 0
                LoadCurrentPic
```

continues

```
            End If
        End If
    Else
        On Error Resume Next

        NewDirectory$ = Mid$(NewItem$, 2, Len(NewItem$) - 2)
        filFiles.Path = TheDrive + NewDirectory$
        lblPattern.Caption = filFiles.Path
```

`LB_RESETCONTENT` clears the list quickly; `LB_DIR` specifies the type of list box, and the `&HC010` parameter specifies only drives and subdirectories:

```
        Y& = SendMessage(ListHandle, LB_RESETCONTENT, 0, ByVal "")
        X& = SendMessage(ListHandle, LB_DIR, &HC010, _
            ByVal CreateFileSpec((filFiles.Path)))

        If Err Then
            MsgBox Error$ + Chr$(13) + Chr$(10) + filFiles.Path, 16, _
                ControllerCaption
            txtCurrentfile.Text = filFiles.Pattern
        End If
    End If
End If

CheckFiles ' Sub to check contents of new directory.

If filFiles.Listcount > 0 Then ' Files found!
    filFiles.SetFocus
    filFiles.ListIndex = 0
    Viewer.Visible = TRU
Else ' No files in this directory...

    txtCurrentfile.Text = LCase$(filFiles.Pattern)
    txtCurrentfile.SetFocus

    'Update the label displaying the current drive,
    ' directory, and filespec.
    If Len(filFiles.Path) = 3 Then
        Newlbl$ = filFiles.Path + filFiles.Pattern
    Else
        Newlbl$ = filFiles.Path + "\" + filFiles.Pattern
    End If
    lblPattern.Caption = Newlbl$
    Viewer.picViewer.Picture = LoadPicture()
    Viewer.Visible = FALS
End If

End Sub
```

Round Robin, or Who Gets Told What

When the user selects a file, drive, or directory—whether by clicking with the mouse or typing in a drive, directory and/or filespec—a complicated operation begins among four controls: the file list box filFiles, the drive/directory list box lstDirectories, the file specification display label lblPattern, and the text box txtCurrentFile. Each informs the other when it receives events, and all work together to ensure that their respective contents accurately reflect the current situation and that the Viewer is correctly updated.

When the user clicks a new file, txtCurrentFile is changed; when the user clicks a new drive or directory, filFiles is informed of the change and updates itself accordingly.

When the user types text into txtCurrentFile and presses Enter, the process can get more difficult. A complex process is set into motion to determine whether the typed entry is valid. The process starts in txtCurrentFile_KeyPress() when the user presses the Enter key:

```
Sub txtCurrentFile_Keypress (KeyAscii As Integer)
' Process whatever the user typed in txtCurrentFile.

If KeyAscii = 13 Then KeyAscii = 0

If KeyAscii = 0 Then
    Temp$ = RemoveSpaces((txtCurrentfile.Text))
```

First the code checks to see if the typed string is present in the file list box:

```
    For ind% = 0 To filFiles.Listcount
        If filFiles.List(ind%) = Temp$ Then
            FileName = Temp$
            Foundit = TRU
            Exit For
        End If
    Next ind%
```

Next, check to see if the user specified the root directory with a single backslash:

```
    If Left$(Temp$, 1) = "\" Then ' User is going for the root.
        DriveLtr$ = Left$(CurDir$, 2)
        Temp$ = DriveLtr$ + Temp$
    End If
```

If the file is not in `filFiles.List`, the code tries to determine what the user is trying to do, using the `ChangeDrive()` and `ChangeDir()` subroutines:

```
If Foundit <> TRU Then
    ColonPos% = InStr(Temp$, ":")      'Drive?
    BslashPos% = InStr(Temp$, "\")     'Subdirectory?
    StarPos% = InStr(Temp$, "*")       'Wildcards?
    QueryPos = InStr(Temp$, "?")

    ErrState% = FALS        'Flag used by ChangeDrive.

    If ColonPos% Then       'If we found a drive, change to it.
        ChangeDrive (Mid$(Temp$, ColonPos% - 1, 1)), ErrState%
    End If
```

If changing to the drive didn't cause any errors or if a drive wasn't specified, check to see if the user entered a directory name:

```
If Not ErrState% Then    ' A subdirectory was specified.
    If BslashPos% Then   ' Evaluate the text string entered.
        TempFileName$ = Temp$
            While InStr(TempFileName$, "\")
                NewDrive$ = NewDrive$ + Left$(TempFileName$,
                    InStr(TempFileName$, "\"))
                TempFileName$ = Right$(TempFileName$,
                    Len(TempFileName$) - InStr(TempFileName$, "\"))
            Wend
```

At this point, `NewDrive$` holds everything to the left of the last backslash while `TempFileName$` holds the rest. Now process them with a call to `EvalTextEntered()`:

```
        Result% = EvalTextEntered(NewDrive$, TempFileName$)
    End If

    ' Did the user specify only a new pattern?
    If Result% = FALS Then
        If StarPos% Or QueryPos Then
            If ColonPos% Then
                filFiles.Pattern = Right$(Temp$,
                    Len(Temp$) - 2)
            Else
                filFiles.Pattern = Temp$
            End If
            txtCurrentfile.Text = filFiles.Pattern
```

```
                End If
            End If
        End If
End If
```

The following code highlights the text box regardless of the results of the activity in the form:

```
txtCurrentfile.SelStart = 0
txtCurrentfile.SelLength = Len(txtCurrentfile.Text)
If Visible Then txtCurrentfile.SetFocus
X% = DoEvents()
```

Finally, issue a call to `CheckFiles()` and set the contents of `lblPattern`:

```
CheckFiles

If Len(filFiles.Path) = 3 Then
   Newlbl$ = filFiles.Path + filFiles.Pattern
Else
   Newlbl$ = filFiles.Path + "\" + filFiles.Pattern
End If
lblPattern.Caption = Newlbl$

End If


End Sub
```

The `EvalTextEntered()` function evaluates the text string the user typed in the `Controller`'s text box. The API call `OpenFile()` checks for the presence of the file:

```
Function EvalTextEntered (NewDrive As String, TempFileName As String) _
   As Integer

  Dim TheStruct As OfStruct  ' Structure passed to openfile.

  If NewDrive <> "" Then       ' If a NewDrive is specified, change to it.
     If Len(NewDrive) > 1 Then
        NewDrive = Left$(NewDrive, Len(NewDrive) - 1)
        ChangeDir (NewDrive)
     End If
  End If

  If Len(TempFileName) > 0 Then 'Evaluate it.
```

continues

```
    If InStr(TempFileName, "*") > 0 Or InStr(TempFileName, "?") >
        0 Then 'NEW FILESPEC.
        filFiles.Pattern = TempFileName
        txtCurrentfile.Text = filFiles.Pattern
        EvalTextEntered = TRU
        Exit Function
    Else
```

If we get to this point in the program, there are no wildcard characters in the string (which means the nature of the typed entry is unknown), so we assemble a string to test with the `OpenFile()` API call. The call opens the file, which obtains the file handle. If the handle is 0, you know the file doesn't exist. It must, therefore, be a subdirectory:

```
        If Right$(filFiles.Path, 1) <> "\" Then
            TestName$ = filFiles.Path + "\"
        Else
            TestName$ = filFiles.Path
        End If
        TestName$ = TestName$ + TempFileName

        FileHandle% = OpenFile(TestName$, TheStruct, OF_EXIST)
        Result% = lclose(FileHandle%)
' A file handle was obtained; it's a file!
            If FileHandle% > 0 Then
                CurrentPath = filFiles.Path
                FileName = TempFileName
                FullFileName = TestName$
            Else ' No handle. Assume it's a directory.
                ChangeDir (TestName$)
            End If
        EvalTextEntered = TRU
    End If
  End If

End Function
```

At Last, the Picture...

Another advantage to Visual Basic is the `LoadPicture()` function. It enables you to read any of several graphic file formats and insert the resulting images in picture controls. In addition, `LoadPicture()` supports Windows bitmap (.BMP) files and their generically named cousins .DIB (device-independent bitmaps) and .ICO (icon) files, which are just another sort of bitmap.

Visual Basic also supports *run length encoded* (.RLE) files, although this isn't documented in the Visual Basic manuals. .RLE files take up less space on your hard disk than .BMP files do. This size savings is also realized internally; if you have a large .BMP file loaded into the picture property of a form or picture box, use `WinGif`, `BitEdit`, or some other conversion program to convert your .BMP file to an .RLE file and load that file instead. Forms with .RLE images actually take up less disk space than the same forms with .BMP images.

Windows metafiles aren't drawings as such; they contain instructions to the loading program on how to draw the metafiles. This means they are resizeable in Visual Basic. If you change a metafile's size, the metafile draws itself to the new larger size. ViewPoint Jr. takes advantage of this; if the string .WMF is present in the file name, the `Viewer.picViewer.AutoSize` property is set to FALS so that the image resizes to fit the picture. If the file isn't a metafile, the picture's `AutoSize` property is set to TRU so that the picture control resizes to fit the image.

When you click or change to a file name in the `filFiles` control, the subroutine launches `LoadCurrentPic()`:

```
Sub LoadCurrentPic ()

    If Controller.FilFiles.FileName = "" Then Exit Sub

    If Len(Controller.FilFiles.Path) = 3 Then
    ' It's the root directory - don't add  \
        FileToLoad$ = UCase$(Controller.FilFiles.Path +
            Controller.FilFiles.FileName)
    Else
        FileToLoad$ = UCase$(Controller.FilFiles.Path + "\" +
            Controller.FilFiles.FileName)
    End If

    'AlreadySizing = TRU
    Controller.FileOpen.Enabled = TRU
    Controller.EditCopy.Enabled = TRU
```

The following code fragment is where you load the picture into the `Viewer`:

```
    Viewer.picViewer.visible = 0
    Screen.MousePointer = 11
    Viewer.picViewer.Picture = LoadPicture(FileToLoad$)
    Screen.MousePointer = 0
```

continues

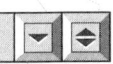

```
If Err Then
    ErrMsg$ = "Error Loading  " + UCase$(FileToLoad$) +
        ": " + Error$(Err) + "."
    Beep: MsgBox ErrMsg$, 64, "Viewer Error"
    Exit Sub
End If
```

At this point, you determine if you have not loaded a Windows metafile. If not, size the picture to fit the image. Otherwise, the image is sized to fit the picture:

```
If InStr(FileToLoad$, ".WMF") = 0 Then 'BITMAP. size to picture.
    Viewer.picViewer.Autosize = TRU
    Viewer.Caption = UCase$(Controller.FilFiles.FileName)
    Viewer.picViewer.Autosize = TRU
    Viewer.Height = Viewer.picViewer.Height + VHOffset
    Viewer.Width = Viewer.picViewer.Width + VWOffset

Else ' METAFILE:  Size to Form.
    Viewer.picViewer.Autosize = FALS
    Viewer.Caption = UCase$(Controller.FilFiles.FileName) +
        " (Resizeable)"
    Viewer.picViewer.Autosize = 0
    Viewer.picViewer.Height = Viewer.ScaleHeight
    Viewer.picViewer.Width = Viewer.ScaleWidth
End If

End Sub
```

Other Goodies Explained

ViewPoint Jr. offers several other features that make it a great choice for managing graphical files. The `FileOpen()` function enables you to edit the file you're currently viewing using the graphics editor of your choice. Simply double-click the current file name (or press Enter), and your graphics editor is launched with the selected file. The code to perform this task is in the `FileOpen_Click` menu item, which in turn can be called from `Controller.FilFiles_DblClick()` and `Controller.FilFiles_KeyPress()`.

If Paintbrush is your editor of choice, ViewPoint Jr. offers additional functionality. The program uses the `GetActiveWindow()` API call when you load Paintbrush, and loops until that program ends. When the API call `IsWindow()`

returns zero, ViewPoint Jr. knows that Paintbrush has ended and returns focus to the `Controller`:

```
Sub FileOpen_Click ()

    On Error GoTo BadLaunch
    If filFiles.ListIndex = -1 Then Exit Sub

    ' Get the full name of the file to be edited...
    file$ = UCase$(filFiles.List(filFiles.ListIndex))
    If Len(filFiles.Path) = 3 Then  ' Root directory.
                                    ' Backslash not needed.
        FullFile$ = UCase$(filFiles.Path +
            filFiles.List(filFiles.ListIndex))
    Else
        FullFile$ = UCase$(filFiles.Path + "\" +
            filFiles.List(filFiles.ListIndex))
    End If

    Screen.MousePointer = 11
```

The following code assembles the string you'll eventually send to the `Shell()` statement. Start by determining which editor to use:

```
    If Right$(FullFile$, 4) = ".ICO" Then
        If IconEditor = "" Then
            MsgBox "No Icon Editor specified to edit " + file$ +
                ".", MB_ICONEXCLAMATION
            On Error GoTo 0
            Exit Sub
        End If
        EditorName$ = IconEditor
    Else
        If GraphicsEditor = "" Then
            MsgBox "No Graphics Editor specified to edit " + file$ +
                ".", MB_ICONEXCLAMATION
            On Error GoTo 0
            Exit Sub
        End If
        EditorName$ = GraphicsEditor
    End If

    ShellStr$ = EditorName$ + " " + FullFile$

    CState% = Controller.WindowState
    Controller.WindowState = 1 'Will minimize Viewer.
```

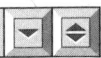

If Paintbrush is the editor but a file other than .BMP is specified, the user has the option of editing a copy of the image. ViewPoint Jr. does this by copying the image to the Clipboard, launching Paintbrush, and pasting the image into it:

```
If InStr(file$, ".BMP") = 0 And InStr(file$, ".ICO") =
    0 And InStr(EditorName$, "PBRUSH.EXE") <> 0 Then
    Msg$ = file$ + " is not a Bitmap file." + Chr$(13) + Chr$(10)
    Msg$ = Msg$ + "Edit a COPY using PaintBrush?"
    Confirm% = MsgBox(Msg$, 36, "")
      If Confirm% = 7 Then
          On Error GoTo 0
          Screen.MousePointer = 0

          Controller.WindowState = CState%
          X% = DoEvents()
          Controller.SetFocus
          Exit Sub
      Else
          Screen.MousePointer = 11
          Clipboard.Clear
          Clipboard.SetData Viewer.picViewer.image
          Viewer.Hide
          Viewer.picViewer.Picture = LoadPicture(FullFile$)
          X% = Shell("PBRUSH.EXE", 1)
          Screen.MousePointer = 0
          X% = DoEvents()
          AppActivate "Paintbrush - (Untitled)"
          pBrushhWnd% = GetActiveWindow()
          SendKeys "%OI%D{ENTER}", -1
          SendKeys "%" + Chr$(32) + "X", -1
          SendKeys "%EP", -1
          While IsWindow(pBrushhWnd%)
          X% = DoEvents()
          Wend
          Controller.WindowState = CState%
          X% = DoEvents()
          Controller.SetFocus
          Viewer.Show
          Exit Sub
      End If
End If

Result% = Shell(ShellStr$, 1)
Screen.MousePointer = 0
```

Chapter 12: ViewPoint Jr.

If Paintbrush is the editor, the following code gets its handle and loops until the program has ended, at which time focus returns to the `Controller`:

```
If InStr(UCase$(EditorName$), "PBRUSH.EXE") Then
    GedithWnd% = GetActiveWindow()
    While IsWindow(GedithWnd%): X% = DoEvents(): Wend
    Controller.WindowState = CState%
    X% = DoEvents()
    Controller.SetFocus
    Viewer.Show
End If

On Error GoTo 0
Exit Sub
```

The following is a good example of a subroutine. The statement at the beginning directs the program to drop down to the `BadLaunch()` subroutine in the event of an error. If anything goes wrong, control passes down to this subroutine, and this code handles the errors. Note that `BadLaunch()` also resets the error trap to the default, `GoTo 0`. This isn't a *real* `GoTo`; it's just a way to tell Visual Basic to resume its handling of errors as they occur:

```
BadLaunch:
    Screen.MousePointer = 0
    Msg$ = "Error Launching " + EditorName$ + ".  Check to see" + LF
    Msg$ = Msg$ + "if it exists and is on your PATH."
    MsgBox Msg$, 32, "Graphics Editor Error"
    Controller.WindowState = CState%
    X% = DoEvents()
    Controller.SetFocus
    On Error GoTo 0
    Exit Sub

End Sub
```

Another feature of this program is that the user can specify what graphics and icon editors to use. The code, which is quite simple, uses both the `InputBox$()` function and the `StringToINI()` wrapper function discussed earlier. If the user enters a string, that value is written to the .INI file:

```
Sub OptGraphEd_Click ()
    P$ = "Enter the file name of your graphics editor.  "
    P$ = P$ + "If it's not on your PATH, include it's drive
        and directory:"
    T$ = "Graphics Editor"
    D$ = GraphicsEditor
```

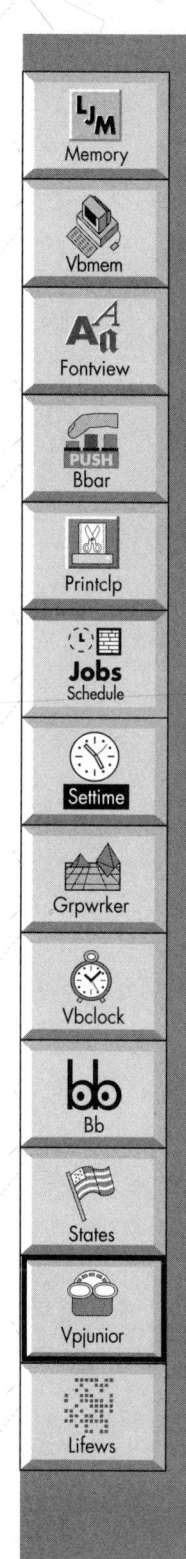

continues

```
    Editor$ = InputBox$(P$, T$, D$)
    If UCase$(Editor$) = UCase$(GraphicsEditor) Or Editor$ =
        "" Then Exit Sub
    GraphicsEditor = UCase$(Editor$)
    r% = StringToINI("Editors", "Graphics", GraphicsEditor,
        INIFileName)
End Sub
```

The `picViewer_MouseMove()` event reports the X and Y coordinates of the mouse on the picture in the caption of the `Viewer` window. This can help professionals like graphics designers and artists who need exact measurements of the image. When any of the main controls on the `Controller` receive the focus, the `Viewer` caption reverts to the name of the file you are viewing. The mouse movement code is simple, but the results are impressive:

```
Sub picViewer_MouseMove (Button As Integer, Shift As Integer,
    X As Single, Y As Single)
    Viewer.Caption = " X = " + Format$(X, "0") + "  Y = " +
        Format$(Y, "0")
End Sub
```

The Poor Man's Help System

Basic help is included in the system. The Help menus are a control array under `HelpMain`, called `HelpSub()`. Code in the `HelpSub()` procedure displays one of several message boxes based on the index, in other words, the number of the menu item that the user clicked.

This method of providing help is practical only when the information to be presented is simple and there's not much need for fancy formatting. The `MsgBox()` function in Visual Basic can accept a surprisingly large amount of text, but line breaks can change with the screen resolution; text that looks good on a Super VGA screen may look terrible when displayed on a regular VGA screen. If you use this method, check your formatting at regular 640 by 480 resolution. If you can make it there, you can make it anywhere!

Assemble your strings before sending them to the `MsgBox()` function. You can insert tabs and linefeeds, which work well as long as you take formatting into consideration as mentioned earlier. There is some formatting in this code, achieved with the global variables LF and TABB, which are two very good friends of mine:

Chapter 12: ViewPoint Jr.

```
Sub HelpSub_Click (Index As Integer)
    Dim Msg As String, Title As String

    Select Case Index
    Case 0 'File Operations
        Title = "File Menu"
        Msg = ""
        Msg = Msg + "Open:" + TABB +
            "Open the current file with your editor. " + LF
        Msg = Msg + "New:" + TABB + "Create a new file." + LF
        Msg = Msg + "Reset:" + TABB +
            "Reset the filespec to the default." + LF
        Msg = Msg + "Exit" + TABB + "Leave ViewPoint Jr."

    Case 1 'Edit Options
        Title = "Edit Menu"
        Msg = "Copy:" + TABB + "Copy the image to the Clipboard."

    Case 2 'View Options
        Title = "View Menu"
        Msg = "Max Viewer:" + TABB + "Maximize the Viewer Window." + LF
        Msg = Msg + "Clipboard:" + TABB +
            "Run or Activate CLIPBRD.EXE." + LF
        Msg = Msg + "Home Windows:" + TABB +
            "Both Windows to top left corner." + LF
        Msg = Msg + "Fetch Viewer:" + TABB +
            "Bring Viewer to Controller's side."

    Case 3 'Options
        Title = "Options Menu"
        Msg = Msg + "Graphics Editor:" + TABB +
            "Specify graphics editor." + LF
        Msg = Msg + "Icon Editor:" + TABB + "Specify icon editor."

    Case 4 'About ViewPoint Junior
        Title = "        About ViewPoint Junior        "
        Msg = "ViewPoint Jr. is a quick and easy way to browse
            graphics files.  "
        Msg = Msg + "With ViewPoint, you can select the drive
            and directory you "
        Msg = Msg + "want, then view each file with a single
            mouse click.  " + LF + LF

        Msg = Msg + "Bitmaps, Icons, Run Length Encoded,
            Device Independent Bitmaps "
```

continues

```
    Msg = Msg + "and Windows Metafiles are all
        viewable.  For BMP, RLE, DIB  "
    Msg = Msg + "and ICO files the Viewer resizes to
        fit the size of the image.  "
    Msg = Msg + "You can view WMF files at different "
    Msg = Msg + "sizes simply by resizing the viewer." + LF + LF

    Msg = Msg + "Watch for VIEWPOINT, ViewPoint Jr's
        big brother, coming soon!  "
    Msg = Msg + "ViewPoint offers file management
        capabilities such as rename, copy, "
    Msg = Msg + "move and delete and comes with full
        online help." + LF + LF

    Msg = Msg + "---------------------------------------
        ---------------------------------------------
        ---------------------------------" + LF
    Msg = Msg + "Marquette Computer Consultants" + LF
    Msg = Msg + "22 Sirard Lane" + LF
    Msg = Msg + "San Rafael, CA 94901-1066" + LF
    Msg = Msg + "(415) 459-0835" + LF
    Msg = Msg + "CompuServe 70413,3405" + LF + LF
    Msg = Msg + "
        Copyright (c) 1992 Barry Seymour."
End Select

If Index = 4 Then IconKey% = 64 Else IconKey% = 0

    MsgBox Msg, IconKey%, Title
End Sub
```

You can set each option as desired in the Case statement that evaluates the index. Finally, you can display your message with one call to MsgBox().

ViewPoint Jr. is a great way to manage graphical files on your hard disk, whether for business presentations, multimedia, or slide shows. More enhancements are on the way, but always remember—you saw it here first!

Life Workshop

from Ivory Tower Software

13

Chapter 13: Life Workshop

Overview

Welcome to the Life Workshop. This Windows program enables you to experiment with two-dimensional cellular automata (simple artificial life forms). You can modify the rules and observe the evolution of large colonies of artificial life, or assign life to specific cells in the "workbench" and watch different patterns evolve with different sets of rules.

All you need is a Windows system (800 × 600 pixel resolution or better is recommended, but standard 640 × 480 VGA will work), a mouse or other pointing device, the LIFEWS.EXE file, and the VBRUN100.DLL dynamic link library. The VBRUN100.DLL should be in the same directory as the LIFEWS.EXE file or in any directory in your PATH. Your Windows directory is a good place to keep all your dynamic link libraries (.DLL files). You should install the LIFEWS.EXE in a Program Manager group and double-click its icon to run Life Workshop.

Cellular Automata

Cellular automata are very simple, simulated, single-cell life forms. Each cell exists autonomously and lives, dies, or is born depending on a set of rules that the user defines. The cellular automata in Life Workshop are two-dimensional; however, systems with one or three or more dimensions have been used.

The "Game of Life" was invented in 1970 by John Horton Conway, a professor of mathematics. You can play Life with a pencil and paper, but playing it with a computer is easier and much more fun. Life is played on a two-dimensional grid. Each cell in the grid can be in one of two states—alive or dead. There are three laws (also called rules) to Life: the laws of survival, death, and birth. These rules are applied according to the number of living neighbors a cell has. The number of living neighbors determines the future state of any particular cell.

Life Workshop includes two options for the two dimensional grid plane where the cellular automata live: a classic grid and a hexagonal grid. The classic grid is a rectangular matrix made up of rows and columns, and is the type of grid on which the game was first defined. Each cell not on a grid border has eight neighbors. A cell in the classic grid is arranged in the manner shown in Figure 13.1.

Chapter 13: Life Workshop

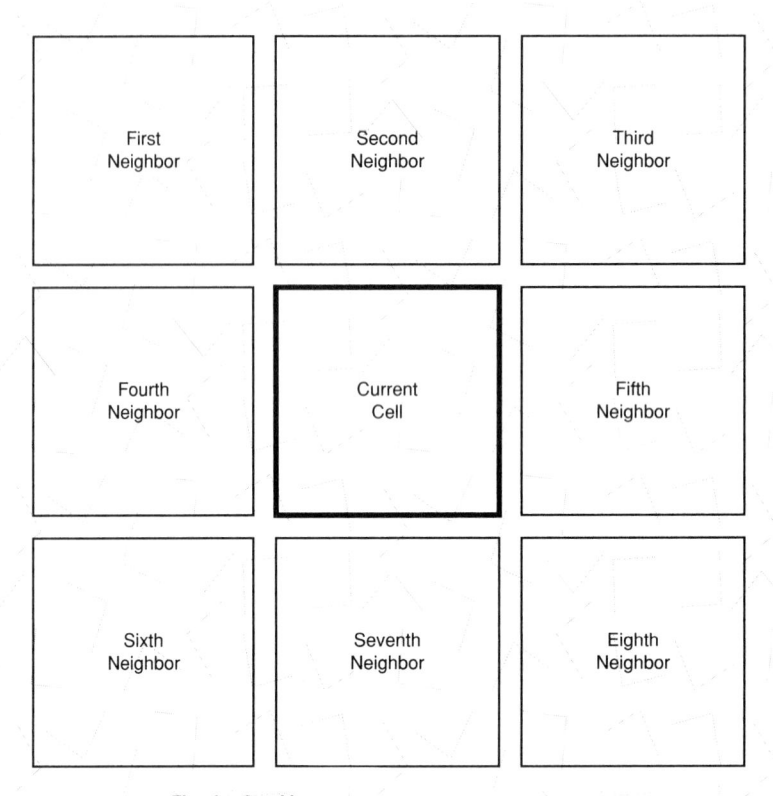

First Neighbor	Second Neighbor	Third Neighbor
Fourth Neighbor	Current Cell	Fifth Neighbor
Sixth Neighbor	Seventh Neighbor	Eighth Neighbor

Figure 13.1. The classic grid.

In the classic grid, a cell's corner neighbor has two of the cell's other neighbors in common with it, whereas a cell's left, right, top, or bottom neighbor has four of its other neighbors in common. This fact lends a kind of hidden complexity to the classic grid, not unlike the complexity inherent in the chess board. This hidden complexity can be illustrated by considering the light and dark squares of the chess board. Each chess player starts with two bishops: one that always stays on the light squares and another that always stays on the dark squares. The player's bishops can never communicate. The chess board has light and dark squares to help us visualize the diagonal paths of the bishops. A computer that plays chess does not have "light and dark" perceptions to make the distinction; however, the computer knows the bishops cannot communicate just the same. This barrier to bishop communication is a result of the inherent complexity of the classic grid.

Chapter 13: Life Workshop

The hexagonal grid looks more complicated because it has three row/columns oriented on 60 degree angles. It's actually a simpler system because each cell's neighbor is identical in properties to all the cell's other neighbors. The hexagonal grid is arranged in the manner shown in Figure 13.2.

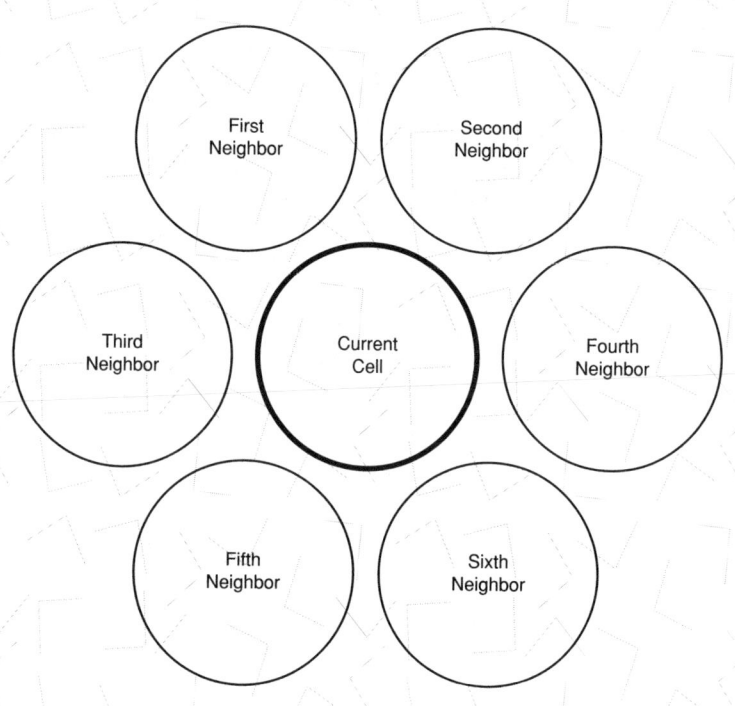

Figure 13.2. The hexagonal grid.

The hexagonal grid is also called an *isogrid*. Because of the sameness of all of a particular cell's neighbors, an isogrid is also more appropriate for the modeling of some physical phenomena. For instance, some combinations of atoms arrange themselves into hexagonal patterns when they form crystals.

The cellular automata discussed so far have existed in two dimensions and have had two available states, life and death. They have also lived by *summation* rules; in other words, the laws of birth, survival, and death have been based on the total number (sum) of neighbors. Many more types of cellular automata, some very useful for modeling physical phenomena, are possible.

For instance, cellular automata with a large number of states can be defined. Users can assign these states by very complex sets of rules. What makes the Game of Life so interesting is that some very complex behavior results from the very simple rules of the game, as you will see.

Using Life Workshop

Start Life Workshop by double-clicking its icon in the Windows Program Manager. When the program has finished loading, you will see the main control window in the upper-left corner of the screen (see Figure 13.3).

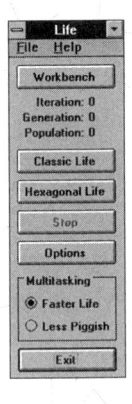

Figure 13.3. The Life Workshop main control window.

The main control window has several buttons that control program modes, a pair of multitasking option radio buttons, and an exit button at the bottom of the window. There are also some pulldown menus for exiting and getting help and information about the program. The main control window is tall and narrow so that it can remain on the screen while the workbench and life windows are displayed.

Click the Workbench button, which is the top button in the window. A new window appears just to the right of the main control window. This is the workbench window for experimenting with life patterns and rules on a small scale for fast performance. In its default mode, the workbench microcosm displays a classic grid of 16 × 16 cells. There is also a pair of radio buttons for toggling between the classic and hexagonal grids, and buttons for starting and stopping evolution, clearing the grid, and exiting the workbench.

Classic Life Experiments

Use the mouse to click a cell in the classic grid. The cell turns black, indicating that it is assigned a state of being alive. Proceeding in this manner, you can establish initial patterns of living cells. As soon as you click the first cell, the Start button is enabled. Pressing Start begins the evolutionary process. The main control window displays the iteration and the generation that are currently being processed. The population (total number of living cells) is also updated for each generation.

Try setting the first pattern shown in Figure 13.4. If you make a mistake, just press the Clear button and start over. (The pattern in Figure 13.4 is the famous "glider" from classic life, so named because it appears to slowly glide across the window during the life process.)

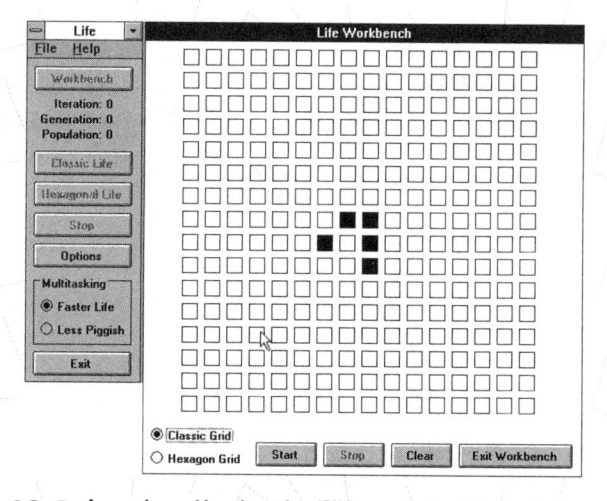

Figure 13.4. A sample workbench setting (Glider—use the default rules).

With the default classic life rules (two or three neighbors are needed for continued life, and exactly three neighbors are needed for birth), the glider reconstitutes itself every four generations, but in an offset position, giving the appearance of gliding across the grid.

Figure 13.5 shows more initial patterns that produce interesting results.

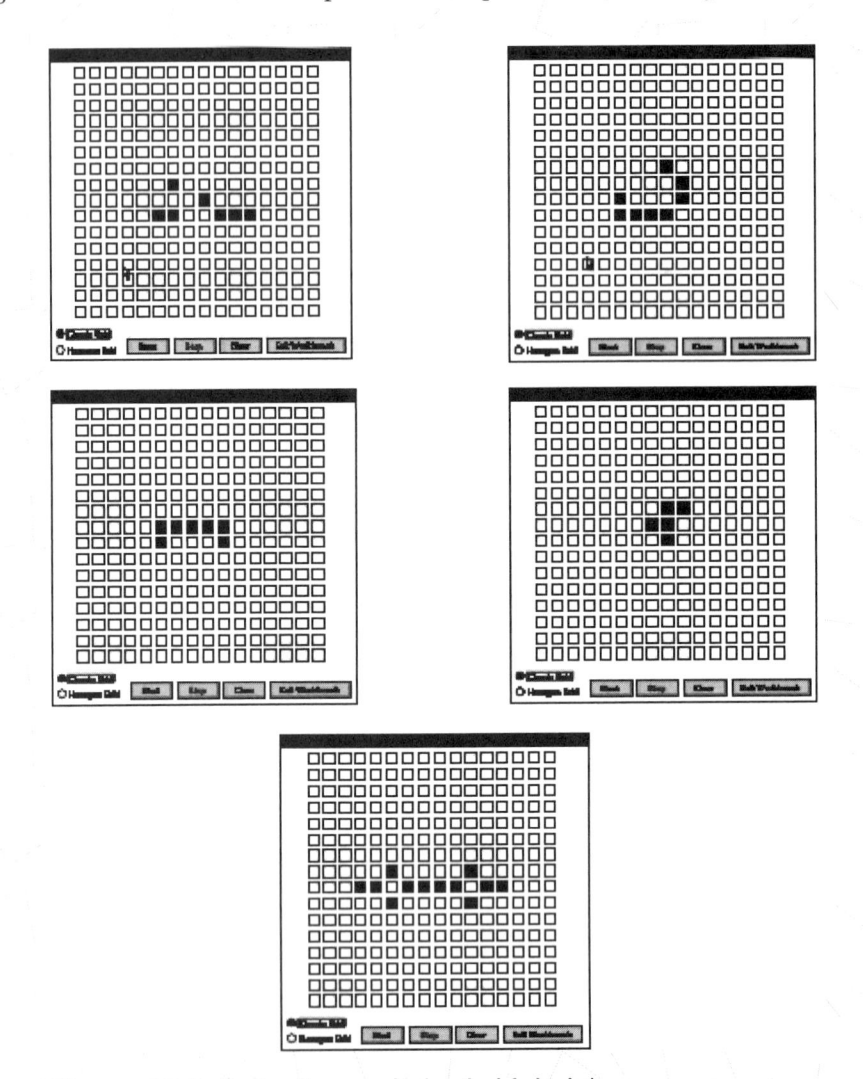

Figure 13.5. Classic pattern examples (use the default rules).

After you have experimented for a while with the initial patterns shown in the preceding figures, you may wish to try some of your own, and to try new sets of rules. You can also change the rules "on the fly," while the evolution is running. In the main control window, click the Options button. A modal window appears, overlapping both the main control window and the workbench

Chapter 13: Life Workshop

window. (*Modal* means that once the window is opened, the user must close it before taking any other action within Life Workshop.)

The Life Options window has a pair of radio buttons at its top for toggling between setting options for classic life and setting options for hexagonal life. The default is for setting classic life options. You will see a number of check boxes for enabling the rules you desire. There are also three radio buttons for selecting the initial density for the random sprinkling of life in the macroscopic life modes (described in the following section). When you have selected the rules you want, click the Done button to make them take effect. Note that there are two complete sets of rules: one for classic life and one for hexagonal life. Changing the rules of one form of life does not affect the rules for the other form of life.

Hexagonal Life Experiments

In the workbench, if you click the Hexagonal Grid option button, the classic grid is replaced by a grid of cells in the form of a hexagon. The operation of the workbench controls is the same for the hexagonal grid as for the classic grid. However, the default rules are different. If you click the Options button to return to the options modal window and then click the Hexagon Life Options radio button, you will see that the default hexagonal grid rules are for continued life with three neighbors and birth with two neighbors. Use these default rules to try the initial pattern shown in Figure 13.6.

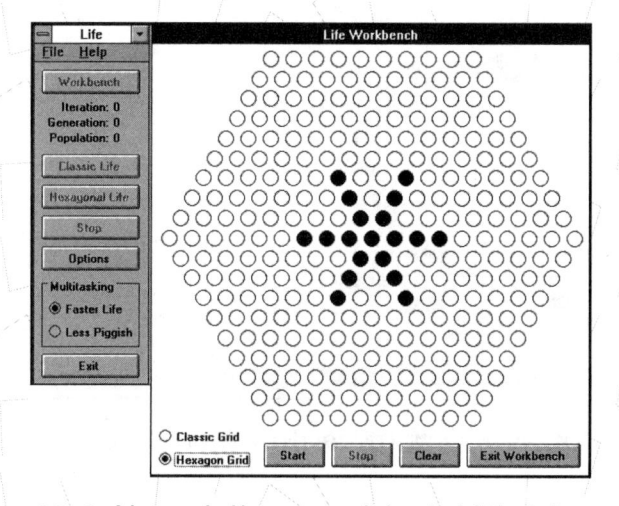

Figure 13.6. A hexagonal grid pattern example (use the default rules).

289

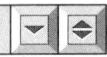

After several generations, the starting pattern illustrated in Figure 13.6 evolves to the pattern shown in Figure 13.7.

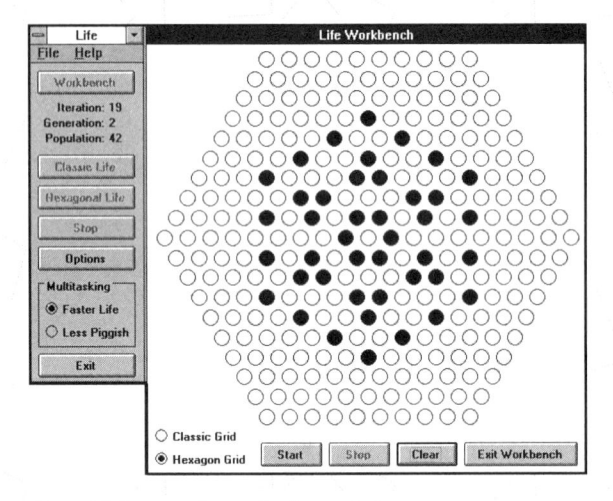

Figure 13.7. The hexagonal example after evolution.

Now, go to the Life Options window and add the Life with two neighbors rule for hexagonal life, and try the example shown in Figure 13.8.

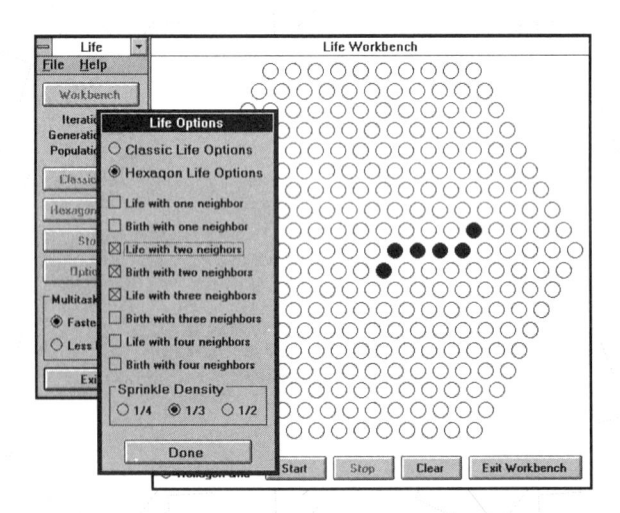

Figure 13.8. Another hexagonal grid example (use the rules shown).

Chapter 13: Life Workshop

With the modified rules, life in the example in Figure 13.8 grows to cover the hexagonal area and stabilizes in a random-looking oscillating pattern after 96 generations. After observing evolution in the hexagonal grid microcosm for a while, you will be ready to experiment with life on the macrocosmic level.

Macrocosmic Experiments

Life Workshop has another cellular automata investigative mode, the macrocosmic mode. This mode provides a large (10,000 cell) life plane on which you can watch the evolution of two-dimensional life with variable life rules. The macrocosm is initially sprinkled in its center portion (2,500 cells) with random life. You can change the random sprinkling density in the Life Options window with the Sprinkle Density radio buttons. To enter the macrocosmic modes, click either the Classic Life or Hexagonal Life button in the main control window.

The macrocosm automatically is sprinkled with random life, which will evolve according to the rules that you set in the Life Options window. Each set of rules you select will lead to different types of population growth, decay, or stabilization. The screen in Figure 13.9 shows classic life after eight generations.

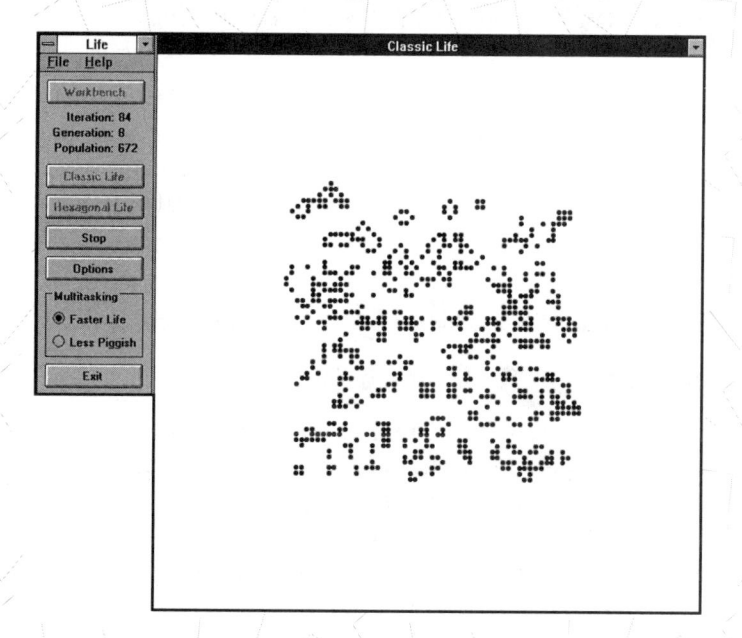

Figure 13.9. Classic life after eight generations (default rules).

Figure 13.10 shows hexagonal life after eight generations.

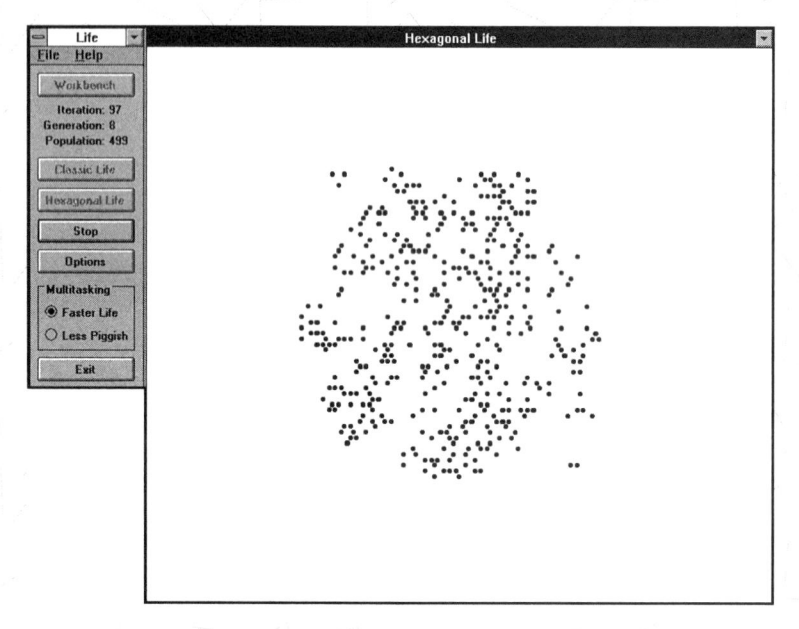

Figure 13.10. Hexagonal life after eight generations (default rules).

Life will continue to evolve when the Life Workshop is minimized. Change multitasking to Less Piggish if you want to use other Windows programs. Change it back to Faster Life for better performance. You can run several sessions of Life Workshop to explore various rules and options simultaneously.

Understanding the Life Workshop Program

I developed the Life Workshop program just for fun and the challenge of making it work. Other people to whom I showed the program enjoyed it, so I posted the executable file on CompuServe as shareware so that more people would be able to explore cellular automata using Microsoft Windows. I have been interested in cellular automata for several years, and I experimented with some character mode programs for the Game of Life. Although character mode programs typically have snappy performance, the grid area available is limited to a character display of 80 columns by 40 rows (3200 cells).

Chapter 13: Life Workshop

When Microsoft published Visual Basic in 1991, I saw the programming environment as ideal for developing Life Workshop, not only because of the graphic functions available, but also because of the user-friendly event-driven interfaces Windows makes possible and the Windows multitasking capability. I was interested in long evolutions of large random populations, but I did not want to tie up my computer with a single program for long periods.

As I was developing the Classic Life display, I began to think more deeply about the nature of the grid itself. The game of chess is played on a 64 × 64 square grid, with alternating cells painted light and dark, to help players visualize the diagonal moves of chess pieces. Two bishops of one color—one on the light squares and one on the dark squares—can never communicate. However, two rooks, which move on the horizontal and vertical paths, can communicate. This indicated to me that there is something inherently different about a cell's corner neighbors compared to the cell's side neighbors.

A proper description of this phenomenon is available from the mathematics of sets. The set of a cell's neighbor cells has eight elements (set N). Four of those neighbors are *corner cells,* and four are *side cells.* Each neighbor cell has its own set of neighbors. Let the corner neighbor's set of its own neighbors be designated by C, and let the side neighbor's set of its own neighbors be designated by S. The intersection of N with C has two elements, whereas the intersection of N with S has four elements. This difference in neighbor set intersections shows that a level of complexity is inherent in the rectangular grid itself.

The philosophical interest in the Game of Life is that such a simply defined world can result in such complex evolution, as shown in the example starting patterns in the early figures in this chapter. I began to wonder if there wasn't a simpler two-dimensional world that would demonstrate evolutionary complexity as well. The hexagonal grid, where each cell has six identical neighbors, is such a simpler world. Any bishop on a hexagonal chess board will communicate with any other bishop (if you can imagine such a chess board). Each of a hexagonal grid cell's neighbors has exactly the same relationship to it as every other neighbor cell. There is no hidden complexity. Thus, if evolutionary patterns of complexity similar to those obtained with classic life could be found with hexagonal life, the demonstration of cellular automata evolutionary complexity would be even more compelling. As the example patterns for hexagonal life show, that seems to be the case.

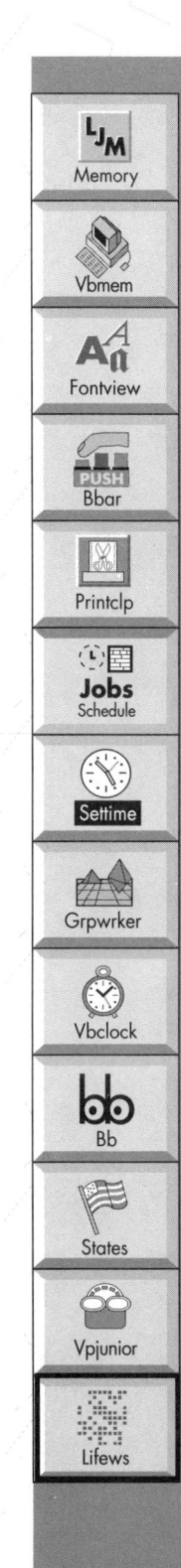

In keeping with the theme of this book, the "fun" aspects of programming, I concentrate here on the challenging or tricky aspects of Life Workshop. Fundamental Visual Basic issues—such as the use of controls and forms, naming conventions, or event-driven user interface design—I leave to the reader to explore.

In the following discussions of the programming aspects of Life Workshop, I suggest that you run Visual Basic and open the project LIFEWS5.MAK so that you can follow along with the text and examine the forms and code examples as you go.

Program Organization

When you load LIFEWS5.MAK, you see that the Life Workshop project consists of seven files in addition to the .MAK file. There is the global module, a `MainForm` form, a `WorkBench` form, the `ClassicLife` and `HexGrid` forms, and the `OptionsForm` and `HelpForm` forms. There is no separate code module. Some of the key subroutines are in the general section of the `MainForm` form, which is also the startup form.

Program Startup Events

Because the `MainForm` form is designated as the startup module, the `MainForm` load event procedure is the first code to be executed on startup. This procedure puts the form into the upper-left corner of the screen with the `move` statement, sets a few variables, and then loads the `OptionsForm` form.

After the `MainForm` load procedure execution completes, the next event to occur is the form resize event. The Visual Basic documentation is not very clear on this, but a form's resize event occurs at least once, right after a form is loaded. The resize event also occurs every time a form is minimized, normalized, or maximized. I do not use any form paint events in this program, but it is of interest to note that if a form's `autoredraw` property is set to true, the form's paint event will never occur. The `MainForm` form resize event procedure makes the other program forms invisible whenever the `MainForm` form is minimized. After the form load and resize event procedures are completed, the user sees the main program control window in the upper-left corner of the screen. Nothing more occurs without user input.

Programming the Workbench

The Workbench button is placed at the top of the main control window to invite the user to click this one first. The Exit button is on the bottom of the form for the opposite reason. Let's examine what happens when the user presses the Workbench button. An easy way to get to the `WorkBenchButton_Click()` event procedure is to double-click the `MainForm` file in the project window to display the form, then double-click the command button control. The appropriate procedure code is then displayed in the `MainForm` edit window.

Aside from setting some button-enabled states, the `WorkBenchButton_Click()` event procedure shows the `WorkBench` form. Now close the `MainForm` form and code window, and double-click the `WorkBench` form in the project window to display the `WorkBench` form. Double-click the form, and the form's load event procedure code is displayed. This code sets the left and top properties of the form and calls the `PaintClassic()` subroutine, which is in the "general" section of the form's code window.

`PaintClassic()` first sets the form's `MousePointer` property to the hourglass, clears the form, and then runs a nested 32 × 32 `For` loop. The `For` loop initializes the A integer array and draws the boxes that represent the empty (non-living) cells of the classic grid. The `MousePointer` is then set back to the default. The A array contains the states of the current generation. These states are logical values, with 0 being false and –1 being true, in keeping with the Visual Basic convention. The living state is indicated by a cell being painted black, and the dead state is indicated by a cell being painted white. There is no reason that the reader cannot extend this program to recognize a larger number of states, with different states being represented by other integers and other colors.

When a user clicks any cell in the workbench, the cell becomes "living," and the Start and Clear buttons are enabled. To see how this occurs, let's examine the `Form_MouseDown()` event. The `MouseDown()` event passes the form X and Y coordinates of the mouse when the mouse button is pressed. If the Stop button is enabled, it means that the workbench evolution is "running," so nothing happens. If the Stop button is not enabled, it means that the workbench is idle, so it can receive user input. Depending on the state of the Classic Grid and Hexagon Grid radio buttons, one of two nested loops is run. These loops test every cell to see if it is the one in which the mouse button came down. If the loop finds the cell, it is repainted with the fill color (black) and the Start and Clear buttons are enabled.

If the user makes a mistake in clicking cells to life in the workbench, he has to clear the entire pattern and start over. Notice that it would be fairly easy for the reader to improve this program by testing for the right mouse button `MouseDown()` event and erasing a cell in that case.

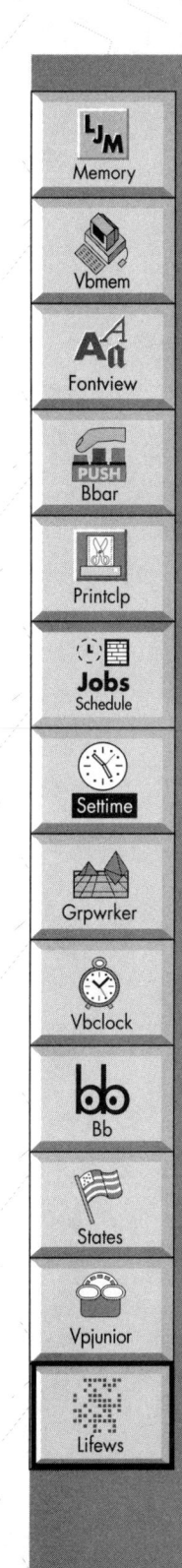

The hexagrid portion of the `MouseDown()` procedure is a bit more complicated than the classic grid part because the circles are positioned differently for the odd and even rows. Only those cells that fit into the hexagon shape are to be drawn. The summation procedure is different, too. When the user stops clicking cells and presses the Start button, the cellular automata evolution begins. Double-click the Start button on the workbench form to see the code for that event procedure.

The `StartButton_Click()` event procedure sets some control properties and, depending on which grid is displayed, runs either the `ClassCompute()` or the `HexCompute()` subroutines, both of which are in the "general" section of the workbench code window. Let's examine the `ClassCompute()` subroutine first.

The first thing `ClassCompute()` does is set the generation counter, `GenCount%`, to zero, and puts this number on the main control window (`MainForm`). `ClassCompute()` then goes into a `While` loop that executes as long as the workbench Stop button is enabled. When the user wants to stop execution, he presses the Stop button, which disables itself. I have tried other ways to communicate with running subroutines, and this technique works well.

The `While` loop contains two nested `For` loops, the first of which sums the living neighbors of each cell (array A), and then sets the future state (array B) depending on the rules that have been enabled (`Rule1` through `Rule8`). Using two arrays (A and B) allows the future generation to be drawn in the same nested loop as the state evaluation. The second nested `For` loop repeats the process with array B representing the current states. Let's look a little closer at the neighbor summation code for the A array:

```
Sum% = 0
If iA(I% - 1, J% - 1) = -1 Then Sum% = Sum% + 1
If iA(I% - 1, J%) = -1 Then Sum% = Sum% + 1
If iA(I% - 1, J% + 1) = -1 Then Sum% = Sum% + 1
If iA(I%, J% - 1) = -1 Then Sum% = Sum% + 1
If iA(I%, J% + 1) = -1 Then Sum% = Sum% + 1
If iA(I% + 1, J% - 1) = -1 Then Sum% = Sum% + 1
If iA(I% + 1, J%) = -1 Then Sum% = Sum% + 1
If iA(I% + 1, J% + 1) = -1 Then Sum% = Sum% + 1
```

First, the sum is set to zero. Then each of the current cell's neighbors is tested for aliveness (a value of –1). If a neighbor cell is alive, the sum is incremented by 1. The value of cells outside the 16 × 16 grid is always zero. In some implementations of cellular automata worlds, the left and right and top and bottom edges of the grid are connected. The reader might want to consider implementing edge communication as a user option for enhancing this software. Such an edge-connected grid is a *torus*.

The equivalent subroutine for the hexagrid (HexCompute()) is similar to ClassCompute(), except it evaluates neighbors differently, uses rules Rule9 through Rule16, has provisions for staggering the drawing of circles, and suppresses the drawing of cells outside the hexagon shape.

Macrocosmic Life

When a user presses the Classic Life button on the main control window, the ClassicLife form is shown and is then painted with an initial random sprinkling of life. The evolution then begins, and continues until the user stops it with the Stop button or exits the program. There are two key subroutines that accomplish this: ClassicSprinkle() and ClassicCompute(). To see the code for ClassicSprinkle(), go to the general section of the MainForm code window and click ClassicSprinkle().

ClassicSprinkle() sets some control properties and "randomizes" so that each time the program is run, a different random order is obtained. A nested loop is then entered that determines the life states of the 50×50 center portion of the grid, based on the user-definable global variable sfSprinkle. After the nested loop completes, ClassicSprinkle() calls ClassicCompute(), where the real evolutionary work takes place.

ClassicCompute() is an endless loop that starts with Do While Flag% = 0. Flag% will always be zero, so the only way out of the loop is for the global integer variable iStopNow to become true, which is what happens when the user presses the MainForm Stop button. The reason there are no controls on the ClassicLife form is to provide as much room as possible for drawing the 100×100 grid. If the circles are drawn too small, they look distorted due to the "aliasing" effect of pixel drawing.

Inside the endless loop are two sets of nested loops, each for a complete generation. These two nested loops alternate between arrays A and B. The neighbor summation and state rule testing are very similar to those described for ClassCompute for the workbench window. HexSprinkle() and HexCompute() for the macrocosm share similarities to their classic counterparts, and I leave their examination to the reader.

Help and Miscellaneous

Indexed help is available to the user from the main control form pull-down menu. The menu option shows HelpForm, which contains a simple list box for selecting help topics. For each topic selected, the appropriate text is loaded in a MsgBox. There is no hypertext capability with this arrangement, but this help format is easy to program and works well for simple applications like Life Workshop.

Performance issues always surface in any cellular automata program. There is always the tendency to "push the envelope" as with Life Workshop's 100×100 macrocosmic grids. Each generation requires updating 10,000 cells. Each update requires the summation of up to eight neighbor states, and the testing of this sum against all the rules. Although the workbench runs well on a fast computer, the macrocosms can make even a 33 MHz 486 seem a bit sluggish.

My primary objective in developing this program was to provide as much functionality for the user as possible, whereas performance was initially of a secondary concern. After I had enabled the basic algorithms to work without errors, I began some fine-tuning and was able to improve performance. The algorithms are still far from performance-optimized, and I have a feeling that many readers will be able to find numerous improvements. If you are able to find ways to make the software run faster, I will appreciate hearing from you.

Life Workshop Source Code

The following listing is the complete text of the source code for Life Workshop. As with all Visual Basic programs, there is significant content in the VB forms themselves, which is accessible only by running the Visual Basic programming environment and loading the source project files that are included with this book on the accompanying disk.

```
Sub Form_Load ()
  left = MainForm.Width + 30
  top = 0
End Sub


Sub FileExit_Click ()
```

Chapter 13: Life Workshop

```
    End
End Sub

Sub HexSprinkle ()

  On Error GoTo HexSprinkleHandler

  Randomize
  MainForm.Label2.Caption = Str$(GenCount%)
  MainForm.Label3.Caption = Str$(Population%)

  'Set all cells to dead except for center hexagon,
  'which is sprinkled with life.
  For J% = 26 To 75
  np% = DoEvents()
  If iStopNow = -1 Then Exit Sub
  MainForm.Label1.Caption = Str$(J%)
  MainForm.Label3.Caption = Str$(Population%)
    For I% = 1 To 100
      If MainForm.Friendlier.Value = -1 Then np% = DoEvents()
        Slope% = Int(J% / 2)
        If J% / 2 = Int(J% / 2) Then
           UpperLeft% = (51 - (Slope%))
           UpperRight% = (50 + Slope%)
           LowerLeft% = (Slope% + 0)
           LowerRight% = (101 - Slope%)
        Else
           UpperLeft% = (51 - (Slope%))
           UpperRight% = (51 + Slope%)
           LowerLeft% = (Slope% + 1)
           LowerRight% = (101 - Slope%)
        End If
        iA(I%, J%) = 0
        If I% >= UpperLeft% And I% <= UpperRight% And I% >=
           LowerLeft% And I% <= LowerRight% Then
           If Rnd < sfSprinkle Then iA(I%, J%) = -1
        End If

      If Int(J% / 2) <> J% / 2 Then
         X! = I% * iHPitch
      Else
         X! = I% * iHPitch + iHPitch / 2
      End If
```

continues

Chapter 13: Life Workshop

```
      Y! = J% * iHPitch * .866

    If iA(I%, J%) = -1 Then
       Population% = Population% + 1
       HexGrid.FillColor = QBColor(0)
       HexGrid.Circle (X!, Y!), iHRadius, QBColor(0)
    Else
       HexGrid.FillColor = QBColor(15)
       HexGrid.Circle (X!, Y!), iHRadius, QBColor(15)
    End If
  Next I%
Next J%

MainForm.Label3.Caption = Str$(Population%)

HexCompute

Exit Sub

HexSprinkleHandler:

  MsgBox "Error in Sprinkle " + Str$(Err)
  Resume Next

End Sub

Sub Form_Load ()

  Move 0, 0
  iHRadius = 31
  iHPitch = 99
  iCRadius = 31
  iCPitch = 87
  sfSprinkle = 1 / 3
  Rule3 = -1
  Rule5 = -1
  Rule6 = -1
  Rule12 = -1
  Rule13 = -1
  Load OptionsForm

End Sub

Sub HexCompute ()

  On Error GoTo HexComputeHandler
```

Chapter 13: Life Workshop

```
GenCount% = 1
Label2.Caption = Str$(GenCount%)

Do While Flag% = 0
  Population% = 0
  For J% = 1 To 100
    MainForm.Label1.Caption = Str$(J%)
    np% = DoEvents()
    If iStopNow = -1 Then Exit Sub
    For I% = 1 To 100
      If MainForm.Friendlier.Value = -1 Then np% = DoEvents()
      Sum% = 0

      If Int(J% / 2) = J% / 2 Then
        If iA(I% + 1, J% - 1) = -1 Then Sum% = Sum% + 1
        If iA(I% + 1, J% + 1) = -1 Then Sum% = Sum% + 1
      Else
        If iA(I% - 1, J% - 1) = -1 Then Sum% = Sum% + 1
        If iA(I% - 1, J% + 1) = -1 Then Sum% = Sum% + 1
      End If

      If iA(I% - 1, J%) = -1 Then Sum% = Sum% + 1
      If iA(I%, J% - 1) = -1 Then Sum% = Sum% + 1
      If iA(I%, J% + 1) = -1 Then Sum% = Sum% + 1
      If iA(I% + 1, J%) = -1 Then Sum% = Sum% + 1

      iB(I%, J%) = 0
      If Rule9 = -1 And Sum% = 1 And iA(I%, J%) = -1
          Then iB(I%, J%) = -1
      If Rule10 = -1 And Sum% = 1 And iA(I%, J%) = 0
          Then iB(I%, J%) = -1
      If Rule11 = -1 And Sum% = 2 And iA(I%, J%) = -1
          Then iB(I%, J%) = -1
      If Rule12 = -1 And Sum% = 2 And iA(I%, J%) = 0
          Then iB(I%, J%) = -1
      If Rule13 = -1 And Sum% = 3 And iA(I%, J%) = -1
          Then iB(I%, J%) = -1
      If Rule14 = -1 And Sum% = 3 And iA(I%, J%) = 0
          Then iB(I%, J%) = -1
      If Rule15 = -1 And Sum% = 4 And iA(I%, J%) = -1
          Then iB(I%, J%) = -1
      If Rule16 = -1 And Sum% = 4 And iA(I%, J%) = 0
          Then iB(I%, J%) = -1

      If Int(J% / 2) <> J% / 2 Then
        X! = I% * iHPitch
```

continues

```
      Else
         X! = I% * iHPitch + iHPitch / 2
      End If

      Y! = J% * iHPitch * .866

      If iB(I%, J%) = -1 Then
         Population% = Population% + 1
         HexGrid.FillColor = QBColor(0)
         HexGrid.Circle (X!, Y!), iHRadius, QBColor(0)
      Else
         HexGrid.FillColor = QBColor(15)
         HexGrid.Circle (X!, Y!), iHRadius, QBColor(15)
      End If

   Next I%
Next J%

GenCount% = GenCount% + 1
MainForm.Label2.Caption = Str$(GenCount%)
MainForm.Label3.Caption = Str$(Population%)

Population% = 0
For J% = 1 To 100
   MainForm.Label1.Caption = Str$(J%)
   np% = DoEvents()
   If iStopNow = -1 Then Exit Sub
   For I% = 1 To 100
      If MainForm.Friendlier.Value = -1 Then np% = DoEvents()
      Sum% = 0

      If Int(J% / 2) = J% / 2 Then
         If iB(I% + 1, J% - 1) = -1 Then Sum% = Sum% + 1
         If iB(I% + 1, J% + 1) = -1 Then Sum% = Sum% + 1
      Else
         If iB(I% - 1, J% - 1) = -1 Then Sum% = Sum% + 1
         If iB(I% - 1, J% + 1) = -1 Then Sum% = Sum% + 1
      End If

      If iB(I% - 1, J%) = -1 Then Sum% = Sum% + 1
      If iB(I%, J% - 1) = -1 Then Sum% = Sum% + 1
      If iB(I%, J% + 1) = -1 Then Sum% = Sum% + 1
      If iB(I% + 1, J%) = -1 Then Sum% = Sum% + 1

      iA(I%, J%) = 0
      If Rule9 = -1 And Sum% = 1 And iB(I%, J%) = -1
         Then iA(I%, J%) = -1
```

Chapter 13: Life Workshop

```
        If Rule10 = -1 And Sum% = 1 And iB(I%, J%) = 0 _
            Then iA(I%, J%) = -1
        If Rule11 = -1 And Sum% = 2 And iB(I%, J%) = -1 _
            Then iA(I%, J%) = -1
        If Rule12 = -1 And Sum% = 2 And iB(I%, J%) = 0 _
            Then iA(I%, J%) = -1
        If Rule13 = -1 And Sum% = 3 And iB(I%, J%) = -1 _
            Then iA(I%, J%) = -1
        If Rule14 = -1 And Sum% = 3 And iB(I%, J%) = 0 _
            Then iA(I%, J%) = -1
        If Rule15 = -1 And Sum% = 4 And iB(I%, J%) = -1 _
            Then iA(I%, J%) = -1
        If Rule16 = -1 And Sum% = 4 And iB(I%, J%) = 0 _
            Then iA(I%, J%) = -1

        If Int(J% / 2) <> J% / 2 Then
          X! = I% * iHPitch
        Else
          X! = I% * iHPitch + iHPitch / 2
        End If
        Y! = J% * iHPitch * .866

        If iA(I%, J%) = -1 Then
          Population% = Population% + 1
          HexGrid.FillColor = QBColor(0)
          HexGrid.Circle (X!, Y!), iHRadius, QBColor(0)
        Else
          HexGrid.FillColor = QBColor(15)
          HexGrid.Circle (X!, Y!), iHRadius, QBColor(15)
        End If
      Next I%
    Next J%

    GenCount% = GenCount% + 1
    MainForm.Label2.Caption = Str$(GenCount%)
    MainForm.Label3.Caption = Str$(Population%)

  Loop
  Exit Sub

HexComputeHandler:
  MsgBox "Error in Compute " + Str$(Err)
  Resume Next

End Sub
```

continues

Chapter 13: Life Workshop

```
Sub ClassicSprinkle ()

  On Error GoTo ClassicSprinkleHandler

  ClassicButton.Enabled = 0
  HexButton.Enabled = 0
  StopButton.Enabled = -1
  Randomize
  MainForm.Label2.Caption = Str$(GenCount%)
  MainForm.Label3.Caption = Str$(Population%)

  'Set all cells to dead except for center 50 x 50 square,
  'which is sprinkled with life.
  For J% = 26 To 75
    MainForm.Label1.Caption = Str$(J%)
    MainForm.Label3.Caption = Str$(Population%)
    np% = DoEvents()
    If iStopNow = -1 Then Exit Sub
    For I% = 26 To 75
      If MainForm.Friendlier.Value = -1 Then np% = DoEvents()
      iA(I%, J%) = 0
      If Rnd < sfSprinkle Then iA(I%, J%) = -1
      X! = I% * iCPitch
      Y! = J% * iCPitch
      If iA(I%, J%) = -1 Then
        ClassicLife.FillColor = QBColor(0)
        ClassicLife.Circle (X!, Y!), iCRadius, QBColor(0)
        Population% = Population% + 1
      Else
        ClassicLife.FillColor = QBColor(15)
        ClassicLife.Circle (X!, Y!), iCRadius, QBColor(15)
      End If
    Next I%
  Next J%

  MainForm.Label3.Caption = Str$(Population%)
  ClassicCompute

Exit Sub

ClassicSprinkleHandler:

  MsgBox "Error in Sprinkle " + Str$(Err)
  Resume Next

End Sub
```

Chapter 13: Life Workshop

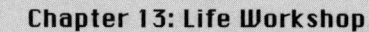

```
Sub ClassicCompute ()

  On Error GoTo ClassicComputeHandler

  GenCount% = 1
  Label2.Caption = Str$(GenCount%)

  Do While Flag% = 0
    Population% = 0
    For J% = 1 To 100
    np% = DoEvents()
    If iStopNow = -1 Then Exit Sub
    MainForm.Label1.Caption = Str$(J%)
      For I% = 1 To 100
        If MainForm.Friendlier.Value = -1 Then np% = DoEvents()
        Sum% = 0
        If iA(I% - 1, J% - 1) = -1 Then Sum% = Sum% + 1
        If iA(I% - 1, J%) = -1 Then Sum% = Sum% + 1
        If iA(I% - 1, J% + 1) = -1 Then Sum% = Sum% + 1
        If iA(I%, J% - 1) = -1 Then Sum% = Sum% + 1
        If iA(I%, J% + 1) = -1 Then Sum% = Sum% + 1
        If iA(I% + 1, J% - 1) = -1 Then Sum% = Sum% + 1
        If iA(I% + 1, J%) = -1 Then Sum% = Sum% + 1
        If iA(I% + 1, J% + 1) = -1 Then Sum% = Sum% + 1

        iB(I%, J%) = 0
        If Rule1 = -1 And Sum% = 1 And iA(I%, J%) = -1 ↵
            Then iB(I%, J%) = -1
        If Rule2 = -1 And Sum% = 1 And iA(I%, J%) = 0 ↵
            Then iB(I%, J%) = -1
        If Rule3 = -1 And Sum% = 2 And iA(I%, J%) = -1 ↵
            Then iB(I%, J%) = -1
        If Rule4 = -1 And Sum% = 2 And iA(I%, J%) = 0 ↵
            Then iB(I%, J%) = -1
        If Rule5 = -1 And Sum% = 3 And iA(I%, J%) = -1 ↵
            Then iB(I%, J%) = -1
        If Rule6 = -1 And Sum% = 3 And iA(I%, J%) = 0 ↵
            Then iB(I%, J%) = -1
        If Rule7 = -1 And Sum% = 4 And iA(I%, J%) = -1 ↵
            Then iB(I%, J%) = -1
        If Rule8 = -1 And Sum% = 4 And iA(I%, J%) = 0 ↵
            Then iB(I%, J%) = -1

        X! = I% * iCPitch
```

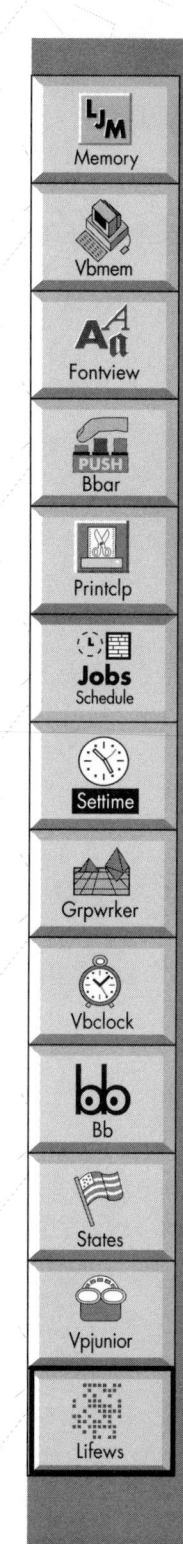

continues

```
      Y! = J% * iCPitch
      If iB(I%, J%) = -1 Then
        ClassicLife.FillColor = QBColor(0)
        ClassicLife.Circle (X!, Y!), iCRadius, QBColor(0)
        Population% = Population% + 1
      Else
        ClassicLife.FillColor = QBColor(15)
        ClassicLife.Circle (X!, Y!), iCRadius, QBColor(15)
      End If
    Next I%
  Next J%
  GenCount% = GenCount% + 1
  MainForm.Label2.Caption = Str$(GenCount%)
  Label3.Caption = Str$(Population%)

  Population% = 0
  For J% = 1 To 100
  np% = DoEvents()
  If iStopNow = -1 Then Exit Sub
  MainForm.Label1.Caption = Str$(J%)
    For I% = 1 To 100
      If MainForm.Friendlier.Value = -1 Then np% = DoEvents()
      Sum% = 0
      If iB(I% - 1, J% - 1) = -1 Then Sum% = Sum% + 1
      If iB(I% - 1, J%) = -1 Then Sum% = Sum% + 1
      If iB(I% - 1, J% + 1) = -1 Then Sum% = Sum% + 1
      If iB(I%, J% - 1) = -1 Then Sum% = Sum% + 1
      If iB(I%, J% + 1) = -1 Then Sum% = Sum% + 1
      If iB(I% + 1, J% - 1) = -1 Then Sum% = Sum% + 1
      If iB(I% + 1, J%) = -1 Then Sum% = Sum% + 1
      If iB(I% + 1, J% + 1) = -1 Then Sum% = Sum% + 1
      If Sum% < 2 Then iA(I%, J%) = 0
      If Sum% > 3 Then iA(I%, J%) = 0
      If Sum% = 2 And iB(I%, J%) = -1 Then iA(I%, J%) = -1
      If Sum% = 3 Then iA(I%, J%) = -1

      iA(I%, J%) = 0
      If Rule1 = -1 And Sum% = 1 And iB(I%, J%) = -1
          Then iA(I%, J%) = -1
      If Rule2 = -1 And Sum% = 1 And iB(I%, J%) = 0
          Then iA(I%, J%) = -1
      If Rule3 = -1 And Sum% = 2 And iB(I%, J%) = -1
          Then iA(I%, J%) = -1
      If Rule4 = -1 And Sum% = 2 And iB(I%, J%) = 0
          Then iA(I%, J%) = -1
      If Rule5 = -1 And Sum% = 3 And iB(I%, J%) = -1
          Then iA(I%, J%) = -1
```

Chapter 13: Life Workshop

```
      ↪ If Rule6 = -1 And Sum% = 3 And iB(I%, J%) = 0
            Then iA(I%, J%) = -1
      ↪ If Rule7 = -1 And Sum% = 4 And iB(I%, J%) = -1
            Then iA(I%, J%) = -1
      ↪ If Rule8 = -1 And Sum% = 4 And iB(I%, J%) = 0
            Then iA(I%, J%) = -1

        X! = I% * iCPitch
        Y! = J% * iCPitch
        If iA(I%, J%) = -1 Then
           ClassicLife.FillColor = QBColor(0)
           ClassicLife.Circle (X!, Y!), iCRadius, QBColor(0)
           Population% = Population% + 1
        Else
           ClassicLife.FillColor = QBColor(15)
           ClassicLife.Circle (X!, Y!), iCRadius, QBColor(15)
        End If
      Next I%
    Next J%
    GenCount% = GenCount% + 1
    MainForm.Label2.Caption = Str$(GenCount%)
    Label3.Caption = Str$(Population%)
  Loop
  Exit Sub

ClassicComputeHandler:
  MsgBox "Error in Compute " + Str$(Err)
  Resume Next

End Sub

Sub StopButton_Click ()

  iStopNow = -1
  ClassicButton.Enabled = -1
  HexButton.Enabled = -1
  StopButton.Enabled = 0
  WorkBenchButton.Enabled = -1
  ClassicLife.Hide
  HexGrid.Hide

End Sub

Sub ClassicButton_Click ()
  iStopNow = 0
  ClassicButton.Enabled = 0
```

continues

```
    HexButton.Enabled = 0
    StopButton.Enabled = -1
    WorkBenchButton.Enabled = 0
    StopButton.SetFocus
    If ClassicLife.Visible = -1 Then ClassicLife.Hide
    If HexGrid.Visible = -1 Then HexGrid.Hide
    ClassicLife.Cls
    ClassicLife.Show
    ClassicSprinkle

End Sub

Sub HexButton_Click ()

    iStopNow = 0
    ClassicButton.Enabled = 0
    HexButton.Enabled = 0
    StopButton.Enabled = -1
    WorkBenchButton.Enabled = 0
    StopButton.SetFocus
    If ClassicLife.Visible = -1 Then ClassicLife.Hide
    If HexGrid.Visible = -1 Then HexGrid.Hide
    HexGrid.Cls
    HexGrid.Show
    HexSprinkle

End Sub

Sub Form_Resize ()

    Static PState1 As Integer
    Static PState2 As Integer
    Static PState3 As Integer
    EndButton.SetFocus
    If MainForm.WindowState = 1 Then
      PState1 = ClassicLife.Visible
      PState2 = HexGrid.Visible
      PState3 = WorkBench.Visible
      ClassicLife.Visible = 0
      HexGrid.Visible = 0
      WorkBench.Visible = 0
    Else
      ClassicLife.Visible = PState1
      HexGrid.Visible = PState2
      WorkBench.Visible = PState3
    End If
```

Chapter 13: Life Workshop

```
End Sub

Sub EndButton_Click ()
  End
End Sub

Sub Form_Unload (Cancel As Integer)

  End

End Sub

Sub HelpAbout_Click ()

  Msg$ = "Life Workshop, version 1.3, copyright 1992 by Ivory
    Tower Software" + Chr$(13) + Chr$(13)
  Msg$ = Msg$ + "This software product is shareware. After a
    reasonable evaluation period,"
  Msg$ = Msg$ + " continued use of this software requires
    the purchase of a user"
  Msg$ = Msg$ + " license. Registered users will receive
    a copy of the latest version"
  Msg$ = Msg$ + " of this program."
  Msg$ = Msg$ + " To register send $10 to:" + Chr$(13) + Chr$(13)
  Msg$ = Msg$ + "Ivory Tower Software" + Chr$(13)
  Msg$ = Msg$ + "3419 W. 180th St." + Chr$(13)
  Msg$ = Msg$ + "Torrance, CA 90504" + Chr$(13) + Chr$(13)
  Msg$ = Msg$ + "Be sure to specify the program, version,
    and your disk size preference."
  Msg$ = Msg$ + " Your comments and suggestions for
    improving this software are welcome."
  Msg$ = Msg$ + " You may also contact ITS via CompuServe
    76427,2611."

  MsgBox Msg$, 0, "About Life Workshop"

End Sub

Sub WorkBenchButton_Click ()

  WorkBenchButton.Enabled = 0
  ClassicButton.Enabled = 0
  HexButton.Enabled = 0
  WorkBench.Show

End Sub
```

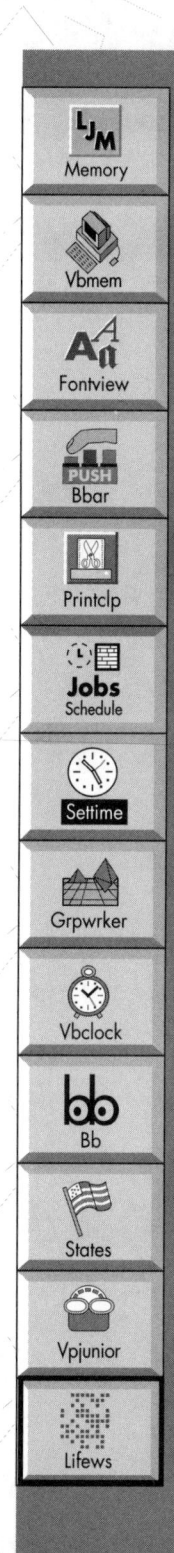

continues

```
Sub OptionsButton_Click ()

  OptionsButton.Enabled = 0
  OptionsForm.Show 1

End Sub

Sub HelpIndex_Click ()

  HelpForm.Show

End Sub

'Global Module of Life Workshop from

'Ivory Tower Software.

'Copyright 1992, all rights reserved.

Global iCPitch As Integer
Global iCRadius As Integer
Global iHPitch As Integer
Global iHRadius As Integer
Global iHexGrid As Integer
Global iA(101, 101) As Integer
Global iB(101, 101) As Integer
Global iStopNow As Integer
Global sfSprinkle As Single

Global Rule1 As Integer
Global Rule2 As Integer
Global Rule3 As Integer
Global Rule4 As Integer
Global Rule5 As Integer
Global Rule6 As Integer
Global Rule7 As Integer
Global Rule8 As Integer
Global Rule9 As Integer
Global Rule10 As Integer
Global Rule11 As Integer
Global Rule12 As Integer
Global Rule13 As Integer
Global Rule14 As Integer
Global Rule15 As Integer
Global Rule16 As Integer
```

Chapter 13: Life Workshop

```
Sub Form_Load ()
  left = MainForm.Width + 30
  top = 0
End Sub

Sub DoneButton_Click ()

  Rule1 = 0
  Rule2 = 0
  Rule3 = 0
  Rule4 = 0
  Rule5 = 0
  Rule6 = 0
  Rule7 = 0
  Rule8 = 0
  Rule9 = 0
  Rule10 = 0
  Rule11 = 0
  Rule12 = 0
  Rule13 = 0
  Rule14 = 0
  Rule15 = 0
  Rule16 = 0

  If Check1.Value = 1 Then Rule1 = -1
  If Check2.Value = 1 Then Rule2 = -1
  If Check3.Value = 1 Then Rule3 = -1
  If Check4.Value = 1 Then Rule4 = -1
  If Check5.Value = 1 Then Rule5 = -1
  If Check6.Value = 1 Then Rule6 = -1
  If Check7.Value = 1 Then Rule7 = -1
  If Check8.Value = 1 Then Rule8 = -1
  If Check9.Value = 1 Then Rule9 = -1
  If Check10.Value = 1 Then Rule10 = -1
  If Check11.Value = 1 Then Rule11 = -1
  If Check12.Value = 1 Then Rule12 = -1
  If Check13.Value = 1 Then Rule13 = -1
  If Check14.Value = 1 Then Rule14 = -1
  If Check15.Value = 1 Then Rule15 = -1
  If Check16.Value = 1 Then Rule16 = -1

  MainForm.OptionsButton.Enabled = -1
  Hide

End Sub
```

continues

Chapter 13: Life Workshop

```
Sub Option2_Click ()

  Check9.Visible = -1
  Check10.Visible = -1
  Check11.Visible = -1
  Check12.Visible = -1
  Check13.Visible = -1
  Check14.Visible = -1
  Check15.Visible = -1
  Check16.Visible = -1

  Check1.Visible = 0
  Check2.Visible = 0
  Check3.Visible = 0
  Check4.Visible = 0
  Check5.Visible = 0
  Check6.Visible = 0
  Check7.Visible = 0
  Check8.Visible = 0

End Sub

Sub Option1_Click ()
  Check1.Visible = -1
  Check2.Visible = -1
  Check3.Visible = -1
  Check4.Visible = -1
  Check5.Visible = -1
  Check6.Visible = -1
  Check7.Visible = -1
  Check8.Visible = -1

  Check9.Visible = 0
  Check10.Visible = 0
  Check11.Visible = 0
  Check12.Visible = 0
  Check13.Visible = 0
  Check14.Visible = 0
  Check15.Visible = 0
  Check16.Visible = 0

End Sub

Sub Fourth_Click ()
```

```
    sfSprinkle = 1 / 4

End Sub

Sub Third_Click ()

    sfSprinkle = 1 / 3

End Sub

Sub Half_Click ()

    sfSprinkle = 1 / 2

End Sub

Sub ClassOption_Click ()
  MainForm.Label1.Caption = " 0"
  MainForm.Label2.Caption = " 0"
  MainForm.Label3.Caption = " 0"
  StartButton.enabled = 0
  FillStyle = 1
  PaintClassic
End Sub

Sub HexOption_Click ()
  MainForm.Label1.Caption = " 0"
  MainForm.Label2.Caption = " 0"
  MainForm.Label3.Caption = " 0"
  StartButton.enabled = 0
  FillStyle = 1
  PaintHex
End Sub

Sub Form_Load ()
  left = MainForm.Width + 30
  top = 0
  PaintClassic
End Sub

Sub PaintClassic ()
  MousePointer = 11
  Cls
  For J% = 1 To 16
    For I% = 1 To 16
```

continues

```
      iA(I%, J%) = 0
      Line ((I% - 1) * 360 + 600, (J% - 1) * 360 + 120)-((I% - 1) _
        * 360 + 840, (J% - 1) * 360 + 360), , B
    Next I%
  Next J%
  MousePointer = 0
End Sub

Sub PaintHex ()
  Cls
  MousePointer = 11
  For J% = 1 To 19
    For I% = 1 To 19
    iA(I%, J%) = 0
    Slope% = Int(J% / 2)
    If J% / 2 = Int(J% / 2) Then
      UpperLeft% = (6 - (Slope%))
      UpperRight% = (14 + Slope%)
      LowerLeft% = (Slope% - 4)
      LowerRight% = (24 - Slope%)
    Else
      UpperLeft% = (5 - (Slope%))
      UpperRight% = (14 + Slope%)
      LowerLeft% = (Slope% - 4)
      LowerRight% = (23 - Slope%)
    End If
    If I% >= UpperLeft% And I% <= UpperRight% And I% >= _
        LowerLeft% And I% <= LowerRight% Then
      If J% / 2 = Int(J% / 2) Then
        Circle ((I%) * 360 - 90, (J%) * 360 * .866 - 90), 120
      Else
        Circle ((I%) * 360 + 90, (J%) * 360 * .866 - 90), 120
      End If
    End If    Next I%
  Next J%
  FillColor = QBColor(0)
  FillStyle = 0
  MousePointer = 0
End Sub

Sub ExitButton_Click ()

  StopButton.enabled = 0
  For J% = 1 To 19
    For I% = 1 To 19
      iA(I%, J%) = 0
```

```
      iB(I%, J%) = 0
    Next I%
  Next J%
  Unload WorkBench
  MainForm.ClassicButton.enabled = -1
  MainForm.HexButton.enabled = -1
  MainForm.WorkBenchButton.enabled = -1

End Sub

Sub Form_MouseDown (Button As Integer, Shift As Integer,
    X As Single, Y As Single)
  If StopButton.enabled = 0 Then
    MousePointer = 11
    If ClassOption.Value = -1 Then
      For J% = 1 To 16
        For I% = 1 To 16
          If X > (I% - 1) * 360 + 600 And X < (I% - 1) * 360 + 840 Then
            If Y > (J% - 1) * 360 + 120 And Y < (J% - 1) *
                360 + 360 Then
              iA(I%, J%) = -1
              Line ((I% - 1) * 360 + 600, (J% - 1) * 360 + 120)
                  -((I% - 1) * 360 + 840, (J% - 1) * 360 + 360), , BF
              StartButton.enabled = -1
              ClearButton.enabled = -1
            End If
          End If
        Next I%
      Next J%
    Else
      For J% = 1 To 19
        For I% = 1 To 19
          Slope% = Int(J% / 2)
          If J% / 2 = Int(J% / 2) Then
            UpperLeft% = (6 - (Slope%))
            UpperRight% = (14 + Slope%)
            LowerLeft% = (Slope% - 4)
            LowerRight% = (24 - Slope%)
          Else
            UpperLeft% = (5 - (Slope%))
            UpperRight% = (14 + Slope%)
            LowerLeft% = (Slope% - 4)
            LowerRight% = (23 - Slope%)
          End If
          If I% >= UpperLeft% And I% <= UpperRight% And I% >=
              LowerLeft% And I% <= LowerRight% Then
```

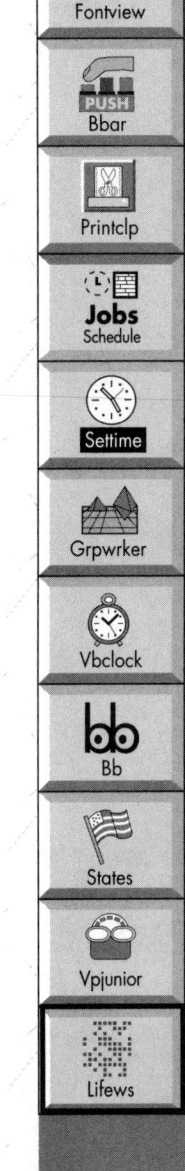

continues

```
              If J% / 2 = Int(J% / 2) Then
                If X > I% * 360 - 210 And X < I% * 360 + 30 Then
                  If Y > J% * 360 * .866 - 210 And
                ↳   Y < J% * 360 * .866 + 30 Then
                    Circle ((I%) * 360 - 90, (J%) * 360 * .866 - 90), 120
                    iA(I%, J%) = -1
                    StartButton.enabled = -1
                    ClearButton.enabled = -1
                  End If
                End If           Else
                If X > I% * 360 - 30 And X < I% * 360 + 210 Then
                  If Y > J% * 360 * .866 - 210 And Y < J% * 360 *
                ↳   .866 + 30 Then
                    Circle ((I%) * 360 + 90, (J%) * 360 * .866 - 90), 120
                    iA(I%, J%) = -1
                    StartButton.enabled = -1
                  End If
                End If
              End If
            End If
          Next I%
        Next J%
      End If
    End If
    MousePointer = 0

End Sub

Sub StartButton_Click ()
    WorkBench.StopButton.enabled = -1
    WorkBench.ClearButton.enabled = 0
    WorkBench.StartButton.enabled = 0
    WorkBench.ClassOption.enabled = 0
    WorkBench.HexOption.enabled = 0
    If ClassOption.Value = -1 Then
        ClassCompute
    Else
        HexCompute
    End If
End Sub

Sub StopButton_Click ()

    StartButton.enabled = -1
    ClearButton.enabled = -1
    StopButton.enabled = 0   ClassOption.enabled = -1
    HexOption.enabled = -1
```

```
End Sub

Sub ClassCompute ()
  On Error GoTo ClassComputeHandler
  GenCount% = 0
  MainForm.Label2.Caption = Str$(GenCount%)
  Do While WorkBench.StopButton.enabled = -1
    Population% = 0
    For J% = 1 To 16
    np% = DoEvents()
    If WorkBench.StopButton.enabled = 0 Then Exit Do
    MainForm.Label1.Caption = Str$(J%)
      For I% = 1 To 16
        If MainForm.Friendlier.Value = -1 Then np% = DoEvents()
        Sum% = 0
        If iA(I% - 1, J% - 1) = -1 Then Sum% = Sum% + 1
        If iA(I% - 1, J%) = -1 Then Sum% = Sum% + 1
        If iA(I% - 1, J% + 1) = -1 Then Sum% = Sum% + 1
        If iA(I%, J% - 1) = -1 Then Sum% = Sum% + 1
        If iA(I%, J% + 1) = -1 Then Sum% = Sum% + 1
        If iA(I% + 1, J% - 1) = -1 Then Sum% = Sum% + 1
        If iA(I% + 1, J%) = -1 Then Sum% = Sum% + 1
        If iA(I% + 1, J% + 1) = -1 Then Sum% = Sum% + 1

        iB(I%, J%) = 0
        If Rule1 = -1 And Sum% = 1 And iA(I%, J%) = -1
            Then iB(I%, J%) = -1
        If Rule2 = -1 And Sum% = 1 And iA(I%, J%) = 0
            Then iB(I%, J%) = -1
        If Rule3 = -1 And Sum% = 2 And iA(I%, J%) = -1
            Then iB(I%, J%) = -1
        If Rule4 = -1 And Sum% = 2 And iA(I%, J%) = 0
            Then iB(I%, J%) = -1
        If Rule5 = -1 And Sum% = 3 And iA(I%, J%) = -1
            Then iB(I%, J%) = -1
        If Rule6 = -1 And Sum% = 3 And iA(I%, J%) = 0
            Then iB(I%, J%) = -1
        If Rule7 = -1 And Sum% = 4 And iA(I%, J%) = -1
            Then iB(I%, J%) = -1
        If Rule8 = -1 And Sum% = 4 And iA(I%, J%) = 0
            Then iB(I%, J%) = -1

        If iB(I%, J%) = -1 Then
          Line ((I% - 1) * 360 + 600, (J% - 1) * 360 + 120)-((I% - 1)
            * 360 + 840, (J% - 1) * 360 + 360), , BF
```

continues

```
        Population% = Population% + 1
      Else
        Line ((I% - 1) * 360 + 600, (J% - 1) * 360 + 120)-((I% - 1)
↳           * 360 + 840, (J% - 1) * 360 + 360), QBColor(15), BF
        Line ((I% - 1) * 360 + 600, (J% - 1) * 360 + 120)-((I% - 1)
↳           * 360 + 840, (J% - 1) * 360 + 360), , B
      End If
    Next I%
  Next J%
  GenCount% = GenCount% + 1
  MainForm.Label2.Caption = Str$(GenCount%)
  MainForm.Label3.Caption = Str$(Population%)

  Population% = 0
  For J% = 1 To 16
    If WorkBench.StopButton.enabled = 0 Then Exit Do
    np% = DoEvents()
    MainForm.Label1.Caption = Str$(J%)
    For I% = 1 To 16
      If MainForm.Friendlier.Value = -1 Then np% = DoEvents()
      Sum% = 0
      If iB(I% - 1, J% - 1) = -1 Then Sum% = Sum% + 1
      If iB(I% - 1, J%) = -1 Then Sum% = Sum% + 1
      If iB(I% - 1, J% + 1) = -1 Then Sum% = Sum% + 1
      If iB(I%, J% - 1) = -1 Then Sum% = Sum% + 1
      If iB(I%, J% + 1) = -1 Then Sum% = Sum% + 1
      If iB(I% + 1, J% - 1) = -1 Then Sum% = Sum% + 1
      If iB(I% + 1, J%) = -1 Then Sum% = Sum% + 1
      If iB(I% + 1, J% + 1) = -1 Then Sum% = Sum% + 1
      If Sum% < 2 Then iA(I%, J%) = 0
      If Sum% > 3 Then iA(I%, J%) = 0
      If Sum% = 2 And iB(I%, J%) = -1 Then iA(I%, J%) = -1
      If Sum% = 3 Then iA(I%, J%) = -1

      iA(I%, J%) = 0
      If Rule1 = -1 And Sum% = 1 And iB(I%, J%) = -1
↳        Then iA(I%, J%) = -1
      If Rule2 = -1 And Sum% = 1 And iB(I%, J%) = 0
↳        Then iA(I%, J%) = -1
      If Rule3 = -1 And Sum% = 2 And iB(I%, J%) = -1
↳        Then iA(I%, J%) = -1
      If Rule4 = -1 And Sum% = 2 And iB(I%, J%) = 0
↳        Then iA(I%, J%) = -1
      If Rule5 = -1 And Sum% = 3 And iB(I%, J%) = -1
↳        Then iA(I%, J%) = -1
```

Chapter 13: Life Workshop

```
      If Rule6 = -1 And Sum% = 3 And iB(I%, J%) = 0
          Then iA(I%, J%) = -1
      If Rule7 = -1 And Sum% = 4 And iB(I%, J%) = -1
          Then iA(I%, J%) = -1
      If Rule8 = -1 And Sum% = 4 And iB(I%, J%) = 0
          Then iA(I%, J%) = -1

        If iA(I%, J%) = -1 Then
          Line ((I% - 1) * 360 + 600, (J% - 1) * 360 + 120)-((I% - 1)
             * 360 + 840, (J% - 1) * 360 + 360), , BF
          Population% = Population% + 1
        Else
          Line ((I% - 1) * 360 + 600, (J% - 1) * 360 + 120)-((I% - 1)
             * 360 + 840, (J% - 1) * 360 + 360), QBColor(15), BF
          Line ((I% - 1) * 360 + 600, (J% - 1) * 360 + 120)-((I% - 1)
             * 360 + 840, (J% - 1) * 360 + 360), , B
        End If
      Next I%
    Next J%    GenCount% = GenCount% + 1
    MainForm.Label2.Caption = Str$(GenCount%)
    MainForm.Label3.Caption = Str$(Population%)
  Loop
  Exit Sub

ClassComputeHandler:
  MsgBox "Error in ClassCompute " + Str$(Err)
  Resume Next

End Sub

Sub HexCompute ()
  On Error GoTo HexCompHandler
  GenCount% = 0
  MainForm.Label2.Caption = Str$(GenCount%)
  Do While WorkBench.StopButton.enabled = -1
    Population% = 0
    For J% = 1 To 19
      np% = DoEvents()
      If WorkBench.StopButton.enabled = 0 Then Exit Do
      MainForm.Label1.Caption = Str$(J%)
      For I% = 1 To 19
        If MainForm.Friendlier.Value = -1 Then np% = DoEvents()
        Sum% = 0

        If Int(J% / 2) <> J% / 2 Then
          If iA(I% + 1, J% - 1) = -1 Then Sum% = Sum% + 1
```

continues

```
      If iA(I% + 1, J% + 1) = -1 Then Sum% = Sum% + 1
   Else
      If iA(I% - 1, J% - 1) = -1 Then Sum% = Sum% + 1
      If iA(I% - 1, J% + 1) = -1 Then Sum% = Sum% + 1
   End If

   If iA(I% - 1, J%) = -1 Then Sum% = Sum% + 1
   If iA(I%, J% - 1) = -1 Then Sum% = Sum% + 1
   If iA(I%, J% + 1) = -1 Then Sum% = Sum% + 1
   If iA(I% + 1, J%) = -1 Then Sum% = Sum% + 1

   iB(I%, J%) = 0
   If Rule9 = -1 And Sum% = 1 And iA(I%, J%) = -1
      Then iB(I%, J%) = -1
   If Rule10 = -1 And Sum% = 1 And iA(I%, J%) = 0
      Then iB(I%, J%) = -1
   If Rule11 = -1 And Sum% = 2 And iA(I%, J%) = -1
      Then iB(I%, J%) = -1
   If Rule12 = -1 And Sum% = 2 And iA(I%, J%) = 0
      Then iB(I%, J%) = -1
   If Rule13 = -1 And Sum% = 3 And iA(I%, J%) = -1
      Then iB(I%, J%) = -1
   If Rule14 = -1 And Sum% = 3 And iA(I%, J%) = 0
      Then iB(I%, J%) = -1
   If Rule15 = -1 And Sum% = 4 And iA(I%, J%) = -1
      Then iB(I%, J%) = -1
   If Rule16 = -1 And Sum% = 4 And iA(I%, J%) = 0
      Then iB(I%, J%) = -1

   Slope% = Int(J% / 2)
   If J% / 2 = Int(J% / 2) Then
     UpperLeft% = (6 - (Slope%))
     UpperRight% = (14 + Slope%)
     LowerLeft% = (Slope% - 4)
     LowerRight% = (24 - Slope%)
   Else
     UpperLeft% = (5 - (Slope%))
     UpperRight% = (14 + Slope%)
     LowerLeft% = (Slope% - 4)
     LowerRight% = (23 - Slope%)
   End If
   If I% >= UpperLeft% And I% <= UpperRight% And I% >=
      LowerLeft% And I% <= LowerRight% Then
     If J% / 2 = Int(J% / 2) Then
       If iB(I%, J%) = -1 Then
         Population% = Population% + 1
```

```
            FillColor = QBColor(0)
            Circle ((I%) * 360 - 90, (J%) * 360 * .866 - 90), 120,
                QBColor(0)
          Else
            FillColor = QBColor(15)
            Circle ((I%) * 360 - 90, (J%) * 360 * .866 - 90), 120,
                QBColor(0)
          End If
        Else
          If iB(I%, J%) = -1 Then
            Population% = Population% + 1
            FillColor = QBColor(0)
            Circle ((I%) * 360 + 90, (J%) * 360 * .866 - 90), 120,
                QBColor(0)
          Else
            FillColor = QBColor(15)
            Circle ((I%) * 360 + 90, (J%) * 360 * .866 - 90), 120,
                QBColor(0)
          End If
        End If
      Else
        iB(I%, J%) = 0
      End If
    Next I%
  Next J%

  GenCount% = GenCount% + 1
  MainForm.Label2.Caption = Str$(GenCount%)
  MainForm.Label3.Caption = Str$(Population%)

  Population% = 0
  For J% = 1 To 19
  If WorkBench.StopButton.enabled = 0 Then Exit Do
  MainForm.Label1.Caption = Str$(J%)
  np% = DoEvents()
    For I% = 1 To 19
      If MainForm.Friendlier.Value = -1 Then np% = DoEvents()
      Sum% = 0

      If Int(J% / 2) <> J% / 2 Then
        If iB(I% + 1, J% - 1) = -1 Then Sum% = Sum% + 1
        If iB(I% + 1, J% + 1) = -1 Then Sum% = Sum% + 1
      Else
        If iB(I% - 1, J% - 1) = -1 Then Sum% = Sum% + 1
        If iB(I% - 1, J% + 1) = -1 Then Sum% = Sum% + 1
      End If
```

continues

Chapter 13: Life Workshop

```
      If iB(I% - 1, J%) = -1 Then Sum% = Sum% + 1
      If iB(I%, J% - 1) = -1 Then Sum% = Sum% + 1
      If iB(I%, J% + 1) = -1 Then Sum% = Sum% + 1
      If iB(I% + 1, J%) = -1 Then Sum% = Sum% + 1

      iA(I%, J%) = 0
      If Rule9 = -1 And Sum% = 1 And iB(I%, J%) = -1
         Then iA(I%, J%) = -1
      If Rule10 = -1 And Sum% = 1 And iB(I%, J%) = 0
         Then iA(I%, J%) = -1
      If Rule11 = -1 And Sum% = 2 And iB(I%, J%) = -1
         Then iA(I%, J%) = -1
      If Rule12 = -1 And Sum% = 2 And iB(I%, J%) = 0
         Then iA(I%, J%) = -1
      If Rule13 = -1 And Sum% = 3 And iB(I%, J%) = -1
         Then iA(I%, J%) = -1
      If Rule14 = -1 And Sum% = 3 And iB(I%, J%) = 0
         Then iA(I%, J%) = -1
      If Rule15 = -1 And Sum% = 4 And iB(I%, J%) = -1
         Then iA(I%, J%) = -1
      If Rule16 = -1 And Sum% = 4 And iB(I%, J%) = 0
         Then iA(I%, J%) = -1

   Slope% = Int(J% / 2)
   If J% / 2 = Int(J% / 2) Then
     UpperLeft% = (6 - (Slope%))
     UpperRight% = (14 + Slope%)
     LowerLeft% = (Slope% - 4)
     LowerRight% = (24 - Slope%)
   Else
     UpperLeft% = (5 - (Slope%))
     UpperRight% = (14 + Slope%)
     LowerLeft% = (Slope% - 4)
     LowerRight% = (23 - Slope%)
   End If
   If I% >= UpperLeft% And I% <= UpperRight% And I% >=
      LowerLeft% And I% <= LowerRight% Then
     If J% / 2 = Int(J% / 2) Then
       If iA(I%, J%) = -1 Then
         Population% = Population% + 1
         FillColor = QBColor(0)
         Circle ((I%) * 360 - 90, (J%) * 360 * .866 - 90), 120,
            QBColor(0)
       Else
         FillColor = QBColor(15)
```

```
              Circle ((I%) * 360 - 90, (J%) * 360 * .866 - 90), 120,
                 QBColor(0)
            End If
          Else
            If iA(I%, J%) = -1 Then
              Population% = Population% + 1
              FillColor = QBColor(0)
              Circle ((I%) * 360 + 90, (J%) * 360 * .866 - 90), 120,
                 QBColor(0)
            Else
              FillColor = QBColor(15)
              Circle ((I%) * 360 + 90, (J%) * 360 * .866 - 90), 120,
                 QBColor(0)
            End If
          End If
        Else
          iA(I%, J%) = 0
        End If
      Next I%
    Next J%

    GenCount% = GenCount% + 1
    MainForm.Label2.Caption = Str$(GenCount%)
    MainForm.Label3.Caption = Str$(Population%)

  Loop
  FillColor = QBColor(0)
  Exit Sub

HexCompHandler:
  MsgBox "Error in HexCompute " + Str$(Err)
  Resume Next

End Sub

Sub ClearButton_Click ()
  MainForm.Label1.Caption = " 0"
  MainForm.Label2.Caption = " 0"
  MainForm.Label3.Caption = " 0"
  StartButton.enabled = 0
  ClearButton.enabled = 0
  FillStyle = 1
  If HexOption.Value = -1 Then
    PaintHex
  Else
    PaintClassic
```

continues

Chapter 13: Life Workshop

```
    End If
End Sub

Sub Form_Resize ()
  Command1.SetFocus
End Sub

Sub Command1_Click ()
  Hide
End Sub

Sub List1_Click ()
  Msg0$ = "'Classic Life' is a cellular automata 'game' invented
    by mathematics professor"
  Msg0$ = Msg0$ + " John H. Conway in 1970 and described
    by A. K. Dewdney in"
  Msg0$ = Msg0$ + " Scientific American magazine's Computer
    Recreations column in several"
  Msg0$ = Msg0$ + " issues in the 1980s. Each cell in the two
    dimensional Cartesian matrix"
  Msg0$ = Msg0$ + " has eight neighbor cells. The life state
    (live or dead) of any cell in the next"
  Msg0$ = Msg0$ + " generation is determined by the number of
    living neighbors in the current"
  Msg0$ = Msg0$ + " generation. This type of cellular automaton
    rule is called a summation rule"
  Msg0$ = Msg0$ + " because cell states are found by summing
    the neighbor states. Cellular"
  Msg0$ = Msg0$ + " automata are interesting, in part, because
    they demonstrate how highly complex"
  Msg0$ = Msg0$ + " systems can arise from fairly simple rules."

  Msg1$ = "Follow this example for a quick introduction to Life
    Workshop:" + Chr$(13) + Chr$(13)
  Msg1$ = Msg1$ + "1. Start Life Workshop by double clicking
    its icon in the program manager." + Chr$(13) + Chr$(13)
  Msg1$ = Msg1$ + "2. Click the 'Workbench' button." +
    Chr$(13) + Chr$(13)
  Msg1$ = Msg1$ + "3. Click the 'Hexagonal Grid' radio button." +
    Chr$(13) + Chr$(13)
  Msg1$ = Msg1$ + "4. Click a random assortment of grid
    cells, turning them on." + Chr$(13) + Chr$(13)
  Msg1$ = Msg1$ + "5. Click the 'Start' button and watch
    the cellular automata evolve." + Chr$(13) + Chr$(13)
  Msg1$ = Msg1$ + "6. After the generations have cycled for
    a while, click the 'Stop' button." + Chr$(13) + Chr$(13)
```

Chapter 13: Life Workshop

```
Msg1$ = Msg1$ + "7. Click the 'Classic Grid' radio button
    and repeat the steps for the 'Hexagonal Grid' (above)." +
    Chr$(13) + Chr$(13)
Msg1$ = Msg1$ + "8. Click the 'Exit Workbench' button." +
    Chr$(13) + Chr$(13)
Msg1$ = Msg1$ + "9. Click the 'Classic Life' button to
    watch life evolve on a large scale." + Chr$(13) + Chr$(13)
Msg1$ = Msg1$ + "10. While you are watching you can change
    the rules of the game by"
Msg1$ = Msg1$ + " clicking on the 'Options' button." +
    Chr$(13) + Chr$(13)
Msg1$ = Msg1$ + "11. If you have real work to do, change
    multitasking to 'Less Piggish,'"
Msg1$ = Msg1$ + " minimize Life Workshop, do your real work,
    and then change back"
Msg1$ = Msg1$ + " 'Faster Life.'"
Msg2$ = "Clicking the 'Exit' button causes the Life Workshop
    program to completely terminate"
Msg2$ = Msg2$ + " immediately. So does clicking the 'Exit'
    option on the 'File' menu."

Msg3$ = "'Hexagonal Life' is similar to 'Classic Life'
    except that it plays on a hexagonal"
Msg3$ = Msg3$ + " grid. A hexagonal grid is also called an
    isogrid. In a hexagonal grid"
Msg3$ = Msg3$ + " each cell has only six neighbors, like a
    cell in a honeycomb. The hexagonal"
Msg3$ = Msg3$ + " grid is more regular than the Cartesian
    grid, and in some ways, is more"
Msg3$ = Msg3$ + " interesting. The inherent simplicity of
    the isogrid cell provides a"
Msg3$ = Msg3$ + " demonstration of the way complex systems can arise
    from very"
Msg3$ = Msg3$ + " simple rules which is more profound than
    that provided by 'Classic Life.'"
Msg3$ = Msg3$ + " Isogrid cellular automata also have
    potential application in computer"
Msg3$ = Msg3$ + " modeling."

Msg4$ = "Life Workshop computes the next generation life
    states by iteration. That is,"
Msg4$ = Msg4$ + " each row in the grid is looked at one by
    one. The number of the iteration"
Msg4$ = Msg4$ + " shows the progress of Life Workshop as it
    computes the next generation."
```

continues

Chapter 13: Life Workshop

```
Msg5$ = "The 'generation' number is the number of cycles of
    cellular evolution completed."

Msg6$ = "Microsoft Windows is a multitasking environment.
    You can set Life Workshop to be"
Msg6$ = Msg6$ + " very polite by clicking the 'Less Piggish'
    radio button. Life Workshop"
Msg6$ = Msg6$ + " will then relinquish control very
    frequently and allow you to run"
Msg6$ = Msg6$ + " other programs without degraded
    performance, but Life Workshop will run"
Msg6$ = Msg6$ + " quite slowly compared to when the 'Faster
    Life' option is selected. These"
Msg6$ = Msg6$ + " options can be changed at any time,
    depending on your needs."

Msg7$ = "The 'Options' button shows an options selection
    window. In this window, options"
Msg7$ = Msg7$ + " for game rules and initial random life
    sprinkling density can be set."
Msg7$ = Msg7$ + " The game rule options for Classic Life and
    Hexagonal Life are set"
Msg7$ = Msg7$ + " separately. Changing these rules from the
    defaults allows you to"
Msg7$ = Msg7$ + " experiment and see the way different rule
    sets affect evolution."
Msg7$ = Msg7$ + " The life density of the initial random
    sprinkling is set by clicking"
Msg7$ = Msg7$ + " the appropriate radio button. This one
    setting applies to both Classic"
Msg7$ = Msg7$ + " Life and Hexagonal Life. The options
    window must be closed by clicking"
Msg7$ = Msg7$ + " the 'Done' button before the new rules
    take effect."

Msg8$ = "The 'population' number gives a count of the
    living cells in the current generation."

Msg9$ = "The rules of the 'game' are changed from the
    'Options' window. Each cell in the"
Msg9$ = Msg9$ + " game has a number of cells which border
    it, called neighbors. An interior"
Msg9$ = Msg9$ + " cell in the classic grid has eight
    neighbors. A cell can be alive or dead."
Msg9$ = Msg9$ + " A cell cannot move. If a cell is dead,
    it can be 'born' in the next"
```

Chapter 13: Life Workshop

```
Msg9$ = Msg9$ + " generation if it has the 'right' number
    of living neighbors. If a cell is"
Msg9$ = Msg9$ + " alive, it will continue to live in the
    next generation if it has the"
Msg9$ = Msg9$ + " 'right' number of neighbors. You can
    change the numbers for 'life'"
Msg9$ = Msg9$ + " and 'birth.' Set these separately for the
    classic and hexagrids by using"
Msg9$ = Msg9$ + " the radio button selector in the 'Options'
    window. The default rules have"
Msg9$ = Msg9$ + " been selected to provide interesting
    cellular behavior. Other combinations"
Msg9$ = Msg9$ + " of rules will also lead to evolutionary
    complexity. You can experiment"
Msg9$ = Msg9$ + " to find sets of rules that you like."

Msg10$ = "The 'Stop' button halts execution of the current
    life process."
Msg10$ = Msg10$ + " Once stopped, this process cannot be
    restarted, except by starting from"
Msg10$ = Msg10$ + " an initial random sprinkling."

Msg11$ = "Life Workshop was originally written for high
    resolution monitors (800 x 600 pixels"
Msg11$ = Msg11$ + " or better). This version was adapted so
    that Life Workshop is fully"
Msg11$ = Msg11$ + " operational with regular VGA (640 x 480).
    Some of the windows will be"
Msg11$ = Msg11$ + " too large to see all of them at once,
    however."
Msg11$ = Msg11$ + " If you are using regular VGA, and"
Msg11$ = Msg11$ + " you want to move a tall 'Help' window
    up to finish reading it, for instance,"
Msg11$ = Msg11$ + " use the keyboard commands to move it.
    Type <ALT> <space bar>, followed by"
Msg11$ = Msg11$ + " M (for move). Then use the up arrow key
    to move the window up. Hit"
Msg11$ = Msg11$ + " <Enter> when you are done, and resume
    mouse control."

Msg12$ = "The 'Workbench' is a reduced size game grid window
    which allows you to specify"
Msg12$ = Msg12$ + " initial conditions by clicking on
    non-living cells to turn them 'on' to"
Msg12$ = Msg12$ + " the living state. In this way you can
    examine the evolution of particular"
```

continues

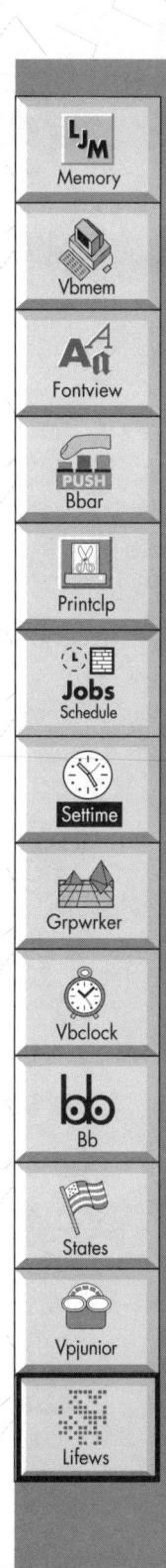

```
  Msg12$ = Msg12$ + " patterns in a faster, interactive mode.
     Execution of the automata can"
  Msg12$ = Msg12$ + " can be halted, modified, and restarted
     at any time. Changing the grid"
  Msg12$ = Msg12$ + " type by clicking on the appropriate
     radio button resets the grid."

    If List1.ListIndex = 0 Then MsgBox Msg0$, 0, "Life Workshop Help"
    If List1.ListIndex = 1 Then MsgBox Msg1$, 0, "Life Workshop Help"
    If List1.ListIndex = 2 Then MsgBox Msg2$, 0, "Life Workshop Help"
    If List1.ListIndex = 3 Then MsgBox Msg3$, 0, "Life Workshop Help"
    If List1.ListIndex = 4 Then MsgBox Msg4$, 0, "Life Workshop Help"
    If List1.ListIndex = 5 Then MsgBox Msg5$, 0, "Life Workshop Help"
    If List1.ListIndex = 6 Then MsgBox Msg6$, 0, "Life Workshop Help"
    If List1.ListIndex = 7 Then MsgBox Msg7$, 0, "Life Workshop Help"
    If List1.ListIndex = 8 Then MsgBox Msg8$, 0, "Life Workshop Help"
    If List1.ListIndex = 9 Then MsgBox Msg9$, 0, "Life Workshop Help"
    If List1.ListIndex = 10 Then MsgBox Msg10$, 0, "Life Workshop Help"
    If List1.ListIndex = 11 Then MsgBox Msg11$, 0, "Life Workshop Help"
    If List1.ListIndex = 12 Then MsgBox Msg12$, 0, "Life Workshop Help"

End Sub

Sub Command2_Click ()

End Sub

Sub Form_Load ()
   CurrentX = 120   CurrentY = 360
   FontSize = 12
   Print "Click index list item for help!"
   List1.AddItem "Classic Life"
   List1.AddItem "Example"
   List1.AddItem "Exit"
   List1.AddItem "Hexagonal Life"
   List1.AddItem "Iteration"
   List1.AddItem "Generation"
   List1.AddItem "Multitasking"
   List1.AddItem "Options"
   List1.AddItem "Population"
   List1.AddItem "Rules"
   List1.AddItem "Stop"
   List1.AddItem "VGA Users"
   List1.AddItem "Workbench"

End Sub
```

Chapter 13: Life Workshop

Conclusion

In this chapter, I have described the installation and operation of Life Workshop, and have given some background information on cellular automata. I have listed the source code and described the operation of the key subroutines. I wrote Life Workshop as a fun challenge, and have suggested some improvements to the software that readers may enjoy implementing on their own. I hope that you have as much fun with Life Workshop as I have had.

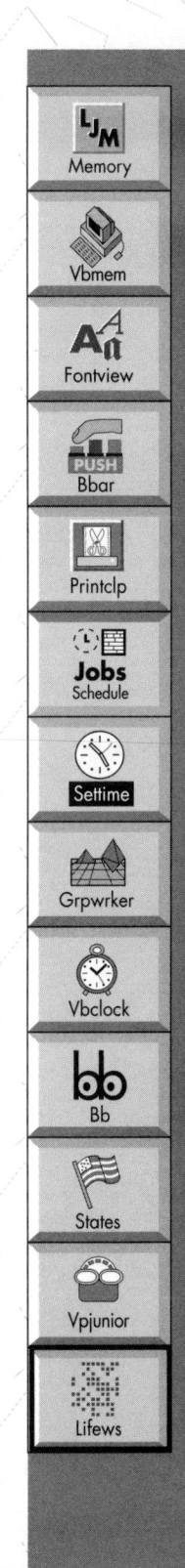

Chapter 13: Life Workshop

Index

Symbols

" " (null string), 56
80-column lines in text, 112

A

A_Icon_Click() subroutine, 95
About dialog box, 10, 60
    form controls, 34
    Memory Match, 33-35
accessing directories, 89-94
adding
    jobs to job list, 139-140
    screen fonts to list boxes, 48, 57
alarm intervals in VBClock utility, 204
AllowFormToMove variable, 204
API calls, 261
    GetFocus(), 267
    GetPrivateProfileString(), 261
    lclose(), 261
    OpenFile(), 261, 271-272
    SendMessage(), 261
    used by VBClock utility, 199-200
    ViewPoint, Jr., 265-266
    WritePrivateProfileString(), 266
Application Error message box, 181
application program interface, see API
applications
    disabling non-sequiturs/ crashes, 143
    proofing, 142-145
ArrangeBar( ) routine, 96
arrays
    controls, clearing, 14, 23
    strings, flag icons, 22

attributes, fonts
    Bold, 55, 59
    Italic, 54, 59
    Normal, 55, 60

B

BARCONFI.FRM ButtonBar module, 68, 84-89
BarConfig form, initializing, 84-86
BarDisplay() routine, 80-82
BBAR.BAS ButtonBar module, 68, 96-104
BBAR.BAS module, 96-104
BBARINT.BAS ButtonBar module, 68-70
beating high scores, 10
Blink Blank! utility, 227
    events, frmGetNewMessage, 239
    forms
        frmAbout, 233
        frmBB, 234-236
        frmBlank, 236-237
        frmDisplay, 237-238
        frmEnterMessage, 238
        frmLunchMessages, 239-240
        frmMessages, 241
        frmPassword, 241-242
        frmPrintReg, 242
        frmRegistration, 242-243
        frmWarning, 242
    Gang screen, 232
    global module, 233
    Hungarian notation, 232
    messages
        controlling display, 230
        custom, 227
        leaving, 229
        lunch, 228-229
        miscellaneous, 228
        retrieving, 230

Index

MODULE1.BAS routine, 243
Windows API functions, 231
.BMP files, 259-260, 272
Board form
   controls, 17-18
   creating, 17-28
Bold font attribute, 55, 59
boxes, *see* list boxes; text boxes
breaking text strings, 113-116
BROWSE.FRM ButtonBar
  module, 68, 89-94
BrowseBox
  form, 89-94
  subroutine, 92-94
BuildCommDCB routine, 152, 160
Button_Click() routine, 71-74
Button_DragDrop() routine, 82-83
Button_GotFocus() routine, 79
Button_KeyDown() subroutine, 83
BUTTON1 MEMORY.GBL variable, 16
BUTTONBA.FRM ButtonBar
  module, 68-83
ButtonBar Plus utility
  forms, 70-83
    BarConfig, 84-86
    BrowseBox, 89-94
    resizing, 97
  modules
    BARCONFI.FRM, 68, 84-89
    BBAR.BAS, 68, 96-104
    BBARINT.BAS, 68-70
    BROWSE.FRM, 68, 89-94
    BUTTONBA.FRM, 68-83
    ICONDISP.FRM, 68, 95
    LICENSE.FRM, 69, 104-105
    THREED.VBX, 69
  relocating, 81
  Windows 3.0, 67
buttons
  Command1, 157-158
  Command2, 157
  Command4, 162
  CommandDelete, 132
  CommandRun, 131
  locations, rearranging, 89
  relocating, 81
  Run, 131
  Set Options, 150
  versus menu entries, 158
  Workbench, 286, 294

C

calls, API, *see* API calls
CancelButton_Click() function, 93
CARD$ MEMORY.GBL variable, 16
CARDBACK$ MEMORY.GBL variable, 16
cells
  corner, 293
  living, initial patterns of, 287-289
  side, 293
cellular automata, 283-286, 292-298
ChangeDir() subroutine, 270
ChangeDrive() subroutine, 270
character mode programs, 292
characters, Chr$(0) null, 265
checking free memory, 41
  mode programs, 292
Chr$(0) null character, 265
ClassCompute() subroutine, 296-297
classic grid, 283, 286-289
classic life
  after eight generations, 291
  experiments, 287-289
  rules, 287
ClassicLife form, 297
ClassicSprinkle() subroutine, 297
CleanUp() procedure, 158-159
Clear_SystemMenu() routine, 83

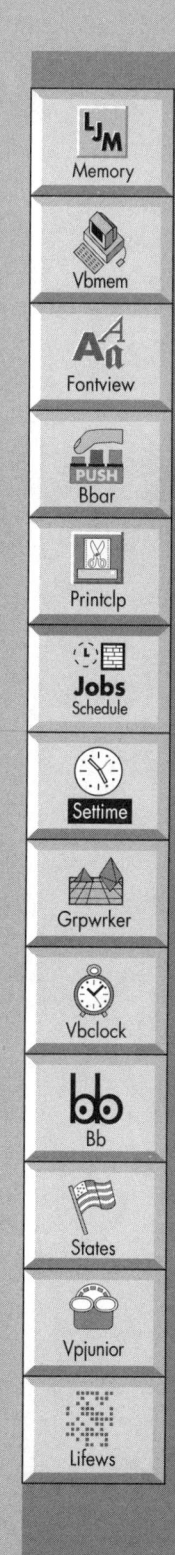

333

clearing
    control arrays, 23
    list boxes, 267
Clipboard text, 111-113
Clock form, 200
    floating on right side of active title bar, 200-201
    moving without title bar, 204
CloseComm() routine, 152
Code menu command, New Procedure, 22, 55
codes
    error checking, 261
    modular, 122
    source
        FontView, 58-63
        GLOBAL.BAS form, 183
        GroupWorker utility, 183-194
        HELPTXT.FRM, 192-193
        MAIN.FRM form, 183-188
        NAGBX.FRM form, 193-194
        PrintClip, 117
        SetTime utility, 164-174
        SETUP.FRM form, 188-192
        VBMem utility, 42-44
    Visual Basic utility
        FRM_Clock.FRM, 211-216
        FRM_Disp.FRM form, 217
        FRM_Opts.FRM form, 217-222
        Global Listing file, 209-211
        VBCLOCK.BAS form, 222-223
colors, choosing for VBCLOCK utility, 203
Command$ function, 182
command-line parameters, specifying, 137
Command1 routine, 157-158
Command1_Click() function, 29, 33
Command1_Click() routine, 84-86
Command1_KeyDown() subroutine, 88
Command2_Click() function, 33

Command2 routine, 157-161
Command3D1_Click() function, 95
Command4 routine, 162
CommandAdd_Click() subroutine, 139
CommandCancel_Click() subroutine, 139
CommandDelete control, 132, 143
CommandDelete_Click() subroutine, 143
CommandModify_Click() subroutine, 140-142
CommandOK_Click() subroutine, 138-139
CommandRun control, 131, 143
commands
    Code menu
        New Procedure, 22, 55
    File menu
        New Form, 28, 34
        New Project, 15
        Properties, 15
        Save File As..., 15
    Fonts menu
        Printer Fonts, 48
        Screen Fonts, 48
    Information menu
        About, 10
        High Scores, 10
    Terminal Edit menu
        Copy, 110
    Window menu
        Menu Design Window, 20
    Windows Control Edit menu
        Copy, 110
CommandStart_Click() subroutine, 144
communications APIs, 152-154
conflicts in programs, preventing, 144-145
constants
    IE_, 155
    WM_USER, 267

control arrays, clearing, 14, 22-23
Controller
   creating, View Point, Jr., 261-262
   `Form_Load()` procedure, 262
   text box, 271
   window, 259
controlling display Blink Blank!
   utility message, 230
controls, 14
   About form, 34
   CommandDelete, 143
   CommandModify, 142
   CommandRun, 143
   drawing for Modify Job form, 137
   file path, linking, 137-138
   High Scores form, 30
   HSENTRY form, 28
   List Box, 121
   ListJob, 125
   lstDirectories, 266-268
   main screen, drawing, 124-125
   Memory Match board form, 17-18
   minimizing use of in VBClock utility, 205-206
   TextBox, 137
   Timer, 121-123
      setting, 133-136
   timer in VBClock utility, 204
converting strings to structures, 127-129
Copy commands
   Terminal Edit menu, 110
   Windows Control Edit menu, 110
corner cells, 293
crashes, preventing, 142-143
creating
   About form in Memory Match, 34-35
   Board form, 17-28

forms
   PrintClip, 110-111
   menu structure, 262
   View Point, Jr., Controller, 261-262
custom messages (Blink Blank!), 227
customizing clock display
   (VBClock utility), 205

D

data
   control block (DCB), 152-154
   loss, preventing, 143-144
   retrieving from system, 41-44
dates, displaying, 123
Day of Week list box, 137
DblClick event, 267
declaring VBMem variables, 41
default
   classic life rules, 287
   hexagonal grid rules, 289
   text, 56
defdir, 182
defining strings, 115
deleting jobs from job list, 132
designing utilities, 121-122
determining string length, 115
device-independent bitmaps, *see* .DIB files
dialog boxes
   About, 10, 33-35
   Display Options, 230
   file open, 261-262
   Lunch Messages, 229
   VBClock Options, 197, 198
.DIB files, 259-260, 272
`DirBox_Change()` subroutine, 90
`DirBox_KeyDown()` subroutine, 93
directories
   accessing, 89-94
   filling list boxes, 259, 266-268
   Windows, 265

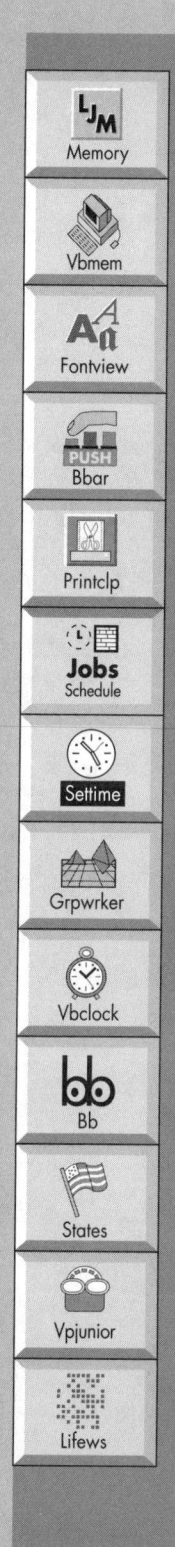

DirJob_Change() subroutine, 137
disabling controls
   CommandDelete, 143
   CommandModify, 142
   CommandRun, 143
DispInfo global array, 143
Display Options dialog box, 230
DisplayFace() function, 60
DisplayFace procedure, 55
DisplayInfo routine, 200-201
displaying
   About Box, 60
   embedded icons, 95
   fonts, 60
   memory in real time, 39
   messages, controlling (Blink Blank! utility), 230
displaying dates and times, 123
DISPLAYSCORES procedure, 31
.DLL files, 283
doo-dads, 232
drawing controls for Modify Job form, 137
DriveBox_Change() subroutine, 90
DriveBox_KeyDown() subroutine, 94
DriveJob_Change() subroutine, 137
drives filling list boxes with, 266-268
dynamic data exchange (DDE), 122
dynamic link libraries, VBRUN100.DLL, 283

E

editing ViewPoint, Jr. graphic files, 259
editors
   graphics, 261
   launching, 261

embedded icons
   displaying, 95
   extracting, 103
enhanced Windows operating mode, 39
Entry_GotFocus() subroutine, 87
Entry_KeyDown() subroutine, 89
Entry_LostFocus() subroutine, 87
errors
   codes, checking, 261
   handling in GroupWorker utility, 180
EvalTextEntered() function, 270-271
events
   DblClick, 267
   Form_MouseDown(), 204
   Form_MouseMove(), 204
   Form_MouseUp(), 204
   GotFocus, 265
   Load, 111
   MainForm
      form resize, 294
      load, 294
   MouseDown(), 295-296
   Resize, 111-116
   StartButton_Click(), 296
   WorkBenchButton_Click(), 295-297
   see also procedures
evolution, 288, 290
   in hexagonal grid microcosm, 291
   of two-dimensional life, 291-292
   process, 287
experiments, macrocosmic, 291-292
ExtFloodFill() function, 249-250
extracting embedded icons, 103
Extractor routine, 103

F

Faster Life, 292
fields, Pgm_Status, 155, 159
File menu
   commands
      New Form, 28, 34
      New Project, 15
      Properties, 15
      Save File As..., 15
   GroupWorker utility, 181
`FileBox_Click()` subroutine, 90
`FileBox_DblClick()` subroutine, 91
`FileBox_KeyDown()` subroutine, 93
`FileBox_PathChange()` subroutine, 91
files
  .BMP, 259-260, 272
  .DIB, 259-260, 272
  .DLL, 283
  Global Listing, Visual Basic code, 209-211
  GLOBAL.BAS, constants defined, 250
  .ICO, 260
  job list
    loading, 145
    saving, 145
  LIFEWS.EXE, 283
  LIFEWS5.MAK, loading, 294
  manipulating, 260
  open dialog box, 261-262
  OPTFORM.FRM, 166-168
  path controls, linking, 137
  private profile (.INI), 149
  .RLE, 259-280
  SETTIME.BAS, 164-166
  SETTIME.FRM, 168-173
  SETTIME.INI, 173-174
  specification display label (lblPattern), 269-272
  VBCLOCK.INI, 202
  viewer, graphics, 259-261
  VPJUNIOR.INI, 261, 265
  .WMF, 260
filFiles file list box, 269-272
filling list boxes with drives and directories, 266-268
flag icons, placing in string arrays, 22
`FLAG$` MEMORY.GBL variable, 16
floating `Clock` form on side of active title bar, 200-201
`FlushComm()`
   functions, 159
   routine, 154
fonts
   attributes
      Bold, 55, 59
      Italic, 54, 59
      Normal, 55, 60
   choosing for VBCLOCK utility, 203
   displaying, 60
   modifying, 48
   printer, 48
   raster, 48
   screen, 48
   sending to printer, 56-57, 61
   TrueType, 47-48
   viewing, 47
Fonts menu commands, 52
   Printer Fonts, 48
   Screen Fonts, 48
FontView utility, 47-63
   commands
      Printer Fonts, 48
      Screen Fonts, 48
   screen, 49-50
   source code, 58-63
`Form_KeyDown()` subroutine, 88, 93
`Form_Load()` routine, 22, 31, 35, 41, 43, 53, 58-59, 74-83, 86-89, 91, 95, 104, 111, 130-131, 156-157, 162, 204

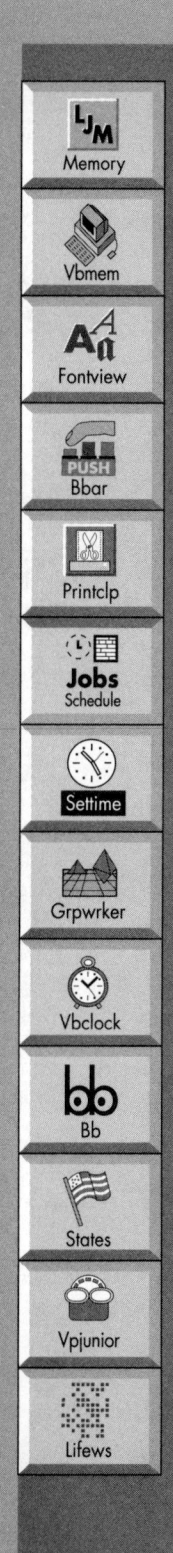

Form_MouseDown() event, 204
Form_MouseMove()
  event, 204
  subroutine, 78
Form_MouseMove routine, 78-79
Form_MouseUp() event, 204
Form_Paint() routine, 54, 59,
  76-77, 92, 95, 105
Form_Resize() routine, 42, 44,
  54, 59, 77, 88, 117
Form_Unload() routine, 144
formats, graphic file, 272-274
FormJobList form, 124
forms
  BarConfig, 84-86
  BrowseBox, 89-94
  ButtonBar Plus
    License, 104-105
    resizing, 70-83, 97
  ClassicLife, 297
  Clock, 200
    floating on right side of
      active title bar, 200-201
    moving without title bar, 204
  declarations/events
    frmAbout, 233
    frmBB, 234-236
    frmBlank, 236-237
    frmDisplay, 237-238
    frmGetNewMessage, 239
    frmLunchMessages, 239-240
    frmMessages, 241
    frmPassword, 241-242
    frmPrintReg, 242
    frmRegistration, 242-243
    frmWarning, 242
  FormJobList, 124
  Memory Match
    About, 33-35
    Board, 17-28
    High Scores, 30-33
    HSENTRY, 28-29

VBMEM.FRM, 39
hiding, 139
main form for GroupWorker
  utility, 177
Main_Form, 249
MainForm, 294
modal, 29
Modify Job, 136
  drawing controls, 137
  linking file path controls, 137
Name the States program,
  248-249
OPTFORM.FRM, 158
OptionsForm, 294
PrintClip, 110-111
Setup, 179-180
source code
  GLOBAL.BAS, 183
  HELPTXT.FRM, 192-193
  MAIN.FRM, 183-188
  NAGBX.FRM, 193-194
  SETUP.FRM, 188-192
Startup, 180
unloading, 139
WorkBench, 295-297
Visual Basic code
  FRM_Clock.FRM, 211-216
  FRM_Disp.FRM, 217
  FRM_Opts.FRM, 217-222
  VBClock, 208-223
  VBCLOCK.BAS, 222-223
free memory, checking, 41
free system resources, 198
FreMem string, 41
FreRes string, 41
FRM_Clock.FRM form, 211-216
FRM_Disp.FRM form, 217
FRM_Opts.FRM form, 217-222
frmAbout form, 233
frmBB form, 234-236
frmBlank form, 236-237
frmDisplay form, 237-238

Index

frmEnterMessage, 238
frmGetNewMessage, 239
frmLunchMessages form, 239-240
frmMessages form, 241
frmPassword form, 241-242
frmPrintReg form, 242
frmRegistration form, 242-243
frmWarning form, 242
functions
   Command$, 182
   Command1_Click(), 29, 33
   Command2_Click(), 33
   DisplayFace(), 60
   EvalTextEntered(), 270, 271
   ExtFloodFill(), 249-250
   FlushComm(), 159
   Form_Load(), 22, 31, 35, 43, 58-59
   Form_Paint(), 59
   Form_Resize(), 44, 59
   GAME_Click(), 26-28
   GetActivewindow(), 261
   GetCommError(), 154-156
   GetFocus(), 261
   GetFormat(), 113
   GetFreeResources(), 80
   GetFreeSystemResources, 41
   GetInfo(), 202
   GetPrivateProfileInt(), 203
   GetPrivateProfileString(), 203
   GetText(), 113
   GetWindowsDirectory(), 202, 261, 265
   GetWinFlags(), 41
   HiWord&(), 80
   housekeeping, 262-265
   ICONRESET(), 23
   InStr, 129
   IsWindow(), 261
   JOKE_Click(), 26
   LoadPicture(), 260, 272-274
   LoWord&(), 80
   Lst_Face_Click(), 54, 59
   Lst_Size_Click(), 59
   M_DText_Click(), 60
   M_Exit_Click(), 60
   M_PFont_Click(), 62-63
   M_PrtLst_Click(), 61
   M_SFont_Click(), 62
   M_SText_Click(), 60
   Mid$, 125
   Mid$(), 115
   MsgBox, 33
   MSText_Click, 56
   Pic_Pc_Click(), 44
   picture-handling, 260
   Picture1_Click(), 60
   Rack, 127
   SendMessage(), 266-268
   SetSysModalWindow(), 231
   SETUP(), 22-23
   Shell(), 121, 123
   ShowCursor(), 231
   Static Sub MEMORY_Click(), 24-25
   StringFromINI(), 264
   system evaluation, 262-265
   TimeStr(), 162
   Tmr_Mem_Timer(), 43
   TrimZeroTerm(), 202
   txtCurrentFile_KeyPress(), 269
   Val(), 154
   WinDir$(), 263
   Windows API in Blink Blank! utility, 231
   WinHelp(), 231
   WritePrivateProfileString(), 261
   see also procedures; routines; subroutines; wrapper functions

G

game grids, Memory Match, 12
Game of Life, 283, 286, 292-293
`GAME_Click()` function, 26-28
`GAMEBOARD MEMORY.GBL` variable, 16
Games menu, 9
Gang screen (Blink Blank! utility), 232
`GetActivewindow()` function, 261
`GetBBarIni()` routine, 101-103
`GetCommError()` function, 154-156
`GetCommState()` routine, 152
`GetFocus()`
   API call, 267
   function, 261
`GetFormat()` function, 113
`GetFreeResources()` function, 80
`GetFreeSystemResources()` function, 41
`GetInfo()` function, 202
`GetMatix()` subroutine, 97
`GetMemory()` subroutine, 80
`GetPrivateProfileInt()` function, 203
`GetPrivateProfileInt()` routine, 154-156, 162
`GetPrivateProfileString()` routine, 154-156, 203, 261
`GetResource()` subroutine, 80
`GetText()` function, 113
`GetWindowsDirectory()` function, 202, 261, 265
`GetWinFlags()` function, 41
global
   arrays, `DispInfo`, 201
   constants
      `MaxItems`, 202
      `NumTypes`, 202
   modules, 15-16
      Blink Blank! utility, 233
      BBARINT.BAS, 69
   variables, scope, 138
Global Listing file, Visual Basic code, 209-211
GLOBAL.BAS
   file, constants defined, 250
   form souce code, 183
   module, 231
`Got_Line()` routine, 161
GotFocus event, 265
graphic files
   editing, ViewPoint, Jr., 259
   formats, reading, 272-274
graphics editor, 261
grids
   classic, 283, 286-289
   default, 289
   hexagonal, 283-285, 289
   patterns, 289
   rules, 289
GroupWorker utility, 177
   error handling, 180
   File menu, 181
   Help menu, 181
   initializing `Sub Form_Load()` program, 182
   main form, 177
   project window, 178
   Setup form, 179-180
   source code, 183-194
   Startup form, 180

H

handles of windows, 199
Help menu (GroupWorker utility), 181
help topics, 298
`Help_Click()` subroutine, 89

Index

HelpForm, selecting help topics, 298
HELPTXT.FRM form source code, 192-193
hexagonal
   grid, 283-285
      microcosm evolution, 291
      patterns, 289
      rules, 289
   life
      after eight generations, 292
      experiments, 289-291
HexCompute() subroutine, 296-297
hiding forms, 139
high scores
   beating, 10
   Memory Match, 9-10
   resetting, 33
   tying, 10
   viewing, 10
High Scores
   command (Information menu), 10
   form
      controls, 30
      Memory Match, 30-33
HiWord&() function, 80
HSENTRY form
   controls, 28
   Memory Match, 28-29
Hungarian notation (Blink Blank! utility), 232

I

.ICO files, 260, 272
icon files, *see* .ICO files
IconArrange_Click() subroutine, 89
IconArrange_Click routine, 89
ICONDISP.FRM ButtonBar module, 68, 95-105
IconDisplay routine, 95
ICONRESET() function, 23
icons
   embedded
      displaying, 95
      extracting, 103
   flag, placing, 22
   PrintClip, 110
IconSelect_Click() subroutine, 94
IE_ constants, 155
implementing Memory Match pull-down menu system, 13, 20
indexed help, 298
Information menu commands
   About, 10
   High Scores, 10
initial patterns of living cells, 287-289
Initialize() procedure, 251
initializing
   BarConfig form, 84-86
   programs, 74-76
input, keyboard, 83
InStr(x,y) string manipulation routine, 114
InStr() function, 129
intervals, job scheduling, 145
isogrid, 285
IsWindow() function, 261
Italic font attribute, 54, 59

J

jobs
   job lists
      adding to, 139-140
      deleting from, 132
      modifying in, 140-142
      processing, 133-136
      saving, 132-133
      unsaved changes, 145

modifying, 138-139
running, 131-132
scheduling intervals, 145
storing, 125
JobScheduler utility, 121
  drawing controls, 124-125, 137
  job lists
    adding, 139-140
    deleting jobs, 132
    processing, 133-136
    saving, 132-133
  linking file path controls, 137
  loading `ListJob` list box, 130-131
  Modify Job form, 136
    modifying jobs in job list, 140-142
    populating list boxes, 137
    preventing unloading form, 139
  proofing applications, 142
    conflicts in programs, preventing, 144-145
    data loss, preventing, 143-144
    disabling non-sequiturs, 143
  running jobs, 131-132
  `Shell()` function, 123
  storing jobs, 125
  structures
    converting strings, 127-129
    creating, 125-126, 138-139
  suggested ultility modifications, 145
  time and date serials, 123
  `Timer` control, 123
`JOKE_Click()` function, 26

K-L

keyboard input, 83
`KeyHandler()` routine, 83
launching
  editor, 261
  Microsoft Windows 3.1 programs, 67
`lblPattern` file specification display label, 269-272
`lclose()` API call, 261
leaving messages (Blink Blank!), 229
`Left$(x,y)` string manipulation routine, 114
`Len(x)` string manipulation routine, 114
length of strings, determining, 115
libraries, dynamic link, VBRUN100.DLL, 283
License forms, ButtonBar Plus, 104-105
LICENSE.FRM ButtonBar module, 69, 104-105
life experiments, classic, 287-291
life forms, simulated single-cell, 283-286
Life Options window, 289-291
Life Workshop utility, 283, 286-298
  cellular automata, 283-286
  minimizing, 292
  source code, 298-328
LIFEWS.EXE file, 283
LIFEWS5.MAK file, loading, 294
linking file path controls, 137
List Box control, 121
list boxes
  clearing, 267
  Day of Week, 137
  directory, 259, 266-268
  `filFiles` file, 269-272
  filling with drives and directories, 266-268
  `lstDirectories` drive/directory, 269-272
  populating, 137

Index

screen fonts, adding, 57
settings, 50
Time of Day, 137
Window Style, 137
list files, job
   loading, 145
   saving, 145
`ListJob`
   control, 125
   list box, loading, 130-131
`ListJob_Click()` subroutine, 143
Load events, PrintClip, 111
loading
   files, LIFEWS5.MAK, 294
   list files, job, 145
   `ListJob` list box, 130-131
   pictures into Viewer, 273-274
   PrintClip, 109
   Windows PIF Editor, 145
loading procedures, ViewPoint, Jr., 262-265
`LoadPicture()` function, 260, 272-274
loops, `While...Wend`, 114-115
loss of data, preventing, 143-144
`LoWord&()` function, 80
`Lst_Face_Click()` subroutine, 54, 59
`Lst_Size_Click()` subroutine, 59
`Lst_Size_Click` procedure, 54
`lstDirectories`
   control, 266-268
   drive/directory list box, 269-272
`lstDirectories_DblClick()` routine, 267
lunch messages (Blink Blank!), 228-229
Lunch Messages dialog box, 229

M

`M_DText_Click` routine, 56, 60
`M_Exit_Click` routine, 56, 60

`M_PFont_Click()` routine, 57, 62-63
`M_PrtLst_Click()` routine, 56, 61
`M_SFont_Click()` routine, 57, 62
`M_SText_Click()` routine, 60
macrocosmic
   experiments, 291-292
   mode, 291-292
main control form, indexed help, 298
main controls
   screen , drawing, 124-125
   window, 286-288, 294, 297
MAIN.FRM form source code, 183-188
`Main_Form` form, 249
`MainForm`
   edit window, 295
   form, 294
   form resize event procedure, 294
   load event procedure, 294
`Makegroup_click()` procedure, 180
manipulating files, 260
MATCHES MEMORY.GBL variable, 16
`MaxItems` global constants, 202
memory
   displaying, 39
   free, checking, 39-41
   statistics, 80
Memory Match utility, 9-36
   commands
      About, 10, 33-35
      Menu Design Window, 20
      New Form, 28
      New Project, 15
      Properties, 15
      Save File As..., 15
   forms
      About, 33-35
      Board, 17-28

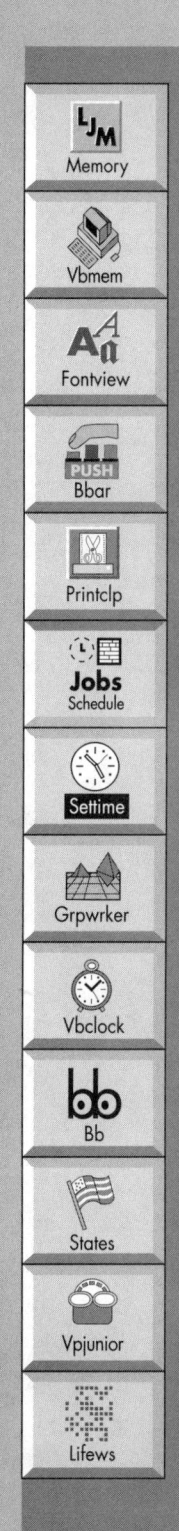

343

    High Scores, 30-33
    HSENTRY, 28-29
game grids, 12
high scores, 9-10
    beating, 10
    tying, 10
picture controls, 13-14
pull-down menu system,
    implementing, 13, 20
variables (MEMORY.GBL)
    BUTTON2, 16
    CARD$, 16
    CARDBACK$, 16
    FLAG$, 16
    GAMEBOARD, 16
    MATCHES, 16
    NUMFLAGS, 16
    PICKED, 16
    SCORERECORD, 16
    TRIES, 16
MEMORY_Click routine, 23
Menu Design Window (Window menu) command, 20
menus
    command buttons versus menu entries, 158
    File (GroupWorker utility), 181
    Fonts, 52
    Games, 9
    Help (GroupWorker utility), 181
    Information, 10
    pop-up (VBClock utility), 205
    structure, 262
    Text, 52
messages
    Blink Blank!
        controlling display, 230
        custom, 227
        leaving, 229
        lunch, 228-229
        miscellaneous, 228
        retrieving, 230

    boxes, Application Error, 181
metafiles, Windows, 274
Microsoft Windows 3.1 programs, launching, 67
Mid$() function, 115, 125
minimizing Life Workshop, 292
miscellaneous messages (Blink Blank!), 228
modal, 130
    forms, 29
    window, 288
modes, macrocosmic, 291-292
Modify Job form, 136
    drawing controls, 137
    linking file path controls, 137
modifying
    fonts, 48
    jobs in job list, 138-142
modular code, 122
MODULE1.BAS routines (Blink Blank! utility), 243
modules
    BBAR.BAS, 96-104
    ButtonBar
        BARCONFI.FRM, 68, 84-89
        BBAR.BAS, 68, 96-104
        BBARINT.BAS, 68, 69-70
        BROWSE.FRM, 68, 89-94
        BUTTONBA.FRM, 68, 70-83
        ICONDISP.FRM, 68, 95
        LICENSE.FRM, 69, 104-105
        THREED.VBX, 69
    global, 15-16
        BBARINT.BAS, 69
        Blink Blank! utility, 233
    GLOBAL.BAS, 231
    MEMORY.GBL global variables, 16
    OPTFORM.FRM, 156-158
    SETTIME.BAS, 151-156
    SETTIME.FRM, 158-163
    SETTIME.INI, 163-164

Index

mouse, positioning, 77-78
MouseDown() event procedure, 295-296
MousePointer property, 295
moving Clock form without title bar, 204
MsgBox function, 33
MSText_Click function, 56
multitasking, Less Piggish, 292

N

NAGBX.FRM form source code, 193-194
Name the States program, 247-248
    Autoredraw, 251
    controlling program flow, 251
    ExtFloodFill() function, 249-250
    forms and purposes, 248-249
    GLOBAL.BAS file, 250
    procedural operation, 251-256
    ScaleMode, 251
New commands
    Form (File menu), 28, 34
    Procedure (Code menu), 22, 55
    Project (File menu), 15
New High Score window, 10
Normal font attribute, 55, 60
null
    characters, Chr$(0), 265
    string (" "), 56
NUMFLAGS MEMORY.GBL variable, 16
NumTypes global constant, 202

O

OK_Click() subroutine, 88
OpenCom routine, 155
OpenComm routine, 152
OpenFile() API call, 261, 271-272

operating modes
    enhanced, 39
    standard, 39
Opt_Bold_Click() subroutine, 55, 59
Opt_Ital_Click() subroutine, 54, 59
Opt_Norm_Click() subroutine, 55, 60
OPTFORM.FRM
    file, 166-168
    form, 158
OPTFORM.FRM module, 156-158
options, Sub, 22
OptionsForm form, 294
organization, Life Workshop, 294
oscillating pattern, 291

P

Paintbrush, 261
PaintClassic() subroutine, 295
parameters, command-line, specifying, 137
passwords for retrieving messages in Blink Blank!, 230
patterns
    initial of living cells, 287-289
    oscillating, 291
Pgm_Status field, 155, 159
Pic_Pc_Click() function, 44
Pic_Pc_Click procedure, 42
PICKED MEMORY.GBL variable, 16
picture box, repainting, 54
picture controls, 13-14
picture-handling functions, 260
Picture1_Click() function, 55, 60
pictures, loading into Viewer, 273-274
placing flag icons in string arrays, 22

pop-up menu (VBClock utility), 205
positioning mouse, 77-78
preventing
    crashes, 142-143
    data loss, 143-144
    program conflicts, 144-145
PrintClip utility
    creating forms, 110-111
    events
        Load, 111
        Resize, 111-116
    icons, 110-112
    loading, 109
    source code, 117
    strings, defining, 115
printer fonts, 48, 56-57, 61
Printer Fonts (Fonts menu)
  command, 48
printing text strings, 109-117
`PrintLabel()` subroutine, 206
private profile (.INI) APIs, 149,
  154-155
procedures
    `CleanUp`, 158-159
    `Controller's Form_Load`, 262
    `DisplayFace`, 55
    `DISPLAYSCORES`, 31
    `Form_Load`, 41, 53, 162, 204
    `Form_Paint`, 54
    `Form_Resize`, 42, 54
    `GAME_Click`, 26
    `Initialize`, 251
    `Lst_Size_Click`, 54
    `M_DText_Click`, 56
    `M_Exit_Click`, 56
    `M_PFont_Click`, 57
    `M_PrtLst_Click`, 56
    `M_SFont_Click`, 57
    `Opt_Norm_Click`, 55
    `Pic_Pc_Click`, 42
    `Picture1_Click`, 55
    `Select_State()`, 253
    `ShowBar()`, 206-207

`Sub Makegroup_click()`, 180
`Sub WorkGroup_DblClick()`,
  180
`Tmr_Mem`, 41-42
see also events; functions;
  routines; subroutines
processing job list, 133-136
profile files, SETTIME.INI, 150
Program Manager, 283, 286
programs
    character mode, 292
    conflicts, preventing, 144-145
    globals, 155
    initializing, 74-76
    launching Microsoft Windows
      3.1, 67
    stabilizing, 142-145
    terminating, 56
    see also utilities
`ProgramSelect_Click()`
  subroutine, 94
Project Window
    OPTFORM.FRM module,
      156-158
    SETTIME.BASE module,
      151-156
    SETTIME.FRM module,
      158-163
    SETTIME.INI module, 163-164
proofing applications, disabling
  non-sequiturs/crashes, 142-145
properties, `MousePointer`, 295
Properties (File menu) command,
  15
pull-down menu system,
  implementing in Memory
  Match, 13, 20

R

Rack function, 127
raster font, 48
`ReadComm()` routine, 152-154

Index

reading graphic file formats, 272-274
real time memory display, 39
rearranging button locations, 89
relocating buttons, 81
repainting picture box, 54
resetting high scores, 33
Resize events, PrintClip, 110-116
resizing ButtonBar form, 97
resources, free, 39
retrieving
    Clipboard text, 112-113
    data from system, 41-44
    messages (Blink Blank!), 230
Right$(x,y) string manipulation routine, 114
.RLE files, 259-280
routines
    ArrangeBar, 96
    BarDisplay, 80-82
    BuildCommDCB, 152, 160
    Button_Click, 71-74
    Button_DragDrop, 82-83
    Button_GotFocus, 79
    Clear_SystemMenu, 83
    CloseComm, 152
    Command1, 157-158
    Command1_Click, 84-86
    Command2, 157-161
    Command4, 162
    DisplayInfo, 200-201
    Extractor, 103
    FlushComm, 154
    Form_Load, 31, 74-83, 86-89, 156-157, 162
    Form_MouseMove, 78-79
    Form_Paint, 76-77
    Form_Resize, 77
    GetBBarIni, 101-103
    GetCommState, 152
    GetMatix, 97
    GetPrivateProfileInt, 154-156, 162
    GetPrivateProfileString, 154-156
    Got_Line, 161
    IconArrange_Click, 89
    IconDisplay, 95
    KeyHandler, 83
    lstDirectories_DblClick(), 267
    MEMORY_Click, 23
    MODULE1.BAS (Blink Blank! utility), 243
    OpenCom, 155
    OpenComm, 152
    ReadComm, 152-154
    SetCommState(), 152-154
    ShadowEffects, 103-104
    string manipulation
        InStr(x,y), 114
        Left$(x,y), 114
        Len(x), 114
        Right$(x,y), 114
    Timer1_Timer, 77-78
    Timer2_Timer, 79
    WriteComm(), 152-154
    WriteDefaultIni, 97-101
    WritePrivateProfileString(), 154, 158
    see also functions; procedures; subroutines
rules, default classic life, 287
Run button, 131
run length encoded files, *see* .RLE files
running jobs, 131-132

S

Save File As... (File menu) command, 15
SaveJobList() subroutine, 143
saving
    job lists, 132-133
    list files, 145

scheduling jobs, intervals, 145
scope, global variables, 138
SCORERECORD MEMORY.GBL
  variable, 16
screen fonts, adding to list boxes,
  48, 57
Screen Fonts (Fonts menu)
  command, 48
screens
  FontView, 49-50
  Gang (Blink Blank! utility), 232
screensaver, see Blink Blank!
Select_State() procedure, 253
SelectButton_Click()
  subroutine, 92
SelectButton_KeyDown()
  subroutine, 93
sending fonts to printer, 56-57, 61
SendMessage()
  API call, 261
  function, 266-268
Set Options button, 150
SetCommState() routine, 152-154
SetSysModalWindow() function,
  231
SetTime utility, source code, 149,
  164-174
SETTIME.BAS
  file, 164-166
  module, 151-156
SETTIME.FRM
  file, 168-173
  module, 158-163
SETTIME.INI
  file, 173-174
  module, 163-164
  profile file, 150
settings, list boxes, 50
Setup form, 179-180
SETUP() function, 22-23
SETUP.FRM form, source code,
  188-192
ShadowEffect() subroutine, 104

ShadowEffects routine, 103-104
Shell() function, 121-123
ShowBar() procedure, 206-207
ShowCursor() function, 231
side cells, 293
single-cell life forms, simulated,
  283-286
source code listings
  FontView, 58-63
  GLOBAL.BAS form, 183
  GroupWorker utility, 183-194
  HELPTXT.FRM, 192-193
  Life Workshop, 298-328
  MAIN.FRM form, 183-188
  NAGBX.FRM form, 193-194
  PrintClip, 117
  SetTime program, 164-174
  SETUP.FRM form, 188-192
  VBMem, 42-44
specifying command-line
  parameters, 137
stabilizing programs, 142-145
standard Windows operating
  mode, 39
StartButton_Click() event
  procedure, 296
starting
  evolution process, 287
  Life Workshop utility, 286
startup events, 294
Startup form, 180
statements, LoadPicture(), 260
states, cellular automata, 286
Static Sub MEMORY_Click()
  function, 24-25
storing jobs, 125
string arrays, flag icons, placing, 22
StringFromINI()
  function, 264
  wrapper function, 265
strings
  defining, 115
  FreMem, 41

Index

FreRes, 41
  length, determining, 115
  Temp$, 265
  text
    breaking, 113-116
    printing, 113-116
StringToINI() wrapper function, 266
structures, converting to strings, 125-129
Sub option, 22
subroutines
  A_Icon_Click(), 95
  ArrangeBar(), 96
  BarDisplay(), 80-82
  BrowseBox, 92-94
  Button_Click(), 71-74
  Button_DragDrop(), 82
  Button_GotFocus(), 79
  Button_KeyDown(), 83
  CancelButton_Click(), 93
  ChangeDir(), 270
  ChangeDrive(), 270
  ClassCompute(), 296-297
  ClassicSprinkle(), 297
  Clear_SystemMenu(), 83
  Command1_Click(), 84
  Command1_KeyDown(), 88
  Command3D1_Click(), 95
  CommandAdd_Click(), 139
  CommandCancel_Click(), 139
  CommandDelete_Click(), 143
  CommandModify_Click(), 140
  CommandOK_Click(), 138, 139
  CommandStart_Click(), 144
  DirBox_Change(), 90
  DirBox_KeyDown(), 93
  DirJob_Change(), 137
  DriveBox_Change(), 90
  DriveBox_KeyDown(), 94
  DriveJob_Change(), 137
  Entry_GotFocus(), 87
  Entry_KeyDown(), 89
  Entry_LostFocus(), 87
  FileBox_Click(), 90
  FileBox_DblClick(), 91
  FileBox_KeyDown(), 93
  FileBox_PathChange(), 91
  Form_KeyDown(), 88
  Form_KeyDown(), 93
  Form_Load(), 75, 86, 91, 95, 104, 111, 130-131, 137-138
  Form_MouseMove(), 78
  Form_Paint(), 77, 92, 95, 105
  Form_Resize(), 77, 88, 117
  Form_Unload(), 144
  GetBBarIni(), 101-103
  GetMatix(), 97
  GetMemory(), 80
  GetResource(), 80
  Help_Click(), 89
  HexCompute(), 296-297
  IconArrange_Click(), 89
  IconSelect_Click(), 94
  KeyHandler(), 83
  ListJob_Click(), 143
  OK_Click(), 88
  PaintClassic(), 295
  PrintLabel(), 206
  ProgramSelect_Click(), 94
  SaveJobList(), 143
  SelectButton_Click(), 92
  SelectButton_KeyDown(), 93
  ShadowEffect(), 104
  Timer1_Timer(), 78
  Timer2_Timer(), 79
  User_Setup_Click(), 87-88
  WriteDefaultIni(), 97-101
  see also functions; procedures; routines
summation rules, 285
system evaluation functions, ViewPoint, Jr., loading procedures, 262-265

T

`Temp$` string, 265
Terminal Edit menu command, Copy, 110
terminating programs, 56
text
    80-column lines, 112
    boxes
        Controller, 271
        `txtCurrentFile`, 269-272
    Clipboard, 111
    default, 56
    Text menu, 52
    printing, 109-117
    retrieving, 112-113
    strings
        breaking, 113-116
        printing, 113-116
TextBox control, 137
THREED.VBX ButtonBar module, 69
time, displaying, 123
Time of Day list box, 137
Timer control, 121-123, 133-136
timer control in VBClock utility, 204
`Timer1_Timer()` routine, 77-78
`Timer2_Timer()` routine, 79
`TimeStr()` function, 162
`Tmr_Mem` procedure, 41-42
`Tmr_Mem_Timer()` function, 43
TRIES MEMORY.GBL variable, 16
`TrimZeroTerm()` function, 202
TrueType fonts, 47-48
Turbo Pascal for Windows, 109
two-dimensional life, evolution of, 291-292
`txtCurrentFile` text box, 269-272
`txtCurrentFile_KeyPress()` function, 269
tying high scores, 10

U

U.S. Naval Observatory, 149
unloading forms, 139
unsaved changes in job lists, 145
`User_Setup_Click` subroutine, 87-88
utilities
    Blink Blank!, 227
        events, `frmGetNewMessage`, 239
        forms, 233-243
        Gang screen, 232
        global module, 233
        Hungarian notation, 232
        messages, 227-230
        MODULE1.BAS routine, 243
        Windows API functions, 231
    ButtonBar Plus
        forms, 70-86, 89-94, 97
        modules, 68-105
        relocating, 81
        Windows 3.0, 67
    designing, 121-122
    FontView, 47-63
        commands, 48
        screen, 49-50
        source code, 58-63
    GroupWorker, 177
        error handling, 180
        File menu, 181
        Help menu, 181
        initializing program [`Sub Form_Load()`], 182
        main form, 177
        project window, 178
        `Setup` form, 179-180
        source code, 183-194
        `Startup` form, 180
    Job Scheduler, 121
        converting strings to structures, 127-129
        creating structures, 125-126

Index

deleting jobs from job list, 132
drawing main screen controls, 124-125
loading `ListJob` list box, 130-131
processing job list, 133-136
running jobs, 131-132
saving job lists, 132-133
`Shell()` function, 123
storing jobs, 125
time and date serials, 123
Timer control, 123

Life Workshop, 283, 286, 292-298
organization, 294
source code, 298-328
startup events, 294

Memory Match, 9-36
commands, 10, 15, 20, 28, 33-35
forms, 17-35
game grids, 12
high scores, 9-10
picture controls, 13-14
pull-down menu system, implementing, 13, 20
variables (MEMORY.GBL)

Name the States, 247
`Autoredraw`, 251
controlling program flow, 251
`ExtFloodFill()` function, 249-250
forms and purposes, 248-256
GLOBAL.BAS file, 250
procedural operation, 251-256
`ScaleMode`, 251

PrintClip
creating forms, 110-111
events, 111-116
icons, 110-112
loading, 109

source code, 117
strings, defining, 115

SetTime, source code, 149, 164-174

VBClock, 197
alarm intervals, 204
API calls used, 199-200
`Clock` form, floating on side of active title bar, 200-201
`Clock` form, moving without title bar, 204
colors, choosing, 203-204
customizing clock display, 205
examples provided, 198
fonts, choosing, 203-204
minimizing use of controls, 205-206
picture box as button bar, 206-207
pop-up menu, 205
storing display options, 201-202
suggested modifications, 207-208
timer control, 204
tips for writing Windows programs, 208
VBCLOCK.INI file, 202-203
Visual Basic code in forms, 208-223
window handles, 199

VBMem, 39-44
data, retrieving, 41-44
free memory, 39
source codes, 42-44
variables, declaring, 41

ViewPoint, Jr., 259-261
API calls, 265-266
`Controller`, creating, 261-262
directory list boxes, 266-268

351

drive/directory list box
(1stDirectories), 269-272
files, 269-274
graphic files, editing, 259
loading procedures, 262-265
`LoadPicture()` function,
272-274
`SendMessage()` function,
266-268
text box (`txtCurrentFile`),
269-272

V

`Val()` function, 154
variables
  `AllowFormToMove`, 204
  global, scope, 138
  MEMORY.GBL
    `BUTTON1`, 16
    `CARD$`, 16
    `CARDBACK$`, 16
    `FLAG$`, 16
    `GAMEBOARD`, 16
    global module, 16
    `MATCHES`, 16
    `NUMFLAGS`, 16
    `PICKED`, 16
    `SCORERECORD`, 16
    `TRIES`, 16
  VBMem, declaring, 41
VBClock Options dialog box,
197-198
VBClock utility, 197
  alarm intervals, 204
  API calls used, 199-200
  `Clock` form, 200
    floating on right side of
active title bar, 200-201
    moving without title bar, 204
  colors, choosing, 203-204
  customizing clock display, 205

  examples provided, 198
  fonts, choosing, 203-204
  minimizing use of controls,
205-206
  picture box as button bar,
206-207
  pop-up menu, 205
  storing display options, 201-202
  suggested modifications,
207-208
  timer control, 204
  tips for writing Windows
programs, 208
  VBCLOCK.INI file, 202-203
  Visual Basic code in forms,
208-223
  window handles, 199
VBCLOCK.BAS form, Visual Basic
code, 222-223
VBCLOCK.INI file, 202
VBMem utility, 39-44
  data, retrieving, 41-44
  free memory, 39
  source codes, 42-44
  variables, declaring, 41
VBMEM.FRM form, 39
VBRUN100.DLL dynamic link
library, 283
Viewer
  loading pictures, 273-274
  window, 259
viewing
  files, 261
  fonts, 47
  graphics, 259
  high scores, 10
ViewPoint, Jr., 259-261
  API calls, 265-266
  Controller, creating, 261-262
  directory list boxes, 266-268
  drive/directory list box
(1stDirectories), 269-272

files
  list box (`filFiles`), 269-272
  reading graphic formats, 272-274
  specification display label (`lblPattern`), 269-272
graphic files, editing, 259
loading procedures
  housekeeping functions, 262-265
  system evaluation functions, 262-265
`LoadPicture()` function, 272-274
`SendMessage()` function, 266-268
text box (`txtCurrentFile`), 269-272
Visual Basic By Example (Que), 14
Visual Basic
  code
    FRM_Clock.FRM, 211-216
    FRM_Disp.FRM form, 217
    FRM_Opts.FRM form, 217-222
    Global Listing file, 209-211
    VBCLOCK.BAS form, 222-223
  development of Life Workshop, 293
VPJUNIOR.INI file, 261, 265

W-Z

`While...Wend` loop, 114-115
`WinDir$()` function, 263
`WinDir()` wrapper function, 265
Window menu command, Menu Design Window, 20
Window Style list box, 137
windows
  Controller, 259
  handles, 199
  Life Options, 289-291
  main control, 286-288, 294, 297
  `MainForm` edit, 295
  modal, 288
  New High Score, 10
  project window in GroupWorker utility, 178
  Viewer, 259
  workbench, 286
Windows
  3.0 version, ButtonBar Plus, 67
  API functions in Blink Blank! utility, 231
  APIs, 149
  bitmap, see .BMP files
  Control Edit menu command, Copy, 110
  directory, 265
  metafile, 274
  PIF Editor, loading, 145
  programs
    Life Workshop, 283
    tips for writing, 208
Windows Software Developer's Kit, 109
`WinHelp()` function, 231
`WM_USER` constant, 267
.WMF files, 260
WorkBench, 283, 289
  button, 286, 294
  form, 295-297
  window, 286
`WorkBenchButton_Click()` event procedure, 295-297
`WorkGroup_DblClick()` procedure, 180
wrapper functions, 264
  `StringFromINI()`, 265
  `StringToINI()`, 266
  `WinDir()`, 265
wrappers, 265-266
`WriteComm()` routine, 152-154

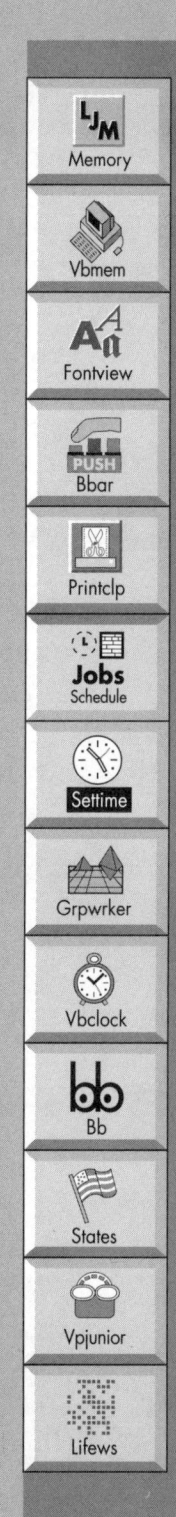

WriteDefaultIni() subroutine, 97-101
WriteDefaultIni routine, 97-101
WritePrivateProfileString()
   API call, 266
   function, 261
   routine, 154, 158
writing
   modular code, 122
   Windows programs, tips, 208

Application and Source Code Disk

By opening this package, you agree to be bound by the following:

This software product is copyrighted, and all rights are reserved by the publisher. You are licensed to use this software on a single computer. You may copy and/or modify the software as needed to facilitate your use of it on a single computer. Making copies of the software for any other purpose is a violation of the United States copyright laws.

This software is sold *as is* without warranty of any kind, either expressed or implied, including but not limited to the implied warranties of merchantability and fitness for a particular purpose. Neither the publisher nor its dealers or distributors assumes any liability for any alleged or actual damages arising from the use of this program. (Some states do not allow for the exclusion of implied warranties, so the exclusion may not apply to you.)

Installation Instructions

> **NOTE:** You will need at least 3 megabytes of disk space to install all the programs and source code for *Fun Programming with Visual Basic*.

1. Make a directory on your hard disk to hold the programs and source code (for example, type MD C:\FUNVB).

2. Copy the contents of the floppy disk to the directory you just created (for example, type COPY B:*.* C:\FUNVB).

3. Make the new directory the active one by typing CD C:\FUNVB.

4. Execute the self-extracting archive file FUNVB.EXE by typing
   C:\FUNVB\FUNVB.EXE /X.

   NOTE: The /X switch is very important. If you do not use it, you will not retain the directory structure of the Visual Basic programs.

5. At this point, you may optionally delete the self-extracting archive file FUNVB.EXE to conserve space on your hard disk (for example, type DEL C:\FUNVB\FUNVB.EXE).

6. If you do not have Visual Basic installed on your computer, you must copy the VBRUN100.DLL file to your WINDOWS\SYSTEM directory (for example, type COPY C:\FUNVB\VBRUN100\VBRUN100.DLL C:\WINDOWS\SYSTEM).

7. Copy C:\FUNVB\BBAR\DLL\THREED.VBX to your WINDOWS\ SYSTEM directory.

The FUNVB directory now has several subdirectories—one for each of the Visual Basic games and utilities covered in this book. You can run any of these via the Windows File Manager by double-clicking the program's executable file icon (.EXE). You can optionally create a new program group via the Windows Program Manager and drag each .EXE icon to the new group. That way, you can simply double-click the program's icon to launch it directly from the Program Manager desktop.

Free Catalog!

Mail us this registration form today, and we'll send you a free catalog featuring Que's complete line of best-selling books.

Name of Book _____

Name _____

Title _____

Phone (___) _____

Company _____

Address _____

City _____

State _____ ZIP _____

Please check the appropriate answers:

1. Where did you buy your Que book?
   - ☐ Bookstore (name: _____)
   - ☐ Computer store (name: _____)
   - ☐ Catalog (name: _____)
   - ☐ Direct from Que
   - ☐ Other: _____

2. How many computer books do you buy a year?
   - ☐ 1 or less
   - ☐ 2-5
   - ☐ 6-10
   - ☐ More than 10

3. How many Que books do you own?
   - ☐ 1
   - ☐ 2-5
   - ☐ 6-10
   - ☐ More than 10

4. How long have you been using this software?
   - ☐ Less than 6 months
   - ☐ 6 months to 1 year
   - ☐ 1-3 years
   - ☐ More than 3 years

5. What influenced your purchase of this Que book?
   - ☐ Personal recommendation
   - ☐ Advertisement
   - ☐ In-store display
   - ☐ Price
   - ☐ Que catalog
   - ☐ Que mailing
   - ☐ Que's reputation
   - ☐ Other: _____

6. How would you rate the overall content of the book?
   - ☐ Very good
   - ☐ Good
   - ☐ Satisfactory
   - ☐ Poor

7. What do you like *best* about this Que book?
   _____
   _____

8. What do you like *least* about this Que book?
   _____
   _____

9. Did you buy this book with your personal funds?
   - ☐ Yes   ☐ No

10. Please feel free to list any other comments you may have about this Que book.
    _____
    _____
    _____

--- Que ---

Order Your Que Books Today!

Name _____

Title _____

Company _____

City _____

State _____ ZIP _____

Phone No. (___) _____

Method of Payment:

Check ☐ (Please enclose in envelope.)

Charge My: VISA ☐   MasterCard ☐

American Express ☐

Charge # _____

Expiration Date _____

Order No.	Title	Qty.	Price	Total

You can **FAX** your order to 1-317-573-2583. Or call 1-800-428-5331, ext. ORDR to order direct.

Please add $2.50 per title for shipping and handling.

Subtotal _____

Shipping & Handling _____

Total _____

--- Que ---

BUSINESS REPLY MAIL
First Class Permit No. 9918   Indianapolis, IN

Postage will be paid by addressee

que®

11711 N. College
Carmel, IN 46032

NO POSTAGE
NECESSARY
IF MAILED
IN THE
UNITED STATES

BUSINESS REPLY MAIL
First Class Permit No. 9918   Indianapolis, IN

Postage will be paid by addressee

que®

11711 N. College
Carmel, IN 46032

NO POSTAGE
NECESSARY
IF MAILED
IN THE
UNITED STATES